Grover Pease Osborne

Principles of Economics

The satisfaction of human wants

Grover Pease Osborne

Principles of Economics
The satisfaction of human wants

ISBN/EAN: 9783337311995

Printed in Europe, USA, Canada, Australia, Japan

Cover: Foto ©Suzi / pixelio.de

More available books at **www.hansebooks.com**

PRINCIPLES OF ECONOMICS

THE SATISFACTION OF HUMAN

WANTS

IN SO FAR AS THEIR SATISFACTION DEPENDS ON

MATERIAL RESOURCES

BY

GROVER PEASE OSBORNE

CINCINNATI
ROBERT CLARKE AND COMPANY
1893

Copyright 1890, 1893.
BY GROVER PEASE OSBORNE.
All Rights Reserved.

PREFACE.

I have long been of the opinion that, in the study of economic science, we can safely start with no narrower subject than the Satisfaction of Human Wants. To avoid a seeming trespass upon the realm of the spiritual, it is necessary to add the limiting qualification, *so far as this satisfaction depends on material resources, or the labor of human beings.* The objection which naturally occurs to the reader is that this subject is too broad, and that it is necessary to take a single division of it; *e. g.,* the science of wealth. But this is not a natural division, and, I am convinced, is too indefinite. For wealth, as defined by the writers who make it the subject of Political Economy, is simply that which has exchange value. Now, exchange value is not solid ground. It depends on four things: the quality of the object, the quantity available, the number of people who want it, and what they have to give for it. It is nothing but a relation between various elements. Water is wealth under some circumstances, and not under others. I believe that the only method which will give us certainty is one that goes back to the wants themselves, and to the resources for their satisfaction. Wants are real things; the resources for their satisfaction are real.

Those in different countries and different ages can be compared. The relations between wants and resources, and between the resources themselves, can be studied under value both in use and in exchange.

No subject is large in outline, which is all that is proposed in the present work. It is something to properly define a subject, and state its natural divisions. Instead of wealth, we consider the resources which the world, or better a single nation, has for the satisfaction of the wants of its people; next the number of people and the wants to be satisfied. Who is to own or control the various classes of these resources, and what are the reasons for such ownership? Then we take up the methods by which the resources can be most economically used; then the principles of their exchange between various owners; and, last, the distribution of such resources as are produced by modern methods, among the various interests which contribute to their production.

The subject does not, after all, seem so much broader than that which political economists attempt to cover under the head of wealth, and it has the advantage of resting on firm ground; we are more likely to see things as they are, and to put them in their right relations. The first object of this work is to present the subject in proper outline. The titles of the various books and chapters are intended to be an analysis of the subject.

The reader will perhaps be struck with the entire omission of all reference to the tariff question, and yet he will see that its treatment does not naturally belong to the subject. It is, of course, one of the many applications of the principles of exchange. But the applications of the principles of exchange, and of those of the other natural divisions of this treatise, are world-wide. I have been the more willing to omit such discussion in order to emphasize the fact that Political Economy is not the science of free trade or protection, as nine out of ten people suppose. Most persons who feel obliged to make some remark to a student of Political Economy will at once ask, "Are you in favor of free trade or protection?" evidently supposing that there are but two kinds of political economists. I should not have hesitated, however, to discuss the tariff question had the plan of this treatise demanded it.

It is not in every respect pleasant to be classed with a "school," because one may not wish to be held responsible for all the views of those with whom he may agree in the main. Many persons suppose that if they know to which of three or four schools a writer belongs, they know all he has to say. I believe, however, that most of the fundamental truths of economic science are to be found in what has been called "the orthodox English school," which includes so many eminent authors in England and the United States. I have sought to make an original investigation on what I believe to be the only true line of study; but truths once discovered, whether by English or German writers, must be used by all who come after them.

Attention is called to the outline of the subject as given in the titles of the various books and chapters;

to the Introduction, the first four chapters of Book I., the first and last chapters of Book II., and the first chapter of Book III. In Book IV. the reader will notice the emphasis put upon the continued employment of labor, and the cost of labor to the laborer. The old and correct view of the distribution of the product between the three elements, "land, capital and labor," is recognized in Book VI., but the larger portion of the space is devoted to the further distribution of the great share of economic labor among the classes of laborers whose interests are naturally opposed, each to all the others. The reader will please notice the share of "good name," a very large share usually overlooked, and the distinction between the laborer who works for himself, the laborer who works for wages in production, and the laborer who satisfies wants directly. The titles of the chapters under "Distribution" give the final shares.

Some portions of this volume were published in 1890 and 1891.

G. P. O.

CINCINNATI, July, 1893.

CONTENTS.

INTRODUCTION—Wants, ... 9

BOOK I.

THE RESOURCES FOR THE SATISFACTION OF WANTS.

CHAPTER I. THE RESOURCES OF NATURE, ... 21
Permanent—Consumable.

CHAPTER II. THE ABILITY TO LABOR, ... 32
Satisfies wants Directly and Indirectly.

CHAPTER III. THE PRODUCTIONS OF HUMAN INDUSTRY, . 38
Permanent or Consumable—Satisfy Wants Directly and Indirectly.

CHAPTER IV. SOCIETY, ... 46
Satisfies Wants Directly and Indirectly.

CHAPTER V. UTILITY OF THE RESOURCES, ... 49

CHAPTER VI. VALUE IN USE, ... 57

BOOK II.

POPULATION—THE NUMBER OF PEOPLE WHOSE WANTS ARE TO BE SATISFIED.

INTRODUCTION—The Relation of Wants to Resources is Shown by Value in Use, ... 65

CHAPTER I. POPULATION AND THE RESOURCES OF NATURE, ... 66

CHAPTER II. POPULATION AND LABOR, ... 87

		PAGE.
CHAPTER III.	POPULATION AND PRODUCED WEALTH,	96
CHAPTER IV.	POPULATION AND SOCIETY,	103
CHAPTER V.	THE LAW OF THE INCREASE OF POPULATION,	116
CHAPTER VI.	APPLICATIONS OF THE LAW OF THE INCREASE OF POPULATION,	135

BOOK III.

OWNERSHIP AND CONTROL OF THE RESOURCES FOR THE SATISFACTION OF WANTS.

CHAPTER I.	PRIVATE PROPERTY OR SOCIALISM,	151
CHAPTER II.	THE OWNERSHIP AND CONTROL OF LABOR,	160
CHAPTER III.	THE OWNERSHIP AND CONTROL OF THE RESOURCES OF NATURE,	165
CHAPTER IV.	THE OWNERSHIP AND CONTROL OF THE RESOURCES PRODUCED BY HUMAN INDUSTRY,	181
CHAPTER V.	CONTROL OF SOCIETY, Individualism and Socialism.	189

BOOK IV.

ECONOMICAL USE OF THE RESOURCES.

INTRODUCTION,		201
CHAPTER I.	THE ECONOMICAL USE OF LABOR,	203
PART I.	The Constant Employment of Labor,	203
PART II.	The Irksomeness of Labor,	209
PART III.	The Division of Labor,	214
PART IV.	The Development of Labor Power, and the Prohibition of Certain Forms of Labor,	221

		PAGE.
CHAPTER II.	ECONOMICAL USE OF THE RESOURCES OF NATURE,	225
PART I.	Permanent Natural Resources,	225
PART II.	Consumable Natural Resources,	231
PART III.	Public and Private Use of the Resources of Nature,	234
CHAPTER III.	ECONOMICAL USE OF PRODUCED WEALTH,	242
CHAPTER IV.	THE USE OF THE RESOURCE OF SOCIETY,	252
CHAPTER V.	THE PURPOSES FOR WHICH THE RESOURCES SHALL BE USED,	256

BOOK V.

EXCHANGE.

CHAPTER I.	HOW EXCHANGE SATISFIES WANTS,	272
CHAPTER II.	THE PRICE OF A DOLLAR,	275
CHAPTER III.	EXCHANGE VALUES,	280
CHAPTER IV.	THE LIMITS OF VALUES IN EXCHANGE ARE FIXED BY VALUE IN USE,	285
CHAPTER V.	SUPPLY AND DEMAND,	289
CHAPTER VI.	COST OF PRODUCTION,	296
CHAPTER VII.	MONOPOLY,	306
CHAPTER VIII.	MONEY,	312
PART I.	Qualities of a Good Money,	313
PART II.	What Determines the Value of Money?	325
PART III.	Efforts to Secure a Money of Uniform Value,	330
CHAPTER IX.	SUBSTITUTES FOR MONEY,	335

BOOK VI.

DISTRIBUTION OF PRODUCED WEALTH.

INTRODUCTION.

			PAGE
CHAPTER	I.	RENT—THE SHARE OF THOSE WHO HAVE POSSESSION OF THE RESOURCES OF NATURE,	355
CHAPTER	II.	INTEREST—THE SHARE OF PRODUCED WEALTH,	363
CHAPTER	III.	THE SHARE OF GOOD NAME,	375
CHAPTER	IV.	THE SHARE OF MONOPOLY,	382
CHAPTER	V.	THE SHARE OF THE PRODUCER—PROFITS OF PRODUCTION,	397
CHAPTER	VI.	THE SHARE OF THE MERCHANT—PROFITS OF EXCHANGE,	406
CHAPTER	VII.	THE SHARE OF THE LABORER WHO WORKS FOR HIMSELF,	411
CHAPTER	VIII.	THE SHARE OF THE LABORER WHO WORKS FOR WAGES,	420
CHAPTER	IX.	THE SHARE OF LABOR WHICH SATISFIES WANTS DIRECTLY,	436
CHAPTER	X.	THE BOOTY OF THE ROBBER, AND THE WINNINGS OF THE GAMBLER,	441
CHAPTER	XI.	THE SHARE OF THE GOVERNMENT,	445

INTRODUCTION.

Economy is the making the most of our resources. The man who gets as much out of an income of five thousand dollars a year as other men from an income of ten thousand, is an economist; while he who lives on five hundred a year, and does not secure the comforts and advantages which other men obtain for three hundred, is a spendthrift. Economy consists in using our resources to the best advantage, in making what we have go as far as possible.

There are more opportunities for the exercise of economy in society or a nation than in the case of a single individual; we have only to call to mind the difference between a civilized nation, such as the United States, and the state of barbarism in which the Indians dwelt, to see how much economy has done toward the promotion of material comfort. The difference is far greater than would at first appear; because, under the uneconomical methods of savage life, the entire territory of the United States could support only a few hundred thousand people; whereas, with such economies as are now employed, the same territory supports more than sixty millions. Even if the people, on the average, had no better living than the savages, the same territory maintains a hundred times as many people. Economical methods result in the supporting of a larger population, quite as often as in giving a better living to the individual members of society. If the resources for the satisfaction of human wants were unlimited; if there were all the food and clothing and dwellings and furniture which the world could possibly use; and if these could all be renewed without effort—then there might be no need of the science of Economics. The fact that the world's resources are limited—that land is limited, that timber and minerals can not be had in a condition fit for use without great labor; that man's power of labor is limited; that there is not, at present, enough of material goods to give to every person in the world a comfortable living—makes it of the highest importance that we use the resources we have to the best advantage.

Economy is the making the most of the resources of an individual, a community, or a nation.

WANTS.

The heaven of the Esquimau is said to be a happy island in a warmer climate, with great kettles of walrus meat, always boiling, beside which a good Esquimau may sit and eat, forever and forever. This is the Esquimau idea of happiness; this is the sum of an Esquimau's wants. The wants of a highly civilized man are a thousand times as great.

There are some needs and desires which belong to man, as man, and which he has in common with the brutes. Air and food and water are necessary to life. There are other wants, such as the desire for personal adornment, which are universal, and as old as the history of the race. Still other wants, such as those which distinguish the civilized man from the savage, have been developed by circumstances, or created by various influences.

THE CREATION, DEVELOPMENT AND SUPPRESSION OF WANTS.—The rudiments of most wants exist in the nature of man; but they are modified and developed and new wants are created, by the circumstances in which individuals and nations are placed. The following influences have been at work in the development of the wants of civilized nations as we find them to-day:

1. *Physical surroundings.*—Climate and the difficulty of obtaining food, the need of shelter, danger from wild beasts and savage men, nearness to the sea, the variety of efforts necessary to secure a livelihood—all these, and many other circumstances, have had much to do with the development of men and nations.

2. *Education, as it is given by man and nature.*—The influence and teaching of the schools, the pulpit and the press, the home education of early life, and the influence of natural surroundings, go to form one's wants. Religious and moral teaching have had an enormous influence in moulding the wants of mankind. Mo-

hammedanism and Christianity have produced different types of nations. The difference between Protestant and Catholic countries must be explained, in part, by the influence of different forms of religion.

3. *The customs and opinions of society.*—By society we mean the people with whom one lives and associates; it may be the other members of an Indian tribe. Men like to do as others do; they are influenced very greatly by what others think of them. Particular methods of living, which may have become established by accident, are adopted by children born into the tribe or society, or who come into it from another locality. Most boys who learn to chew tobacco, do so for no other reason than that it is the fashion of the boys or men with whom they associate. People follow many of the customs of society, simply because they are customs.

4. *Habit.*—A habit is the result of continuing or repeating any act for a sufficient length of time, and it frequently creates a real want. It matters not how the habit is begun, whether by accident, a desire to conform to the customs of society, or through the influence of education. When the habit, good or bad, is once formed, the wants of the man are, so far, changed.

5. *Satisfying wants or leaving them unsatisfied.*—The mere fact of satisfying wants or of leaving them unsatisfied is one of the principal causes of their development, change in character, or complete suppression. Many wants, if regularly satisfied, tend to increase in strength. There are also many which if left unsatisfied will diminish in intensity; and some will die out

entirely. The desire for works of art is strengthened by the study of art. The desire for knowledge is increased by its acquisition. If a person of very simple habits and tastes is suddenly furnished with the means of gratifying them, he will be surprised to see how fast his wants will grow. The direction of their growth may be determined by accident, but it is sure to influence his life for good or evil. On the other hand, if one has not the means of satisfying many of the wants the gratification of which is not necessary to life, he turns toward something else, and in a measure loses his old desires.

Very close to this is the fact that the mere turning of attention to a particular want, and keeping the means of its satisfaction before one, will usually increase its intensity. Merchants and manufacturers know that they must create a demand for some lines of goods before they can be sold. The vender of peanuts locates his stand on the street corner, where the odor of roasting will reach passers-by. The display of goods in shop windows, and most of the various kinds of advertising, are not so much to inform people where they can procure certain commodities, as to create a demand for them. Trade and manufacturers have as much to do with creating wants as with satisfying them; and many wants which manufacturers and merchants have created, die out when these men no longer stimulate them. The saloon-keeper not only satisfies, but creates, wants by an attractive display of his beverages.

The withholding of the means for the satisfaction of wants, tends to keep them in abeyance; but as soon as one is able easily to satisfy the more common wants, a great crop of others will spring up. It is easier to create wants than to suppress them.

6. *Inheritance.*— A powerful factor in fixing the wants of a race is the law of inheritance. It has been said that to educate a man requires at least three generations. The character of the men of New England was determined, not so much by the rocks and the sea and the rugged country, as by the intellectual and moral character of their ancestors in old England. The gain or loss made in life is in a measure fixed, and transmitted from father to son. The nature of the wants of one generation is the most powerful factor in determining the wants of the next.

The historical study of the development of wants is an interesting subject by itself, but is not necessary to an understanding of the means of their satisfaction.

Still more important to the moralist, are the various influences now at work forming the wants of the coming generations. The well-being of the race may be advanced, to the extent of all that lies between the highest civilization and the lowest barbarism, by the development or the suppression of the various wants of its members. What one wants, determines, to a great extent, what he is, and will become. It is, indeed, one of the claims of Christianity that it possesses supernatural power to modify and actually revolutionize the wants of its adherents. This is the highest claim that any system can make. Wants seek their satisfaction, and often find or make a way to it through seeming impossibilities. What a man thinks he wants, is, therefore, of the highest importance; not only to himself, but to those who live in society with him. No field of study can be more inviting to the practical philanthropist. *The history of civilization is the history of the development, the creation, and the suppression of human wants.*

SPIRITUAL AND RELIGIOUS WANTS.—There are mental, spiritual and religious wants which can not be satisfied by material resources; and, to that extent, they do not come under this enquiry. A happy state of mind may give one great comfort in life, even with very indifferent surroundings. It is one of the claims of Christianity, that its followers may receive spiritual help; and that there are wants in the nature of man which only spiritual influences will satisfy. Our science has to do with satisfactions only to the extent that they depend on material resources. So far as a house of worship, an organ, or the labor of a minister, aids in the satisfaction of religious wants, our science takes account of them; but in so far as they must be satisfied by divine power, supernatural or spiritual influences, or the condition of the soul itself, this science does not reach them. Surely, this division between the *material* and the *spiritual* is a natural one.

While we thus put theology and religion first, as the greatest things in the world, there is no question that the Social Sciences hold the second place. A science which helps us to use to better advantage the resources which God has given us, which feeds the hungry, and enables more people to live in cleanliness and decency, and improves the condition of men, stands next to the spiritual element in religion. A true social science is, indeed, one of the fruits of the spiritual power of. Christianity; since it is mainly Christian men who are engaged in the practical work of philanthropy. In "each one for himself," the struggle results in a terrible waste. The remedy is not Socialism. It is the mastery of social problems by those who love their fellow-men, and are ready to sacrifice something for their welfare. The more general, economic knowledge becomes, the more likely we are to adopt methods of justice, and methods which give the best opportunity for the development of the individual. The great interest in the study of Economics is one of the results of Christianity. Let it be understood, however, that it is a science by itself, and that the line between it and the spiritual element of Christianity is distinct and broad.

ALL WANTS SHOULD NOT BE SATISFIED.—It is evidently neither for the interest of the individual nor of society that all wants be satisfied. But to discriminate between the wants which should and should not be satisfied, is the duty of the moralist, rather than of the economist. The same economic principles apply, in the main, to all classes of wants, regardless of the moral element in their satisfaction. As a student of economics, one may seek for the general principles which cover the economical satisfaction of all wants; as a moralist, the same person may be called on to decide what wants ought not to be satisfied. In treating of wants in detail, we should not go out of our way to show how the drunkard can be furnished with liquor at the least cost; but the laws which govern the production of corn are the same, whether it is ground into meal or distilled into whisky. There will be differences of opinion concerning the propriety of satisfying numerous wants. General principles apply to all alike. When it comes to questions of detail, there are large classes of wants that do not call for special treatment. It is necessary, however, to emphasize the fact that there are wants which ought not to be satisfied.

It should be remembered, also, that the word *want* is not synonymous with *wish* or *desire*. Its meaning is more nearly that of need, or something lacking. The term *wants* is not, however, synonymous with *needs;* it has a meaning of its own, including elements from both the others.

The fact that a given desire can be satisfied by economic laws does not make it right to satisfy it. It is not uncommon to hear one attempt to justify a wrong by showing that the act was in accordance with economic laws; but this is no more a justification than for a murderer to say that he killed a man by using his knowledge of the poisonous nature of certain chemical compounds, or of the laws governing the explosion of dynamite. All knowledge is power, and all power is dangerous. But the world is better off for its knowledge of chemistry and electricity, as well as for its knowledge of Political Economy. There is no doubt that oppression exists, and that crimes are committed by the use of economic laws. They are no more frequent because of the knowledge, but the knowledge is sometimes used as an excuse for the crime. One may rob his neighbor, through the action of the laws of supply and demand; but the showing how he did it, is no more a justification than for a desperado to explain how he stabbed a man. This point needs emphasis, because of the fact that some works on Political Economy leave the impression upon the reader that any act is right, if it can be shown to be in accordance with the laws of supply and demand; e. g., that it is right to buy as cheap and sell as dear as one can. Whether it is or not, depends on circumstances, and the question is one of morals rather than of economics.

BOOK I.
THE RESOURCES FOR THE SATISFACTION OF WANTS.

BOOK I.

THE RESOURCES FOR THE SATISFACTION OF WANTS.

CHAPTER   I. THE RESOURCES OF NATURE, ... 21
                  Permanent — Consumable.

CHAPTER   II. THE ABILITY TO LABOR, ... 32
                  Satisfies Wants Directly and Indirectly.

CHAPTER III. THE PRODUCTIONS OF HUMAN INDUSTRY, 38
                  Permanent or Consumable — Satisfy Wants Directly and Indirectly.

CHAPTER IV.   SOCIETY, ... 46
                  Satisfies Wants Directly and Indirectly.

CHAPTER   V.   UTILITY OF THE RESOURCES, ... 49

CHAPTER VI.   VALUE IN USE, ... 57

BOOK I.

THE RESOURCES FOR THE SATISFACTION OF WANTS.

The resources which the world has for the satisfaction of wants are properly divided into four classes:
I. The Resources of Nature.
II. Labor.
III. The Productions of Human Industry.
IV. Society.

CHAPTER I.

THE RESOURCES OF NATURE.

The earth as it was before man appeared, or as it has since been modified by natural causes, with the sun that shines upon it, and all the physical forces connected with it, are natural resources. Man had nothing to do with their creation. They are the gifts of Nature, or of God, to the human race. The earth was created for man, and intended to answer the needs of each generation, as its members are born and die.

Some of the older political economists comprised all the resources of nature under the term "Land," on the theory that land includes the water which covers it, the air above it, the minerals found beneath it, the animals that roam over it, and the forces connected with it. It is a question of names; but names are important, and the attempt to use common words out of their ordinary signification has been productive of great mischief.

1. *Land*, in its common acceptation, is the most important of the natural resources. It is the surface of the earth, whether covered by water or not.

The first utility which land possesses for man is that of a place of residence; a place to stand or lie down upon; a place to build his wigwam or his palace; a door-yard or a lawn for his children's playground or his own enjoyment; a place to give him access to the sunlight and the air; ground to separate him from his neighbors, for, much as he desires society, he likes a little space at times between himself and others. He wants a little ground, a portion of the earth's surface, which he can control, and he never realizes its value until he is deprived of it in a crowded city. This use is wholly apart from anything which the land may produce. The occupant may use it for two purposes, to make a garden or grow fruit; but he desires the land for outdoor space, even if he grows nothing but grass and shade trees.

A great deal of land is needed for strictly resident purposes. Even on the American farm a certain portion is usually set aside for the house lot and grounds, and the whole farm is a range for the farmer's children. It fills to a partial extent the wealthy Englishman's desire for a private park. The farm is not, alone, a place for the production of crops; it is a broad residence property, which in a city or crowded country can be enjoyed only by one with large wealth.

The second use of land is for commerce and manufactures. Factories occupy more land than is often supposed, and some establishments require many times as much outdoor yard room as is covered by buildings. It is not the amount of land, but the location, that makes the site important; and the location is of still more consequence in commerce. The point where land and water commerce meet is vital, and the land available for commerce at favorable points is very limited. Ocean navigation must terminate in a harbor where ships can lie in safety, with a depth of water where railroads and ships can transfer their freight. There must also be room for the breaking up of cargoes and the interchange of goods among different lines of transportation, to reach different countries, and different parts of the same country; in short, room for a commercial city. Land in such localities is not abundant. He who controls it can levy an enormous toll for its use. So, in interior transportation. At Chicago, railroads meet the lake, and a large tract of land is required for commercial purposes. Roads, *i. e.*, facilities for communication and transportation, require land, and a great deal of it. The acreage of the wagon roads in the United States is large. Railroads usually have a hundred feet in width, twelve acres to the mile, and to the land thus used must be added large acreage for yard room in cities, and still more land rendered useless by railroad traffic.

The uses of land for residence, manufactures and commerce were to a great extent overlooked in the past. Ricardo wrought out his principles of "diminishing returns" and the whole theory of "rent" from agricultural land. In a new country, such as the United States was a few years ago, agriculture is the main purpose for which land is needed. The proportion of labor required for the production of raw materials a hundred years ago was many times greater than now. In the early discussion of land, therefore, almost all illustrations were drawn from agricultural land, and almost all reasoning based upon it. While land used for residence, manufactures and commerce is still small in area when compared with that used for agriculture, it is large in the aggregate. The most troublesome questions center about it. Principles which appear abstract in connection with land in the country, become very practical when applied to land in cities.

Land for agriculture, as for all other purposes, should be considered as *mere extension*. The bottom lands of rivers have a wealth of vegetable mould which is a mine to draw upon, and the barren sand or the disintegrating limestone can be made productive by the efforts of man; but without the acreage, no man can make a farm. The natural fertility of the soil, accumulated through ages, should be classed with mines, which can be exhausted in the using. The land is measured by acres, not by fertility. Land is merely the extension of the earth's surface.

2. *Water* may be placed next to land in enumerating the Natural Resources. It covers three-fourths of the earth's surface; it separates continents with advantage to nations; it is a highway for commerce. And this highway is not a canal which is only a line between two points; it is a body of water which affords each country an opportunity for commerce with all the others. No railway system can be so perfect as an ocean over which ships can sail anywhere. By it the cost of carriage is reduced below that of any other possible means. Lakes and rivers, with the opportunity for canals, form a system of interior water transportation of scarcely less importance.

The influence of the oceans and great lakes on climate must not be forgotten. They insure an abundant rainfall, and make the general cultivation of the soil possible. Indeed, the water which covers so much of the earth may be said to make the rest habitable, and to afford to continents and nations that isolation which in the past has been necessary to the highest civilization.

These large bodies of water also satisfy wants, *directly*, by affording countless desirable residence sites. The cottage by the sea or lake, in summer, has become popular because of the water and the air. A city on the ocean harbor or the lake has an advantage over one in the interior. The United States would lose immensely were the great lakes to be filled by some convulsion of nature. There are many persons who would like to see them drained, if they could get possession of the land at the bottom; but the loss to the whole country would be a thousand times the gain of the few.

The use of water-power is also of great advantage. It is true that the real power here is the force of gravitation, and the sun-force which lifts the water from the ocean to fall in rain on high levels, so that the force of gravitation can act on it in its descent to the sea; but the water is a convenient means of using this force, and the water-power of the world enables us to satisfy wants with far less labor. It will, also, endure after the coal has been burned up.

For cleansing purposes no substitute could be found. The earth is washed by the rain, and the use of the hose from water-works is one of the methods of making great cities habitable. For domestic uses the amount of water required is small, but its value is very high. When the quantity is greatly reduced, its value becomes that of life itself. For drinking purposes, it is simply one of the resources of nature, absolutely essential, without which everything else would be worthless. The difficulty of supplying a dense population with pure water, or even with water fit for drinking, is very great.

3. The *Atmosphere* is the next resource which nature furnishes to satisfy wants. It is usually left out of the account, simply because so abundant. In taking an account of stock, in order to see what we have to satisfy wants with, we are not to omit the most important resource of all, simply because there happens to be a good deal of it. We are rather to be thankful that the stock is so large. This resource

might have been placed first, because it is most essential of all to life. One may live for a considerable period with nothing else; but five minutes' deprivation of air is fatal. There are places and times when, notwithstanding its abundance on the earth, air suitable for human beings is difficult to obtain. Some one has imagined that the time will come when it will be pumped into the densely populated parts of cities and distributed as water now is. The problem of supplying it pure to our homes in the winter season, has received much attention. At present, however, we are only taking account of stock, and put down an immense volume of air, comparatively pure over the ocean, and with varying qualities on the land.

4. The fourth group of resources is the *Forces of Nature*, including the power exerted by the sun, its light, heat, and chemical influence; the attraction of gravitation, and the molecular forces. The sun is as much a resource for the production of grain as the land. The power of gravitation is not only utilized in the water-wheel, but holds buildings in their places. All growth of plant life is dependent on natural forces. With the creation of these forces man has had nothing to do; they existed before him; they act continuously with a power beside which the physical power of man is infinitesimal. Man may discover and use, he can not create or increase them. It must not be forgotten, in all our future reasoning, that we have this power of natural forces, great almost beyond human conception, as one of the resources for the satisfaction of wants.

28 RESOURCES FOR SATISFACTION OF WANTS.

5. The *Minerals* of the earth constitute the fifth resource. Man has had nothing to do with their formation; he digs them out when he needs them. It may cost him some labor to find them, but he only discovers, he does not create them. In this respect they are like the natural forces. With minerals must be classed the natural fertility of the soil. This natural fertility, formed by the decay of vegetation in the past, much as the coal is formed from vegetable matter, is something apart from the land; and may be used up, leaving us many acres of land as before. In popular language the land is said to be exhausted; which means that its fertility is exhausted, as a mine is exhausted. The land remains, and can be made productive again.

6. The sixth natural resource is the *Forests* or *Timber*.

7. To the list must be added *Wild Animals and Fish*, which are very important resources for the satisfaction of the wants of a savage.

This completes the list of resources which nature provides for man. It is well to spread them all out before us, that we may see what we have, and not confuse them with other general classes yet to follow. They are:

1. Land.
2. Water.
3. Air.
4. The Forces of Nature.
5. The Minerals and Natural Fertility of the Soil.
6. Timber.
7. Wild Animals and Fish.

THE RESOURCES OF NATURE. 29

PERMANENT AND CONSUMABLE.—The first four of the Natural Resources are *permanent;* that is, they are not destroyed by use. The air and the water and the land are used by the men of each generation as it occupies the earth, and are left to those who follow. The sun shines eternally, and the forces of nature will act forever. The land can not be destroyed by the using; great temporary injury may be inflicted, but not beyond the power of repair.

It is not so with the last three resources. Minerals are consumed in the using. Coal is destroyed in the burning; and although iron continues to exist in another form, the ore from which it is made is destroyed. When the bed of ore is exhausted, it will not be replenished within any time we can take into account. When a substance is transformed, as iron ore into iron, it is said to be *consumed*, in the production of something else. We have a new substance, but no longer the old: we can not have both.

Timber, wild animals and fish, while they are consumed in the using, differ from the minerals, in that they may be speedily reproduced by nature, alone, or with the efforts of man. The difference is, that while the ore is consumed in the production of commercial iron which goes to erect a building, and while the timber is cut down and consumed in the production of lumber for the same building, the timber will grow again. The hard-shot forest is soon replenished with game. Fish may be taken for ages, and nature maintain the supply. All of these three classes of Natural Resources—minerals, timber and fish—are *Consuma-*

ble Resources, because consumed in the using; and the distinction between them and the *Permanent* Resources is quite important.

Our classification will then stand:

I. Resources of Nature—
1. Land.
2. Water. } Permanent Natural
3. Air. } Resources.
4. The Forces of Nature.
5. Minerals. } Consumable.
6. Timber. } Consumable, but can
7. Wild Animals and Fish. } be replaced.

DIRECTLY AND INDIRECTLY.—The Resources of Nature satisfy wants, *directly* or *indirectly*. The air when breathed satisfies a want directly. So, also, land when used for residence purposes. The occupant wants the land, and not something that can be produced from it. The savage satisfies his wants, directly by wild fruits, fish and game.

A resource satisfies wants *indirectly* when it aids in the production of some other resource, or enables some other resource to be used in satisfying a want. It is only a means to an end. Such is land used for agriculture, or a water-power employed in turning the wheels of a factory. Coal satisfies wants, directly, when burned in a parlor grate; indirectly, when used in making steam for a factory.

We shall find that this distinction between the satisfaction of wants *directly*, or *indirectly*, runs through all of our subject, and should never be lost sight of.

It will be convenient often to speak of the Resources

of Nature as *Natural Wealth*. There is a difference of opinion as to the proper use of the term "wealth," but with the qualifying word there is no danger of misunderstanding, and this use of the term is also in accordance with popular language. It is the wealth of nature, or Natural Wealth.

CHAPTER II.

THE ABILITY TO LABOR.

Next to the Resources of Nature comes that of human labor. The Natural Resources are placed first, because they are first in the order of time. Without them the existence of man would be impossible. Labor comes next, because it first makes use of the Natural Resources; and is thus next in the order of time.

We should distinguish the ability to labor from the labor actually put forth. It is the ability which men possess which constitutes the Resource, and this ability may exceed many times the labor actually performed. We are now taking account of stock,—of what the world has to satisfy wants with,—and this account must include all the ability which men possess to perform labor of any kind, of either hand or brain.

Labor, in all works on Politial Economy, includes the efforts of both body and mind. The terms "Working man" and "Laboring man" are used in the popular sense to denote muscular labor, but the simple term "Labor" is used, especially in economic writings, to include mental labor as well as physical. We are obliged to have some general term, and there is no other. It is not a question of the irksomeness of the different kinds of labor; it is only the power to do, to accomplish something in satisfying the world's wants. It is indeed impossible to separate entirely mental and physical labor. The lowest form of labor requires some brains, else the work is better done by a machine; and the more brains, the better. The work of the trainmen on the railway would perhaps be classed as manual labor, yet a high order of mental effort is required. The man who knows nothing, will find that muscular strength will not put him in charge of a locomotive; though some strength and endurance are required in addition to mental ability, in order to run it. The profession of civil engineering would be classed as brain work, yet some branches of it require more muscular exertion than is put forth by a street laborer. What the world wants is results, whether accomplished by manual or mental labor, or both combined. Under the general term "Labor" we therefore include all the ability which men possess to do the world's work.

There is great difference in the mere muscular strength of men, and still more difference in the energy with which they use that strength. One Englishman is worth five or six of the natives of India, even for the most common employment. The skill which some men possess, the knowledge they have, and the intelligence that directs, are of far more importance than the power to lift and carry. We can not separate the knowledge and skill of the man from the man himself. All the power he has to do, the skill of eye or hand, all that he knows, his intellect and judgment, his mental capacity to acquire knowledge and skill,—all these go to make up his ability to labor. The locomotive engineer easily does his work, because of his knowledge and skill and mental make-up. A hundred Indians could not do it; the more there were of them, the worse it would be for the engine. The power of a successful physician consists wholly in his knowledge and skill and judgment. No amount of ignorant labor could do what he does. The management of railways and factories, rendering the physical labor employed many times as efficient, is the result of skill and knowledge and mental qualities. The most valuable ability to labor is that of *superintendence.* One man may save the labor of a thousand. A poor superintendent may cost his company many times the salary of a man competent for the place. The great labor-saving inventions are due to intelligence and knowledge. The power to invent is the power to labor; and one man by an invention may save the labor of a multitude.

Under the ability to labor we must also include all the knowledge and experience gained from past ages. This knowledge and experience can be used only as it is known by living men. There are "Lost arts." What the world possessed in them died with the men who understood them. If they are rediscovered, so much more is added to the power of labor.

Unlike the Natural Resources, which remain the same from age to age, Labor is a continually changing force. For the purpose of satisfying wants, its power has increased many times since civilization began, and is increasing with great rapidity to-day. A hundred men can do the work done by a thousand a century ago, not alone because of machinery; but because of the skill in using it, because of the knowledge of new methods. The high degree of skill and mechanical ingenuity shown in the United States is the result of training for generations. The natural aptitude is largely inherited. The power of the world to work, is the fine hand, and brain, and mind inherited from the past. All the knowledge in the world to-day, even the habit of labor, is inherited; and it is useless to expect to educate a savage race to a high degree of ability to work, except through generations. Labor, as a resource for satisfying wants, is the ability of men to do. It is more mental than physical. In this age, muscular power is the smallest part of it. The knowledge of Nature's resources and laws, as discovered by physical and chemical research, and the practical spirit and power of invention which enable the men of the present day to make use of the idle forces of the past,—to use steam and electricity where past ages employed human muscle,—these make up the greater part of the resource of Labor.

The ability of a people to labor, therefore, does not depend on their number, so much as on their physical and mental qualities. We should also add their moral qualities; since men of moral character, when the comparison is made between large numbers, are able to accomplish much more labor during a lifetime than others. The ability of the native white population of the United States exceeds by a thousand-fold that of an equal number of people in Central Africa. No mistake is greater than to estimate the ability of a nation to labor by the number of its people. The time may come when all the work that is done to-day can be done by one-tenth of the people now engaged. If this should be the case, the result would not be the idleness of the other nine-tenths, but the doing of more work, and the better satisfaction of wants.

DIRECTLY AND INDIRECTLY.—Labor satisfies wants *directly* or *indirectly :* Directly, when one does something for himself or another; indirectly, when he helps to produce some articles for use. As soon as a boy is old enough to wash and dress himself, he has begun to satisfy some of his own wants, *directly*. The amount of labor expended in doing for one's self and by members of a family in caring for one another, is a large part of all the manual labor performed. Most political economists leave it out of the account altogether, because it is not paid for. Such labor is not the only kind for the direct satisfaction of wants. The teacher, preacher, singer, lawyer, and physician satisfy wants *directly*, by teaching, preaching, conducting one's case at law, and prescribing when one is ill.

Farmers, on the other hand, satisfy wants *indirectly*. Their labor is employed in the production of commodities, wheat, corn, cotton, beef, etc., which commodities satisfy wants. Neither is it the labor of the artist, but the picture he has painted, that we want. He satisfies a want indirectly, through his picture.

Many of the older political economists divided laborers into "Producers and non-producers," which division has been very misleading, and was frequently supposed to reflect unfavorably on those classed as

THE ABILITY TO LABOR. 37

non-producers; whereas, many of the so-called non-producers are engaged in the most important work of the world. They do not produce commodities, for the reason that they satisfy wants *directly;* and the object which the world has is not production, but *the satisfaction of wants.* Some of the world's workers satisfy wants *directly*, by a short cut; others satisfy them in a more roundabout way, by producing something which can be used in satisfying wants. A singer satisfies wants, directly, when he sings before an audience; a sculptor satisfies a want, not directly, but by producing a statue from a block of marble, and the statue satisfies the want. Here are two artists, perhaps of equal rank; the one satisfies wants directly, the other indirectly. If it be asked, which class is engaged in the more honorable employment, the reply is, there is no difference so far as this division is concerned; since the employments usually counted the most honorable are divided between the two. The preacher, teacher and lawyer satisfy wants directly; the editor and author of books, indirectly. The distinction is, however, of the greatest economical importance, and of more importance in the consideration of Labor than of the other Resources.

CHAPTER III.

THE PRODUCTIONS OF HUMAN INDUSTRY.

It may at first appear that the goods produced by human industry are of so many kinds as to defy classification; yet a little reflection will show that nearly all of the most important fall at once into very few classes, and that for many reasons it is important that these few classes be sharply defined.

1. *Buildings*. A large part of all the produced wealth in the world is in buildings. They are a *permanent* resource; for while nothing made by man endures forever, these endure for many years. They are permanent in contrast with food, which is consumed in the satisfaction of hunger; or with clothing, which lasts perhaps a year, and when once worn is practically unfitted for other persons. Permanent resources once produced remain to satisfy wants for a long period, often for successive generations; while *consumable* resources must be replaced with new productions each year. One builds a house for a lifetime; he raises a new crop of wheat each year.

Buildings are of two classes: Residences, most public buildings, and others which satisfy wants *directly;* and factories and commercial buildings, which satisfy wants *indirectly*. A house is an object in itself. When one has gained it, perhaps at the cost of many years' labor, he feels that a very important want, both for himself and family, has been satisfied for his lifetime. The resource is permanent, and it satisfies wants *directly*. Dwellings must necessarily form a very large portion of all the produced resources in the world, since every family needs a dwelling of some kind; and most civilized men are willing to expend a large part of their labor in securing the use of one for their families.

Buildings which satisfy wants *indirectly* also compose a large portion of the produced wealth in the world. The costly stores and warehouses of a great city, the factories of cities and factory towns, nearly all the structures in the land, except residences, satisfy wants indirectly. Factories are erected, not as an end in themselves, but to produce something that will satisfy wants.

Buildings are therefore divided into two classes: Dwellings, with a few others satisfying wants directly; and buildings satisfying wants indirectly.

2. *Tools and Machinery.* Next to factories and buildings used for commercial purposes, come tools and machinery. Even tools form a considerable stock, since some must be in the hands of every workman; but the machinery in the modern factory, and all that in use in our present civilization, of itself exceeds the produced wealth of ancient times. With a few exceptions, tools and machinery satisfy wants indirectly; they are not an end, but the means of further production.

3. *Roads.* Roads include all improvements on land or water by which transportation, travel or com-

munication is facilitated; such as common highways, railroads, street railways, river and harbor improvements, canals, telegraph and telephone lines, etc. A lake or ocean needing no improvement is solely a resource of nature; ships sail over it as an emigrant drives his team over a trackless prairie. But when a highway is turnpiked and drained, a railroad bed is graded and blasted and ironed, telegraph lines are erected, rivers are cleared and dredged, and harbors are improved, the improvements are a part of the Productions of Human Industry. Roads are an important element of civilization. They include nothing but the track or the wires of a telegraph line. The wagons driven on the highway, the rolling stock of a railroad, the ship and the canal boat belong to the class of Tools and Machinery.

4. *Improvements on Land.* We must always distinguish sharply between land and its improvements. Land is the gift of nature, and can not be increased; improvements are the work of man. Both buildings and roads are usually regarded as improvements on land, and in law are classed as real estate. Land is so essential that it is impossible to produce many permanent resources without connecting them in some way with it. Buildings can not be erected except upon it; one must get possession of a piece of ground before he can build. Roads can be made only over it. But while buildings and roads are properly enough called improvements on land, they are so distinct, so numerous and important, that it is more convenient to put them in a class by themselves; and to reserve the

title "Improvements on Land" for those more closely connected with the soil.

The most important of these are improvements on agricultural land; such as the drainage of swamps, the increase in the fertility of the soil by well-known methods of cultivation—hedges, orchards, vineyards, fences, and all that goes to make a good farm better than land in a state of nature. Their market value may be more than that of the land itself. An interesting question is that of timber, and one's understanding of it is a good test of his grasp of the relation of land to improvements. In a new and heavily-wooded country the removal of timber is popularly regarded as an improvement. There is no way of making a farm except by clearing the forest. In after years the timber is greatly needed; the land would be more desirable with the timber on. The facts are, that timber is not land, but timber. It is always a blunder to misname anything. Timber is not land; but, like land, is one of the Resources of Nature. Unlike land, it is consumed in the using. As a mine is worked out and exhausted, so a forest is destroyed. A new settler may remove the timber to get at the land; but the simple fact is, he has destroyed the timber. When there is abundance of it, more than his generation wants, its loss will not be felt; and it enables him to get the benefit of the use of the land. When more people come, the timber is wanted and, if standing, would perhaps be worth more in the market than the land from which it was taken.

Improvements on agricultural land, in the main,

satisfy wants *indirectly*. A swamp is drained in order that it may produce better crops. Orchards are planted, not for the trees, but for the fruit they are expected to produce. Improvements on residence and public grounds, on the contrary, usually satisfy wants *directly*. A lawn in city or country is made to please the eye. Trees are planted, not for fruit, but for shade. One wants the lawn and the trees about his dwelling. So, public and private parks are improvements on land which satisfy wants directly.

If the reader will stop to think for a moment, he will see how large a portion of all the resources produced by human industry is included in these four classes. It is much more than half. If we were to stop our classification here, we should find the arranging of the greater part of Produced Resources in these four classes, of inestimable value in our further study. There remain, however:

5. *Finished Goods which Satisfy Wants Directly.* These are of two classes: *permanent*, and those which will be *consumed in the using*. Of the first, are articles like pictures and statuary. It is true, they will not last forever, but thousands of people may look at a painting without injury to it. These goods, like buildings, satisfy a want without being injured thereby. We can, therefore, afford to bestow great labor upon them; knowing that when once produced, they will remain for a long period to satisfy wants, perhaps of many people besides the owner. Some of this class of goods, of which household furniture is the most important example, have only a low-

er degree of permanency. They wear out with use; they cease to satisfy wants because of changes in style, etc. Nevertheless, they are often handed down from father to son, or more often from mother to daughter. Few people expect to furnish a house anew every year; the majority of people regard good furniture as purchased to last for many years, if not for a lifetime.

The second class of finished goods is those that are *consumed in the using*. The most important of these is the food supply. Clothing is not absolutely destroyed with once using, but is practically rendered worthless for the use of any other person, and is rapidly worn out.

Some goods will occur to the reader which seem to fall into one of these two divisions as readily as into the other. They are destroyed in the using, but they last for a considerable time. Since a year is the natural measure of the production of goods, those which are usually replaced year by year should always be classed as *consumable*. To be classed as *permanent*, goods should be capable of lasting, under favorable circumstances, at least the greater part of a lifetime. They should be goods which one does not expect to replace as he does the clothing he wears; they should be like books; while one may intend to buy other books on the same subject, he does not expect to replace the same book.

6. *Materials and Goods in Process of Production.* The aim of all production is to satisfy wants. Finished products may be buildings, or roads or tools

designed to aid in producing something else; but the final object is to produce something which will satisfy wants, *directly*. Thus, our last class was "Finished goods satisfying wants directly." There is a still larger class of goods in the *process of production*. Many of these are finished so far as one producer is concerned. Wool is to the farmer a finished product, but it does not satisfy wants in this condition. Cloth is considered by the manufacturer a finished product, but it is really only a material for further production. Not until it is made into clothing is it ready to satisfy wants. The quantity of materials, and goods which are destined to become materials, is many times greater than the finished products.

Of the completed products of human industry, satisfying wants directly, which are speedily consumed in the using, it is not desirable that the world should have a large stock on hand. The labor of preserving and taking care of these products for even one year is considerable. Wants change with the fashions. These commodities can be produced anew every year, and it is necessary only to have a stock sufficient to last from year to year, and to guard against all danger of failure. Improved land, good roads, good machinery, and skilled labor, are far more important than a stock of provisions and consumable goods; always assuming that there is a sufficient amount of the latter to last until more can be produced by ordinary methods.

Of domestic animals some will become food material, and some are used like machinery in the work of production.

The productions of human industry will, for convenience, frequently be called Produced Wealth. The use of the prefixes *Natural* and *Produced* will avoid any confusion with the idea of wealth as the term is used by some writers. Both Natural and Produced Wealth include many resources not covered by the term *wealth* as used by those who define it by the term *value*. It is not the intention here to enter into a discussion of the meaning of disputed terms. Let the reader attach whatever meaning to the word "Wealth" he has been accustomed; but regard these as two new terms, which are here defined. Natural Wealth is the Resources of Nature. Produced Wealth is the Resources Produced by Human Industry. The question of value does not enter into these definitions.

CHAPTER IV.
SOCIETY.

The fourth resource for the satisfaction of wants is Society. This is the presence and companionship of human beings, considered apart from their ability to labor. Robinson Crusoe led a dreary life, and the society of even his man Friday was appreciated. Society includes the home; and, in addition to the relations of father, mother, wife, brother, sister, the presence of companions, neighbors and friends satisfies many of the noblest wants of humanity. The drift toward the cities is partly to get in a crowd, to see and associate with more people.

The mere presence of human beings does not constitute society; it does not necessarily make society that satisfies the wants of others. Many of the productions of industry are only rubbish which we would pay something to have removed. So, there are men and women who are a curse to the other people of the earth. Some of them we remove to work-houses and prisons. Society may be at fault to some extent for their character—we are not now discussing that point—but, as they are, the earth would be better off without them. Churches and missionary societies succeed in reforming many of them; and one object of philanthropic work is to improve the character of the disagreeable and wicked, for the sake of others as well as for their own sake. It is necessary here only to call attention to the fact that not all human beings satisfy the want of others for society.

This want, indeed, can be met only by persons with habits and tastes to some extent like our own. Chinese may be society for Chinamen; but even if an American desires their labor, he seldom wishes their companionship; and if he has no use for their labor he would pay something to have them removed from his neighborhood. Social circles naturally form among people of the same race and nationality, and are limited to those whose habits are very similar.

The want satisfied by society is so real that it is often expressed by a high money value. A residence lot of a few feet front sells for twenty thousand dollars, when other lots equally near and convenient to the business center of the same city can be had for five thousand. They are equally desirable in every respect except the single one of the neighbors who live on the same street and in the vicinity. Fifteen thousand dollars is, in this instance, the commercial value of the society of a particular neighborhood.

The development of a society which shall better satisfy the wants of its members is as legitimate a subject for discussion in our science as the production of food or dwellings, but it is far more difficult.

Society Satisfies Wants Indirectly. Society satisfies want indirectly by affording opportunity for the division of labor, and by permitting the production of goods in large quantities.

The advantage of the division of labor—a technical
4

phrase made popular by Adam Smith—will be shown further on. Such division, by which each one does a particular kind of work, is possible only where there is a considerable number of people. If each man devotes his entire time to a single branch of labor, the number of workmen must be very large. It must be much larger than the number of trades and branches of trades, since in order that one man may work all the time at so simple a thing as bending piano wires, hundreds or thousands of men must be employed in each branch of the more common trades.

The advantage of producing goods in large quantities is well understood. Cotton prints are now manufactured at a cost of less than five cents a yard; if made in small quantities, they could not be produced at a cost of fifty cents. But cotton prints can not be made in large quantities unless there is a large number of people to use them. One person can teach thirty children of the same age and attainments as well as she could teach one, perhaps with more advantage to each. If there were only one child to be taught, the labor would be proportionately thirty times as great.

It is the satisfaction of human wants, so far as they can be satisfied by these four classes of Resources, that forms the subject of this volume. That is, the satisfaction of wants so far as they can be satisfied by the Resources of Nature, Labor, the Productions of Human Industry, and Society, or the presence and companionship of human beings.

CHAPTER V.

UTILITY OF THE RESOURCES.

Utility is the quality of an object which makes it useful, or fits it to satisfy human wants. Utility resides in the object. It is a quality of the object and not of the user. The quality of sweetness which is in sugar makes it useful and is its utility. This quality is not at all dependent on the number of people who use it, or on the quantity which may be desired. The popular idea of utility is the correct one. Iron, wood, water, air, grain, fruits—these are useful, or have utility. All Resources for the Satisfaction of Wants possess utility. It is the possession of this quality that makes them resources.

It is to be regretted that Professor Jevons, in his admirable work, "The Theory of Political Economy," uses the word "Utility" in the sense of "Value in Use." There are three ideas which we must keep distinct—Utility, Value in Use, and Value in Exchange. It has been the mistake of many political economists to attempt to dispense with one of the three, whereas not one of them can be spared. One who reads Professor Jevons, or other writers who have followed him, should remember that by "Utility" he means precisely what will hereafter be defined as Value in Use; and that the Utility here considered is an entirely different thing. It is a question of names, not of ideas.

50   RESOURCES FOR SATISFACTION OF WANTS.

It should be noticed that an article may have the utility of satisfying wants directly, as food and clothing; or of satisfying them indirectly, as the plow by which the farmer fits the ground for a crop.

An object may have more than one utility, and most objects have. Water, for example, has the utility of satisfying thirst, and thus of preserving life. It has a lower utility of cleansing, and a still lower utility of furnishing the means of navigation. Objects are used for their highest utility first; and when they are sufficiently numerous to satisfy the more important wants, lower utilities come into play. If one had an allowance of only a pint of water per day, it might all be needed for quenching thirst; but where water is abundant, it is used for less important purposes. These different utilities in the same object may be as distinct as different utilities in different objects. New utilities are constantly being discovered, sometimes in objects which have been used for other purposes, and often in objects heretofore useless. It was a great step forward when it was learned that anthracite coal could be burned. A utility of what seemed a black stone was discovered.

The utilities of many objects can be increased by human effort. It is one of the objects of labor to increase them. The knife-blade has a higher utility than the iron ore or the steel from which it was made. Great labor has been put forth to convert the steel into knife-blades; and it was expended solely to give more utility to the steel. Gain in utility is always a benefit to mankind, because it increases the power of

UTILITY OF THE RESOURCES. 51

the Resources in satisfying human wants. The greater the utilities, population remaining the same, the better can wants be satisfied.

1. THE UTILITIES OF THE RESOURCES OF NATURE.
—Strictly speaking, the Utilities of the Resources of Nature can seldom be increased. They are as they were created, and nearly all additions to them are classed as Produced Wealth. The ditch which drains the swamp, the fences and buildings put upon the land by man, are all Produced Wealth. The knife-blade itself is classed as Produced Wealth.

The land, the air and the water remain largely as they are from age to age. To some slight extent they are modified, usually more to their damage than to their improvement. Air may be vitiated by a manufacturing establishment, and its utility decreased. A stream of water may be polluted by the drainage of the factory, and its utility for drinking purposes destroyed. The natural fertility of land may be exhausted, and the forms of consumable natural wealth, such as coal and timber, are actually destroyed with the use, and their utility is gone. On the other hand, the atmosphere is sometimes purified by the drainage of the swamp, but this is a comparatively slight change. The general principle is that the utility of Natural Resources remains much the same from century to century.

There has been a continued discovery of new utilities of the Natural Resources, and this discovery is sometimes mistaken for an increase in the utility of the resources themselves. When it was first found that the red ore could be smelted, and wrought into iron bars, an unsuspected utility in this seeming stone was discovered. The world was so much the richer, just as an individual would be who should discover a buried treasure hidden on the estate he had inherited from his ancestors. There would be no more gold in the world than before, but he discovered that which was hidden. There have been many discoveries of new utilities in well-known objects. When it was learned that water could be converted into steam, and the steam into power, the world was so much the richer.

2. UTILITY OF PRODUCED WEALTH.—The utility of Produced Wealth, on the contrary, can be very greatly increased. Indeed, this is the main object of labor. Take a bar of steel and convert it into watch-springs; the utility is many times as great. Take lumber and brick, and build them into a dwelling; the utility is far greater than that of the materials. The wool produced by the farmer is manufactured, with great labor, into cloth and clothing. Indeed, the object of expending labor upon materials is to increase their utility; and the object of all labor, which does not satisfy wants directly, is to increase the utility of some part of Produced Wealth.

A very considerable portion of Produced Wealth consists in improvements on land, which may seem to be an increase in the utility of Natural Resources. A swamp is drained, and the waste land bears a crop. Sometimes Produced Wealth is so united with land as really to become a part of it, in which case the utility of the land is increased by human labor. It is usually much better to treat of all improvements on land apart from the land. They may be destroyed, but the land will remain forever.

Minerals and timber when once removed from the land are regarded as Produced Wealth. The timber is like a crop which can be grown again in years; and while minerals can not be replaced, their removal from the soil, and their great transformation, make it necessary to treat them as Produced Wealth. We need never lose sight of the element of Natural Wealth in them.

3. UTILITY OF LABOR.—The utility of labor is its power to satisfy wants, either directly or indirectly. We have before seen that great difference exists in the power of men to labor; that the services of some men will accomplish a hundred times as much as those of others; that is, they possess far more utility. There are, however, many utilities of labor. Most men have the power of doing a considerable number of useful things. Under modern civilization, each group of men learns to do things which others can not do; and they acquire skill, which makes their labor many times as useful.

The utility of labor can be very greatly increased. This is one of the objects of education, and almost the only object of learning a trade, or acquiring skill in any department. It would doubtless be profitable to the world to give even more attention to increasing the utility of the labor of the rising generation. With more general education and better training, there is no reason why the next generation might not be able to accomplish much more than the present, with no more exertion.

4. UTILITY OF SOCIETY.—It is one of the distinctive features of this book that it treats, not only of the subject of Economics from the point of view of human wants, and of the resources for their satisfaction, but that it also takes account of Society as one of the great resources for the satisfaction of wants, equal in importance to that of labor and produced wealth. As soon as men are provided with the lowest necessities of life, the desire for society becomes one of the strongest of all. The boy thirsts for companionship. He is not happy unless he can be with other boys. The condition of a single human being on an island is the most pitiable possible to conceive. From the lowest conditions of life to the highest, society is equally desired and equally important.

The utility of Society must be carefully distinguished from the utility of Labor. A good workman may be a thief, or a very undesirable companion. A pleasant companion may have little power of labor. Society and Labor are both embodied in human beings, but have nothing else in common.

As the utility of labor can be greatly increased by the education or training of the workman, the business manager, and the scientific investigator, so the utility of society can be greatly increased by the education of the people in morals and manners, in general intelligence, and in all that goes to make a desirable companion.

The utility of some parts of society is a negative quantity; so much less, or worse, than no society. It was the custom of England, years ago, to transport criminals beyond the high seas, in order to get rid of their society. Undoubtedly, if any village, and especially any city of considerable size, could be free from the presence of a certain portion of its people, it would be a much more desirable place to live in. This sort of society is a negative quantity. It is a damage to the city and the people; and the world would be better off if these undesirable persons did not exist. Occasionally undesirable society is found in connection with considerable labor power, and heartless capitalists are willing to inflict any sort of people upon a nation, if they can thereby secure labor cheaper, and make some money out of it. Such employers are the enemies of the well-being of the human race.

The improvement of society, that is, the increase in its utility for the satisfaction of wants, consists in eliminating undesirable elements, and in preventing their increase. Most of the recent immigration, however much it may add to the labor power of the country, introduces very undesirable elements of society. This is the practical objection to the Chinese. While they have labor power, their utility for the purpose of society is a negative quantity, and lowers the average utility of society as a whole.

Positive efforts for the increase of social utilities are those of the churches and schools, and all moral influences which tend to make men better companions. The present high utility of American society is very largely due to schools and churches, although inherited traits count for a great deal. Improvement in moral, intellectual, and social character is, of course, to be made mainly among the young. A proper education of the children of any country, provided it were free from the influence of immigration, would, in a few generations, greatly increase the utility of the society of the nation. Every city would be a far more desirable place of residence. Contrast life in a convict colony with life in a colony composed of Christian people! Contrast life among idiots, the stupid and ignorant, with life among intelligent and well-informed persons! Contrast life among the Indians with the life of a New England city or village! It is as important that we make provision for desirable society in the future as that we build houses and factories.

CHAPTER VI.
VALUE IN USE.

Value in Use depends both on Utility and the number and wants of the people. Nothing can have value which is not useful, but Value in Use shows how scarce an article is. So long as there are more objects than the people can possibly use, they have no value; but when the number of people increases, so that articles of any kind become scarce, this scarcity is expressed by Value in Use. The scarcer they become, the higher the value.

Value in Use must not be confused with *Value in Exchange.* Exchange Value is merely what one can get for a thing in the open market. There will be no confusion if we remember that Value in Use is what a thing is worth to use; Value in Exchange is what it is worth to sell. "Exchange" will be the subject of a subsequent book, and Exchange Value will, of course, be treated in that place.

Value in Use is the scarcity of useful things. It shows the relation between useful things and the number of people who desire them. Value always means scarcity, and high values are always unfortunate for the world. Let a traveler in the desert be perishing with thirst; an allowance of a quart of water per day would have the value of life to him. Water ordinarily has no value, because it is abundant. One of its *utilities* is that of preserving life, and when it becomes sufficiently scarce its value is equal to this utility. A gallon of water per day would have a higher value to this traveler than a single quart, but not greatly higher. The quart preserves his life. A gallon is convenient for cooling his face and hands, a minor consideration. A hogshead of water per day might have but little more value than a gallon, since a gallon would be all he could use. Where he has a hogshead per day, one quart is practically nothing, because he can spare any particular quart and still have more than he needs. If there were all the wheat that the world could use, its value would be much less than at present, and more people would be able to use wheat as an article of food instead of some cheaper grain. A high value shows great scarcity; that there is insufficient for the satisfaction of all wants. No values mean abundance. High values mean scarcity.

The popular notion that high values are desirable arises from the fact that each man desires a high *Exchange* Value for what he has to sell, in order that he may get as much of other things in return as possible. Value in Use is what a thing is worth to use. Value in Exchange is what it is worth to sell. Now, if one has something to sell, the higher its value, the more of other goods can he get for it. Hence, each man desires that the value of his own possessions be as high as possible, but he also desires that the value of all other things which he has to buy be as low as possible. The things he has to sell can only have a high value when they are scarce. A large crop lowers the price of grain; large production reduces the value of goods, sometimes almost to nothing. It is certainly to the interests of the world that goods be plenty. It would be fortunate for us if many other necessities of life were as plenty as the air and water, which, although they possess the highest Utility, seldom have any Value at all, simply because they are abundant.

It is not easy for us to get this idea firmly in our minds, that Value means scarcity; that is, the scarcity of useful things. Their Value in Use shows how scarce they are. Neither must we forget that the difference between Value in Use and Value in Exchange is that one is what a thing is worth to use, and the other is what it is worth to sell, or what one can get for it. An article may have a very high Value in Use to a particular person, though he could get nothing for it in the market. The Value in Exchange is nothing. So a horse may be worth nothing to a man to use, since he has no use for him; yet he may have a Value in Exchange, since he can be sold for something. Indeed, it is when the Value in Exchange is higher than the Value in Use of the article that exchange takes place.

Measure of Value in Use.—We estimate the Value in Use of any particular object by comparing it with some other with which we are more familiar. The Value in Use is the satisfaction which the object gives to the user. He compares this satisfaction with that from some other object. He says: " The coat is worth more to me than the picture, seeing that in my circumstances it satisfies my wants better." In common language we are continually comparing the wants of things in this way. "This is worth more to me than that; we would rather have this than a dozen of the other."

An Average Value in Use.—It will readily be seen that the Value in Use of an object to one person is sometimes a hundred times as great as to another; perhaps because the first has all he wants of it, and the second has none. Its average Value in Use becomes the basis of Value in Exchange, and will be considered farther on.

Value in Use Decreases with Quantity.—It will also be seen that the more one has of a given object the less its value becomes to him, until, when he has more than he can use, the value of any particular portion is nothing. One suit of clothes is a necessity, and has a very high Value in Use. A second is a convenience, but has a much lower value, since one can very easily get along without it. Ten suits have more value than two, but very little more; while, perhaps, a hundred suits of clothing would have no more Value in Use to most men than ten, since ten would satisfy all their wants. This is also true of money, which represents all purchasable commodities. It is not true that a dollar is worth as much to one man as to another. To the laborer in a city who receives one dollar per day, that one dollar may mean support of himself and his family, and have the Value in Use of life itself, or of life out of the poorhouse. A second dollar per day has also a very high value to him, but not so much as the first. Ten dollars per day would have a still higher value, since it would enable him to satisfy more wants; but not five times as great a value as two dollars per day since the wants satisfied by the additional eight dollars are by no means to be compared with those supplied from the first two. To one whose income is a hundred dollars per day, an addition of a single dollar would have very little Value in Use, since the additional wants which it would enable him to supply would be of small consequence. Compare the additional wants which that dollar would supply with the food and clothing of the man who receives but one dollar a day. The greater one's income, therefore, the less is a dollar worth to him. That is, the Value in Use of money, after one has a certain income, decreases very rapidly.

BOOK II.
POPULATION.

BOOK II.

POPULATION—THE NUMBER OF PEOPLE WHOSE WANTS ARE TO BE SATISFIED.

INTRODUCTION — The Relation of Wants to Resources is
Shown by Value in Use, ... 65

CHAPTER I. POPULATION AND THE RESOURCES OF
NATURE, ... 66

CHAPTER II. POPULATION AND LABOR, ... 87

CHAPTER III. POPULATION AND PRODUCED WEALTH, . 96

CHAPTER IV. POPULATION AND SOCIETY, ... 103

CHAPTER V. THE LAW OF THE INCREASE OF POPULATION, ... 116

CHAPTER VI. APPLICATIONS OF THE LAW OF THE INCREASE OF POPULATION, ... 135

BOOK II.
POPULATION:
THE NUMBER OF PEOPLE WHOSE WANTS ARE TO BE SATISFIED.

It is obvious that the absolute extent of the Resources for the Satisfaction of Wants is of less importance than their relative extent, when compared with the population. A million dollars is a large fortune for a single family; it divides into ten smaller fortunes for ten families. If divided among a hundred families, they have ten thousand each. If there are a thousand families, it means only one thousand for each; if the families number ten thousand, the million becomes only a hundred dollars for each. The satisfaction of the wants of the people depends not so much on the absolute wealth of a country as on its wealth relative to the number of people.

The relation between Wants and Resources shows itself in *Value in Use*. In the last chapter, we saw that Value in Use always means scarcity of useful things; the scarcer an article, the higher the value. But articles become scarce through increase in the number of the people, as well as by the diminution of the goods. Value in Use shows the relation between Wants and Resources.

CHAPTER I.

POPULATION AND THE RESOURCES OF NATURE.

It is obvious that the Resources of Nature can not be increased. Man has had nothing to do with creating them, and as they were in the beginning so will they remain, except so far as Nature, by earthquakes, by upheavals, and the wearing down of the land by wind and rain, and the action of her own powers, changes them. Land, in the sense used in Political Economy, is nothing but the extension of the earth's surface, and the earth's surface can not be increased. The atmosphere remains the same, contaminated and purified by Nature's chemical laws. The water is lifted from the ocean's surface and blown over mountain and prairie, to be carried by the rivers back to the sea; but the volume of water on the earth's surface remains the same. The forces of Nature act continually; gravitation has pulled with the same power since man appeared, and will doubtless continue the same as long as the world shall exist. A few of the less important Resources of Nature, such as timber and wild animals, may be destroyed; but no increase of Nature's resources comes with increase in population.

Let no one suppose, however, that increase of population necessarily means less of the Resources of Nature for each one, because there is enough for a vast multitude. One can drink as much from a pitcher as from a fountain. A mountain spring which feeds a river may supply a hundred families as well as one. If there are few people living by it, the immigration of several more does not mean less water for each. The newcomers use what before was unused. In an earlier day, an emigrant settled on a vast prairie, and could use but a small portion of the land about him. He welcomed neighbors who would take a claim next his own. He had all the land he wanted; and there was plenty for others. The newcomers took from him no Resources of Nature, and added to his resources that of Society.

The earth was made for a great population. It is to be subdued and filled with people. It may be filled, however, or any particular country may be filled, so that all the Resources of Nature are in use by some one. The population about the spring may be so great that there is not water enough for all; and can be supplied only by bringing it from afar, either by hand with great labor, or by elaborate works of engineering, at great expense. The prairie may become so thickly settled that when the farmer's sons want a farm, they must be content with a few acres, where their father had hundreds. There is no more land in a State with ten million people than when there were only ten thousand.

The Resources of Nature do not increase with the population. They seem unlimited so long as there is more than can be used; the pressure begins to be felt as soon as all the land is occupied. It is a very slight pressure at first, and increases as the Resources of

Nature appear scarce, and become more valuable with the increase of population.

DISCOVERY.—While the Resources of Nature are no greater now than when man appeared on the earth, they were not all discovered at once. To the ancients, all beyond the sea was boundless speculation. Little by little, and again by great leaps, man has pressed on to see what treasures nature had for him. He discovered America. He sailed around the globe. He pressed far up into the frozen latitudes of the North. He has crossed the dark continent, and penetrated into darkest Africa. There is not much more for him to discover in the way of mere extension of the earth's surface.

It is not so with the *Forces* of Nature. Here, indeed, great discoveries have been made. The last few years have been a great period of discovery in the methods of using power by means of electricity. We realize now, as our fathers did not, something of the magnitude of the power stored up in nature which belongs to man to use. There is no reason to believe that discoveries on this line are at an end.

There is much mineral wealth yet undiscovered. The world is waiting for a cheap method of producing aluminum from common clay. No one knows whether such cheap extraction is possible. If it is, another resource of nature may be made available.

We must distinguish sharply between discovery and production. The land of the world exists, whether civilized man has explored it or not. Minerals are buried in its depths, whether he has staked out his mines or not. Natural gas filled the porous rock and sand a hundred years ago, as truly as when it was reached by the first drill. The laws which govern the use of electricity were the same a thousand years ago.

When it is said, therefore, that the Resources of Nature can not be increased, it does not follow that provision may not be made for supplying the wants of more people. Natural Resources may be discovered, and we can never tell when we have completed our discoveries. The wealth of nature is great: how great we do not know. It is certainly far greater than any one in the last century imagined.

A very considerable portion of the labor of the world is now engaged in discovery, rather than in production. He who finds more of nature's wealth, and makes it available to mankind, renders a service as truly as he who produces a machine from the crude iron.

A LIMIT TO NATURAL RESOURCES.—It is evident that, notwithstanding discovery, there must be a limit to Natural Resources, though we can not with certainty say where that limit is. We know what we have; each new discovery shows that there has always been something we did not see; but discovery is limited to what there is to discover. When Columbus touched land in the Western hemisphere no one knew what might be found beyond the coast line. We know now that we have reached the limit; that we have found, in outline, all the land there is to find outside the frozen zones. The limit to discovery was the land that actually existed. No explorer can find what is not there. The discovery of the forces of nature must be limited to the forces that exist. We simply find what is.

How Many People will the Resources of Nature Support with Comfort?—*Quantity of Land Required for Residence Purposes.*—Land is used for three purposes: residence, manufacturing and commerce, and agriculture. It might seem to the savage that there could never be so many people in the world as to make the land required for mere residence a matter of any consequence. But not only is the acreage used for residence very considerable when each has all he wants, but the most desirable residence land is extremely limited. A rough measure of the land desired for residence is the common village lot. In cities few families are able to afford the land they need. In the country village, where land is comparatively cheap, so that a little, more or less, does not greatly add to the cost of a home, we are likely to find the average man using all the land he wants. The most common size of lots in such villages is four rods by eight (66 x 132 feet), including, to the center of the street in front, one-fourth of an acre. Many residents desire acre lots. The amount of land one desires in a well-regulated village is limited by the annual expense of maintaining walks and streets in front, lighting streets, etc., and of keeping his own ground in proper order. One such lot is all that the majority of people wish to take care of. If we accept this common village lot as a standard, allow something for cross streets, park, and grounds for school and other public buildings, and something for the few families who desire larger grounds, sometimes five or ten acres, we shall have, in round numbers, two thousand residences to the square mile. This is a convenient, practical estimate of the amount of land desired for residence purposes by the majority of the people, if it costs nothing. Smaller lots than these bring people closer together than most of them desire to live. Larger lots put neighbors farther away than many desire, and add to the expense of maintenance of the ground and streets. It is to be remembered that this measure is not assumed; it is the one found in existence in thousands of villages. It is certain that the average family desires more, rather than less, land than this.

Two thousand residences to the square mile means a population of ten thousand people. Where more than this live within a square mile, the land is overcrowded for the highest welfare of all. In cities there are frequently more than ten times this number—people packed tier above tier, ten stories high; but even when supplied with all modern conveniences, they lack the ground, sunlight, and the air. How desirable is a little land about a residence in a great city, is shown by the price that wealth pays for it. Grounds about a dwelling become a luxury which only the rich can afford. The wants of those who are deprived of them can not be said to be satisfied. The horrible condition of the tenement houses of the poor in the large cities has been so often described that the description need not be repeated. Something of this is due to the habits of the inmates, something to poorly constructed buildings; but more to the lack of land. A little ground about a dwelling is a great sanitary measure, even for those who care nothing for sanitary laws. One of the problems of the modern philanthropist is to break up the population of the densest portion of the cities, and scatter the people over a wide extent of country.

When a residence district is overcrowded, the erection of buildings becomes more costly. A two-story house in a village can be built at a comparatively low cost. Where buildings are ten stories high, foundations must be deep and massive, and walls heavy. They must be nearly fire-proof, to prevent the danger of a whole city being swept away in a night. When buildings are low and isolated, they cost comparatively little; and the space between them, of itself, affords protection against an extensive fire.

In a densely populated residence district, the desire for land can never be perfectly supplied, and the limited satisfaction is had at greatly increased cost.

In round numbers, then, we may say that ten thousand people per square mile is the limit for the simple purpose of residence, where the desire for residence land is satisfied. For other reasons, people may prefer to live where the population is a hundred thousand per square mile, but at a sacrifice of the desire and need of land. In the Jewish quarter of New York the population is estimated at 330,000 to the square mile. The most densely populated portion of London has 170,000 to the square mile. It is to be remembered, also, that the entire country can not be built over in this way. A city implies great stretches of land or water beyond, separating it from other cities. It is because of the free air in this open country around, that the densely populated city is rendered habitable.

On the other hand, where the limit of overpopulation is not passed, a certain density of population is of great advantage. The anxiety of a new country for settlers is due in part to land speculators, but it is also caused by a popular appreciation of the fact that the presence of a considerable number of the right sort of people is a mutual advantage. Nearly all of these advantages are obtained long before overcrowding begins. A good public school has seven or eight grades below the high school. The course in the latter is three or four years, making from ten to twelve distinct classes from the beginning to the end. These classes can be taught to much better advantage when separated. In order that there may be pupils for classes in the higher grades, there must be enough for two or three schools in the lower—at least five hundred pupils in all; and seven or eight hundred could be taught more economically. Since more than one-fourth of the entire population is of school age, schools with five hundred pupils mean only a total population of two thousand, if all persons between the ages of six and eighteen are in school, as they should be. In a high school the classes should not be as large as in the lower grades, and one hundred scholars are sufficient for a four years' course. The number of persons between the ages of fourteen and eighteen, fifteen and nineteen, or sixteen and twenty—a period of four years—is about seven per cent of the entire population. Villages of two thousand will have, on an average, one hundred and forty persons who should be in a high school. A population of two thousand is required to sustain good schools economically. Unfortunately, most pupils are compelled to leave school at an earlier age, so that a somewhat larger population is now required to sustain a good high school in an economical way. We may hope that the day will come, when it will be the exception that any one leaves school under eighteen or twenty years of age.

With the diverse religious views of the people of the United States, several churches are likely to be maintained in each village or city. Any minister prefers to preach to a congregation of three hundred, rather than less. It is pretty well agreed among the clergy that it is better that a church consist of at least four or five hundred members. Some hold that larger churches should be divided, but no one would place the desirable limit below three hundred. To gather churches of this size, of even four religious denominations, means at least four or five thousand people.

There is reason to believe that the fuel of the future, in towns large enough to sustain a plant, will be gas. Rock gas has shown us how convenient such fuel is. It is freely stated in many cities that if the supply of natural gas were to fail, the pipes would be utilized for the distribution of manufactured gas for fuel. The experiment of fuel gas for dwellings is sure to be attempted. To make its success possible, there must be a considerable population. Coal-gas works can not be erected and maintained for a few families.

POPULATION AND THE RESOURCES OF NATURE. 75

What is true of gas is also true of water works. Gas and water, distributed under pressure, are now among the common conveniences of modern life. Neither can be had in a hamlet.

The necessity of a considerable number of people for the maintenance of shops, stores, and the thousand conveniences of a city, is apparent to all. To say just where the line lies between the greatest convenience and overcrowded territory is, of course, impossible. The largest city has some advantages over the next smaller. It must not be forgotten that many of these advantages belong to it simply because it is larger than others. The best of everything is likely to drift to the metropolis. If it were not half as large, the best would still be there, so long as there was no larger place. Oliver Wendell Holmes thought the jealousy of the country village was because the city drained it of its best men. It is not the absolute, but the relative size, that determines where the best men of any calling go, and there can be but one largest.

In round numbers, we may say that a city of five thousand intelligent people, of the same race and general methods of living, make possible *nearly* all the substantial advantages which come from the massing of population. As good public schools may be maintained as are found in the largest city, at far less expense and risk. Churches of the more prominent denominations can be well maintained. Gas and water works can be economically operated. Merchants will not be able to keep as large a variety of some lines of goods, as if there were more people to sell to, but with all the more common goods they can supply their customers as well as any city. We have assumed an intelligent American white population. Cities differ greatly in this respect, and there are many places of ten thousand inhabitants which do not afford the advantages to be found in others of five thousand. It is evident that here, as elsewhere, the greatest advantage is found in the "golden mean," where population is neither too sparse nor too dense.

Only a small part of the land of this nation is now required for residence purposes; but the scarcity is no less real because confined to cities and towns. Some land is not well suited for residences. Some is much more desirable than other on account of natural location. The desire to live in cities is not alone on account of the crowd; it is because of the factories and the opportunity of obtaining employment. The scarcity of residence land in the city may be caused by artificial means; yet with certain methods of factory production it is necessary to bring large numbers of people together during the day. They must live somewhere, and the natural limits of residence land must be taken into account. The production of goods may be carried on with less labor in a densely populated place; but, on account of the scarcity of land in that vicinity, the cost of satisfying the wants of the laborers is far greater. Rapid and cheap transportation, by which persons are carried miles away from their work at the close of the day, is some relief. A better provision is the moving of factories to the country.

Land Required for Factories and Commerce.—

The quantity of the best land for factories and commerce is very limited. In a new country there may be water-power enough for all mills and factories. As population increases, the best mill-sites are soon taken. Where there are but few people, there is plenty of room in the best harbors for all ships which visit their coast. As the people multiply, the best wharf-ground is taken; and that must be very poor which can be had for nothing. Later, any land which can be made available, even with great expense for improvement, commands a high price. All this shows that certain kinds of land, land suitable for manufacturing and commercial purposes, becomes scarcer as population increases. People must use inferior sites, or improve other sites at greater cost. They must do with less room than is desirable. It is not as easy to estimate the actual amount of land needed for manufacturing and commerce as for residence. The needed acreage is not great, but the acres fitted for the purpose are few. There are few harbors on the sea coast, and the wharf lines are limited. Up to a certain limit the pressure is scarcely felt. When that limit is passed, a larger population may be of advantage in some respects; but, for this purpose, it means proportionally less for the people, with great danger of monopoly by the few.

Land Required for Agriculture. — The larger portion of the land in civilized countries is used for agriculture. The Indian wants thousands of acres to roam over. In Great Britain, a considerable portion of the country is enclosed in parks for hunting and private pleasure, showing the desire for great pleasure-grounds. This fact indicates that in the future there may be more great public parks for the people; and, for many reasons, a larger part of the land than is now devoted to that purpose, in the older parts of the United States, might well be maintained in park or forest, for the good of all. No doubt a fair satisfaction of the better wants of mankind would considerably reduce the acreage of land now used for agriculture. Nevertheless, the price of agricultural land shows the scarcity of the more desirable portions. Although the atmosphere is essential to life, it brings no price, because there is more of it than can be used. For the same reason, land is often sold in new countries for less than the cost of surveying; because there is so much land, and so few people. In European countries, it sells for what seems, to an American farmer, an extravagant figure; because there is so little land, and so many people. The Western ranchman likes to measure his ranch in square miles; the Western farmer thinks a hundred and sixty acres a moderate farm. There are more people as we travel from the West to the East, with less land for each. Within a certain limit higher culture produces more, with less labor, from the smaller farm. After this limit is passed, although the amount of produce from an acre can still be increased, it is with greater proportional labor, so that the laborer gets less than before. This is the origin of the famous phrase, "diminishing returns."

DIMINISHING RETURNS.—Diminishing returns does not mean a smaller return from land, but a smaller return from labor; not a smaller return from labor in factories, but a smaller return from labor on land.

The Western cattle king, now passing away, valued land very lightly. One of them, perhaps, owns some hundreds of acres by the streams, and has the title to a strip which shuts others out of a considerable region beyond. He may have used Government land, pasturing his herds in common with the other kings, branding the calves at the annual "round-up," and enforcing the property right of his brand with his Winchester rifle, and a band of determined cowboys. Not that he often had to fight for his rights. There was a mutual understanding that they were to be respected. The returns to labor were enormous; the returns from an acre of land, very small. A dozen men could tend a great herd of cattle that pastured on thousands of acres of land. Great fortunes were made by the owner; which, even if divided equally among all the men employed, would have given each one several times the compensation he could have earned in the older States. It is not surprising that such cattle kings resisted the opening of the country to settlement in farms of one hundred and sixty acres.

The hundred-and-sixty-acre farmer, however, gets a large return from his labor compared with the five-acre farmer. He does not cultivate his land so well, but he cultivates more of it with less labor, and the total return to him is far greater. Illinois has a reputation as a great corn State, but the average yield of corn per acre in Illinois is less than in Ohio. There are more acres planted. The Illinois farmer plants a field of forty or eighty acres, does most of the work by two-horse machinery, and gets a large crop for the labor bestowed. The Ohio farmer plants perhaps ten acres to the other's forty, bestows as much labor on a ten-acre field as an Illinois farmer on forty acres, and gets more corn to the acre, but not four times as much. He does not get as many bushels for each day's work. If one asks why he does not plant more acres, the obvious reply is that he has no more acres to plant. The price of land is so much higher than in Illinois that he can not afford to buy more. There are more people, more farmers, with less land for each.

To the English farmer it is a surprise to see land in Ohio cultivated so poorly. American farming appears slovenly. The reply is, it pays better to work more land than to give the high English culture. The American farmer gets a greater return for his labor, but not so much from an acre of land.

It is a sort of stock argument with some that we ought to cultivate our land better. Part of the apparent force of this statement lies in the pride of a nice farm. A farmer owes it to his neighbors to keep his farm in good order, and to keep down unsightly weeds, whether it pays or not. It is also true that, up to a certain limit, more labor, better cultivation, pays. If the average production of wheat be fifteen bushels per acre, it is possible that if one will bestow twice the labor, and double the cost of fertilizers, etc., he can get thirty bushels. That is, without regard to the price of his land, by doubling the cost of production he can double the product. But how is it, after he reaches the thirty-bushel product? If he now doubles the labor on a single acre, will he get sixty bushels? If so, would again doubling the labor on an acre bring a hundred and twenty bushels? Every farmer can tell the foolishness of such an attempt. He will point to a slovenly farmer, who gets half a crop; and say that if that man would work twice as hard he would get twice as much off his land; but when one has already brought his land up to a certain state of cultivation, which, in this country, is called good farming, it is impossible to get increased returns in proportion to the increase of labor and cost. Every good farmer knows that more work will bring better crops, but not in proportion. Doubling the labor and expense may increase the crops twenty-five or fifty per cent.; but it is more profitable to work more land.

So much effort has been made to break the force of this obvious truth—as certain as the axioms of geometry—that we can afford to look at it from another point of view. A good American farmer who owns one hundred and sixty acres of land is visited by three Englishmen, who tell him that he does not work land as they do in England, and that it would pay him to cultivate it better. They propose that he divide his farm among the four; he to retain the forty acres with dwelling house and buildings, and to give them forty acres of bare land apiece. Say they: "Now, you just put as much labor and capital on this forty acres as you have on the one hundred and sixty, and you will make as much money, and we will all have a farm apiece." An American farmer would not be caught with this chaff. He knows he could get more off any forty acres of his farm, but not four times as much. If he is a good farmer, he has cultivated his land nearly up to the point of diminishing returns; that is, additional labor and capital applied to his land will not bring as great a return as that now bestowed. It would pay him better to work more land, provided the additional land could be had for nothing.

Whenever an accurate calculation shows that it will pay better to cultivate additional land, *rent free*, than to put more work on that under cultivation, the point of *diminishing returns* has been reached.

The limits of diminishing returns may be reached in one country, but not in another; in one State, but not in the entire United States. The only thing that is sure is, that there is a limit to the returns to labor on agricultural land. When it is passed, land is becoming scarce in proportion to the population. It may support twice the present number of people, but at an increased cost of labor. A point would be reached— has been reached in many countries of the world— where the average man must be content with less food, or poorer food and clothing, than if there were fewer people for the land to support. Like Lot and Abraham, the land is not able to bear them. The remedy at that time was emigration. It is the remedy which the Old World is trying, in shipping to us its surplus population.

Calling a Farm by Some Other Name.—The last attempt to break the logic of the law of diminishing returns is to call a farm a factory. There are some people who take great delight in calling a thing by some other name, with the idea that the change of name will change the thing. The object in calling a farm a factory is to assume that agricultural produce can be manufactured like cotton cloth, at less expense for large quantities than for small. The suggestion is to use fertilizers of the highest strength, containing the elements of the crop to be raised. One Frenchman proposes to warm the soil by buried steam-pipes, and to transform the whole land into a reeking swamp of the torrid zone. The answer is that, even if the law of diminishing returns did not apply here, as it does, there is a limit to the power of the air and the sunlight. We may have a few city hotbed vegetable gardens, because of the wide expanse of country between. The air sweeps over the prairie and the farm, and its volume is sufficient to purify the city, and for the hotbed garden. There is a limit to the amount of concentrated fertilizers, and decaying vegetable and animal matter, that may with impunity be heaped on a given space of ground, and transformed into vegetation. The experiment of sewage farms has been tried as a means of disposing of the sewage of cities; the growth of vegetation is rank and unfit for human food; where it has been fed to cows, there have been serious doubts of the wholesomeness of their milk. It is a good way of disposing of the sewage of a city, but it would be most, unfortunate if the whole country were transformed into one vast sewage farm. Great spaces of clear, open country are needed for the sake of densely populated cities—spaces occupied by ordinary farms, with nature's methods of production, not forced much beyond that of the English agriculture.

It is impossible, however, to increase the production of land, even by the most artificial means, beyond certain limits, without increasing the cost of production. It is impossible to get rid of the law of diminishing returns. There is a limit to the number of bushels of wheat that can be raised to the acre, even though the ground be heated by steam-pipes, and overcharged with fertilizers, until the grain is unfit for use. When the limit is reached, the wheat will be produced at ten times the cost to a Dakota farmer.

All improvements in agriculture are to be welcomed. The limitations imposed are found in the extent of the earth's surface, the air, the sunlight, and the natural forces. The earth might have been larger than it is. The extent of land might have been greater, and that of water less; but we have only so many square miles, only so many acres, in a given division. The earth is large enough for vast multitudes, for numbers of which no man can form a vivid conception; but it would be foolish to shut our eyes to the limits of the land and its productive capacity.

The consideration of the law of diminishing returns has been a little tedious to the reader, yet it was scarcely possible to make it shorter or simpler. Without an understanding of it, we should make great mistakes. Ignorance of this natural law has permitted many intelligent men to fall into laughable absurdities.

VALUE IN USE OF THE RESOURCES OF NATURE.—The Value in Use of land is determined by the number and character and condition of the people who desire to use it, or on whom its use depends. The land on which the city of Chicago stands was a few years ago worthless because there was nobody to use it. There was a vast unoccupied territory to the west of it. There were a few settlers, but the land had no value, because value means scarcity. As soon as this Western land was occupied, there was need of a commercial metropolis, and the natural place for this is a harbor on the lake. The site of Chicago now comes into use because of the people west of it. Very little value is given to any particular city lot by the improvements on that lot itself. The value comes from the people who live on other land about it. Improvements on one lot give value to others in the neighborhood, because they ensure a large and better population.

The value of land is not determined alone by the population immediately about it, but often by that thousands of miles distant. The value of land in the Dakotas is influenced by the number and character of the people in London. Dakota land has the utility of producing wheat, but would have no more value than water unless there were people to eat that wheat. The population of the British isles thus increases the value of land in Dakota. Were there fewer people in England, or were they unable to afford wheat as an article of diet, there would be no foreign demand. With the present state of commerce, the value of land is often affected by the population of very distant places, and by the convenience of communication and transportation. Land is no longer scarce or plenty with sole reference to the people in the immediate neighborhood. It may be scarce with reference to those who draw their supplies from it half way round the globe. The value of the land suitable for raising tea in India and China and Japan, will be affected by the number of people in the entire earth, and by their tastes; that is, their wants. The question is not, Is such land scarce with reference to the people in India? but, Is it scarce with reference to the people of the earth? The value of any given piece of land is the scarcity of that kind of land, or of land which people like as well as this; and its scarcity is caused by the number of people who want it. Utility of land remaining the same, it becomes valuable in proportion to its scarcity, and its scarcity is increased with the number of people dependent on it, and with the development of their wants.

VALUE OF OTHER NATURAL RESOURCES.—Fortunately, most of these are so plenty as to have no value, either in use or exchange, except under unusual circumstances. In the well-known story of the Black Hole in Calcutta, there was not air enough for all the prisoners; and those who got the little there was lived, while the others died. The utility of air was no greater than before, but its scarcity gave it the value in use of life itself. The atmosphere is often injured by the exhalations from swamps, or the products of factories. Here pure air, if it could be furnished, would have a Value in Use.

Wild animals, timber, and other useful natural objects, may become valuable as population increases, through their scarcity.

CHAPTER II.

POPULATION AND LABOR.

The Resource of Labor, or rather of the ability to perform labor, differs from the Resources of Nature in almost every respect. It is embodied in the people whose wants are to be satisfied. One of the mistakes of the orthodox English school of political economy, which has done so much for the science, is in considering Labor too much as a machine, or as something apart from the people. It was, of course, assumed that the laborer must eat and be clothed, but the steam-engine must also be supplied with coal, and there was an unconscious tendency to treat of the laborer as if he were an engine rather than a man. This tendency was not because of any heartlessness on the part of the investigators, many of whom would have given their own lives for the welfare of humanity; but was rather the result of incorrect methods of study, and a mistake in the definition of the subject on which they wrote. We are to keep in mind the fact that we are dealing with men — men with wants and power to labor, both embodied in the same individual. We can not separate the laborer from the man whose wants are to be satisfied. We may consider, now his power to labor, and again his wants as man; but in each case we are to remember the other.

The resource of Labor differs from the Natural Resources in that it *can* be increased. We see that there is no more land in the world to-day, no more air, water, or minerals, than there were thousands of years ago. There will be no more thousands of years hence. The extent of the Resources of Nature is entirely unaffected by the increase of population. But the increase of population is likely to bring more laborers into the field. The more people, the more there are to work; and there is no reason why the ability to labor should not keep pace with the increase of population. If the islands of Great Britain were so full that there was not room enough in all the land for a house for each family, there would be great scarcity of Natural Resources (in fact, people would die off long before that point was reached), but there need be no scarcity of labor. Labor would be a drug in the market; there would be more of it than could by any possibility be used. Land, air, sunlight, water, the products of the soil—all these would be at a premium. We are always to guard against the mistaken notion that any one resource is sufficient for the satisfaction of wants. To Adam Smith belongs the glory of bringing into clearer light the importance of Labor, and it has since been the basis of many a treatise on Political Economy. But any system of economics built on Labor alone is false, because Labor alone is useless. So, Natural Resources without Labor are useless. Each is like the half of a pair of shears—they must be riveted together.

But because the ability to labor may be expected to increase with the increase of population, it by no means follows that it always does so. The ability of any nation to labor is never in proportion to the number of its people. It is the *sort* of men, rather than the number of men, which determines the power of a nation. If the reader will recall what was said in an earlier chapter, he will at once see how little the number of people, and how much the character of the people, has to do with determining a nation's ability to do. It is not so much the mere muscular power as the vital energy, which determines its use. Even in this respect, a good American workman is worth five or ten times as much as the men of many nations of the earth; but in intellectual power, the power of adapting means to ends, power of inventing, ability to use the Resources of Nature, he may be worth hundreds or thousands of indolent Africans.

We may imagine, therefore, the population of a country to remain stationary, as does that of France, and the power of labor to increase with great rapidity, perhaps to be multiplied many times during a single generation. Let us suppose a few hundred thousand people, for convenience, isolated on an island. They are people of the average ability of those in the United States, and are living as we do here. Let it be agreed that every boy and girl shall receive the best training and education that can be had from the most competent instructors in the little nation. There are manual training schools, apprenticeship in various trades under the workmen most competent to teach, intellectual culture—in short, all is done that can be done for the development, education, mental, physical, and technical training of each child in the State. Who can doubt that the ability of the second generation to labor would be double that of the first, though its numbers should be exactly the same? There would be some increase in the average physical ability, in muscular power and vital energy; but this would be of little consequence compared with the general and technical knowledge—the knowing how. Even the latter would be small in comparison with the enormous power of invention which would follow so general education, by means of which the Resources of Nature would be used to better advantage, and results accomplished beyond the power of any number of ignorant though muscular men. Labor is something more than muscular exertion. Some one has said that it consists in moving things. It would be nearer the truth to say it consists in moving things to the right place. Knowing what is the right place, and the method of moving with the least exertion, is the greatest part of it. On the other hand, the population might be doubled by the immigration of Poles or Italians, but the power of labor would not be proportionally increased.

It is not alone the efficiency of the laborers, but the proportion of laborers to idlers, that must be taken into account. In some nations, at some times, labor has been counted a disgrace. The citizen lived for war, the hunt and chase. Even at the present day, in European countries, there is a class of wealthy men who do little toward the satisfaction of wants, and procure the services of others, by inherited fortunes. Even in this country, we sometimes hear it regretted that there is no leisure class; that is, no idle class. This is partly because we are a new country, and population is not yet too dense. There is still among us a respect for the man who works by hand or brain. Our most honored citizens have been great lawyers, great physicians, great preachers, and men who have conducted large business enterprises. In England, the most learned physician and the most successful business man are held to occupy a position decidedly inferior to that of an idling nobleman, living on the inheritance of the past or debts contracted in the present. There is a decided tendency in this country toward the same condition of affairs; but, nevertheless, a larger proportion of our people are engaged in some form of active employment than in any other nation in the world.

The power of labor in a nation, other things being equal, is greatest when the largest number of people work. The power of labor in a new country, such as a newly settled State in the West, is likely to be greater than in an older country, because a larger proportion of the people are actively employed. Many of the brightest and most intelligent young men go West. The older, and those unable to endure hardships, are more likely to remain at home. A population composed entirely of men and women between the ages of twenty and fifty, in vigorous health, with high physical and mental powers, would have abundance of labor; perhaps two or three hours a day would be sufficient to secure to all a fairly comfortable living.

With a population of which one-third are children,

a considerable portion aged, a large number sick or feeble, some intellectually incapable of making labor effective, and a certain percentage who refuse to work because possessed of sufficient property to employ others as servants—we have the effective working force greatly reduced, and consequently more hours of labor are required.

The relation of population to labor may be summed up by saying: Labor naturally increases or decreases with the population, but depends on the physical and mental ability of the people, and the proportion of the entire population which is engaged in active work.

The ability of a nation to labor should increase much faster than the population, because of the better education and technical training of each new generation, and the experience it has gained from the past. The time will undoubtedly come when we shall consider the first twenty years of life as sacredly set apart to education; when public opinion will not tolerate the support of parents by minor children; when the State will see that the period of natural growth is used to fit the man for the active work of life. Not that children will do no work; but only so much as is an aid to education, and the learning of a trade or business.

VALUE OF LABOR.—Labor is seldom so plenty as to have no value, because most men dislike to work. When labor has no value, they will not work, and hence the labor offered becomes scarce enough to give it a value. One of the wants we have to satisfy is that of a desire for leisure, and the satisfaction of this reduces the available labor power. Hence, labor that can be had for nothing, that will be put forth whether the man gains anything or not, is so little that it is very scarce as compared with the work to be done. If there were so many men who preferred work to idleness that there was nothing for all of them to do, labor would have no value at all, though the utility would be the same as at present. Such instances are occasionally found. There are just enough of such laborers to make the principle clear. There are a great many people who write very fair poetry, who find so much pleasure in writing it, and seeing it in print, that they prefer to do this kind of work to doing nothing. This grade of poetry has a certain utility. A limited amount of it is printed in various newspapers, but the work possesses no value, because it is not scarce. Poetry of a higher grade, such as Whittier wrote, is scarce. It has, of course, a much higher utility, but it has value also, because of its scarcity.

Value to the Laborer.—The foregoing has reference to the value of the results accomplished, but there is another side, which is the laborer's side. It is the value of labor to him, or rather the value of freedom from toil. Certain kinds of labor are disagreeable, and would be done by no one if it were not to satisfy some want of his own, or to obtain a reward from others. Nearly all forms of labor are disagreeable when carried beyond a certain number of hours per week; so that the laborer, in endeavoring to satisfy his own wants, finds that one of those wants is freedom from exertion. He who has inherited a fortune which gives him control over the labor of others, may spend his time, not in idleness, but in systematic pleasure-seeking. If he labors, it is in some special ways. He does work which he enjoys, or labors from benevolent motives in order to benefit others. It is true that many wealthy men seek to increase their fortunes for various reasons, among them the mere love and satisfaction of increasing them; but the labor they perform is of the kind they enjoy, although it may not seem desirable to others. Most men work more than they wish to. The value of labor is precisely the value of ease. In considering whether he will work a day for a certain reward, a man asks himself whether he prefers it to a day of leisure. Men and nations differ greatly in this respect. Some would prefer a certain number of hours of labor during the year to freedom from toil. They are conscious that work is good for them, that they are better off with a reasonable amount of it than with idleness. The English, Americans, and Germans are types of laboring nations; there are other natural loafing nations, such as the Turks, native Africans, and, in general, people of lower civilization. They love idleness, and value their leisure very highly. They must have sufficient food to prevent starvation, and clothing enough for bodily protection, and will therefore work a little to preserve life; but anything further seems to them a less good than ease. Among them labor has a very high value, because there is so little of it; their laziness makes it very scarce, and the amount of work performed is very small in proportion to their needs.

Labor, from the point of view of the laborer, follows the same law as other values, so fully illustrated before. Its disagreeableness increases very rapidly with its quantity.

Value in Use shows the relation between Wants and Resources. In the case of Labor, value shows the relation of the labor power of the population to the wants of the population. If people are naturally indolent, labor power is small in proportion to wants, and the value of additional hours of work appears to them very great. On the other hand, their labor power may be far in excess of their wants, so that they would willingly assist a neighbor, and the value of labor would be very low. The value of labor is probably higher among civilized nations at the present time than ever before, because of the great increase of wants; so that labor is actually scarce in proportion to the wants it has to satisfy.

The actual power of labor should be raised to its highest point through the development of the individual, and the increase of skill and knowledge. The wants of the people should not increase beyond a point which will require reasonable exertion from the great mass of the population. We may assume that it is desirable that men should have great skill and knowledge, and great labor power, and that wants should increase to the point which will demand such laborers. Such a race of men will certainly rank far above those whose wants are fewer, and powers of labor less.

CHAPTER III.

POPULATION AND PRODUCED WEALTH.

Produced Wealth has no such relation to population as has Labor. Labor is embodied in population; Produced Wealth is entirely independent of the number of people. It may increase with great rapidity when population is decreasing, or it may decrease with great rapidity when population is increasing.

How Much Produced Wealth is Needed?— As with Natural Wealth, it is well to inquire how much Produced Wealth is needed by a given number of people. At first it would seem that there could not be too much; but it is evident that we require only a limited quantity of various classes of goods; but that without a certain quantity of these goods, proportional to the number of people, either want or great suffering must result. Indeed, it is impossible to maintain a large population except by means of vast accumulation of Produced Wealth.

It will be more convenient to notice, first, that which satisfies wants *directly*. The quantity of wheat which can be eaten in a single year is limited; perhaps three hundred and fifty million bushels is sufficient for all the people of the United States. Fortunately, this grain can be stored and carried over into the next year, with some expense; but there is no great advantage in a large supply at the beginning of harvest. Fruit has, however, often been suffered to rot on the ground, because there was more than the people could use. The quantity of clothing required by a nation is also limited. There is no great advantage in a stock sufficient for more than a year; it is better that it be produced as needed. The same is true of dwellings. One or two houses is usually all that a family desires. If we have a house for each family, we may need better dwellings, but not more.

This is one side. On the other hand, if there is too little of any of these goods, or, what is the same thing, too many people in proportion to them, there must be suffering. No matter how great the Natural Resources; no matter how great our labor power—we are compelled to produce for the future rather than the present. Most production requires a year. Unless there is food enough to last until the next crop ripens, there must be suffering, no matter how large a crop may be anticipated. When a shipload of immigrants lands, they require shelter at once. They could not in a densely populated country build them houses, from the beginning, in much less than a year. In a new timbered country one could, with the aid of his neighbors, roll up a very comfortable log house in a few days; but not in New York City or its suburbs. One wants clothing to-day; it will take a long time to raise a flock of sheep, shear the wool and manufacture it into cloth. He can not raise a crop of cotton and turn it into cloth except with many months' labor. We need a vast stock of all this sort of wealth to supply the people until more can be produced. The quantity required is not unlimited; it bears a certain relation to the population.

The articles of luxury which a given population needs are not limited in number, or in the labor which can be bestowed in their production; but the quantity of each sort of goods desired is limited precisely as in the instances before enumerated. Only a certain number of pianos are wanted; although many persons would desire a better instrument. As a nation grows wealthy, the variety of articles of luxury and of art greatly increases; and better quality is sought for. It is seldom that there is enough of these forms of Produced Wealth for all the people. In some periods, and among some peoples, wants have been more nearly satisfied than at present, because the wants were fewer. With the general increase of intelligence and culture, the desire for articles of luxury has greatly increased; and the ability to make use of costly productions is vastly greater than ever before. Wants have, perhaps, developed more rapidly than the means for their satisfaction. With the standard of living desired by educated and cultivated people, the quantity of Produced Wealth required to satisfy wants is so great that it has never been, and perhaps never can be, sufficient for a great population.

The most common type of Produced Wealth which satisfies wants *indirectly*, is machinery. Its purpose is to aid in the production of something, such as clothing, which can be used to satisfy wants, directly. While there is need of a great deal of machinery and many factories in the world, the factories for the production of any one article are limited by the population of a nation, or the market in foreign nations. There can easily be enough cotton factories to produce all the cotton goods that can be worn in the United States. There can be as many railways as are needed. Sometimes a single railway between two points could actually handle all the business at less cost than two.

A large population, however, needs a vast amount of machinery, railroads, etc., and could not be sustained, with even the modern comforts of the poorer classes, without it. Without machinery and factories, a considerable portion of the American people would perish, and the greater portion of the remainder be reduced to the condition of the poor in the middle ages. It is evident that the larger the population, the more machinery and factories are needed.

The limit of profitable accumulation of machinery, satisfying wants indirectly, is greatly increased with each new invention. It is possible for the world to be a great deal richer in proportion to the population than it was a generation or a century ago. What could the world have in early times? Flocks of sheep, herds of cattle, castles, dwellings, and a little rude machinery and works of art. Many utterly useless things, such as the pyramids, were produced with great labor. With the progress of invention, vast wealth is profitable in the form of machinery, and the importance of Produced Wealth is greater than ever before.

It is evident that population can not increase beyond a certain ratio to the Produced Wealth of the land. If there are too many people, some must starve, no matter how great the Natural Resources and the power of labor. Some may starve while others have an abundance, or all may be on short rations, but the weakest or poorest must finally die of hunger. The desirable state of affairs is that there shall be enough for the common wants of all.

VALUE OF PRODUCED WEALTH.—Produced Wealth is not permanent. Time destroys it all, or it is maintained in its original condition only by constant labor in repairs. When destroyed, it can also be replaced. Were it not that men are looking forward to this destruction and replacement, its value would be determined entirely by its scarcity. If there were more dwellings than people could use, they would have no more value than mountain scenery. If there were more clothing of a certain kind than people could wear, it would have no more value than the water of the river. It would be as useful as before, but, like the water, being no longer scarce its value has departed. People look forward to further production; they know that, however great the stock of clothing in the United States may be, it will all be worn out in a few years, and that more must be produced.

When Produced Wealth is scarce, in proportion to the population, and its value therefore high, every effort will be made to increase it. In this respect it differs from Natural Wealth, which can not be increased. When any form of Produced Wealth is so abundant that its value is low, production is diminished, and the stock is reduced by consumption.

All Produced Wealth is the result of saving. As

it is a common saying, "It is not what one earns, but what he saves, that makes him rich;" so it is not what society produces, but what it saves, that constitutes the vast resource of the productions of human industry which were classified in an earlier chapter. A nation may consume during a year the total production of all its people. Here, there is no saving, and no increase in Produced Wealth. The people may even eat up and wear out the stock of goods saved over from former years. The stock of goods deteriorates by mere lapse of time, and, unless replaced from year to year, will naturally diminish; buildings grow old and fall into decay; machinery rusts out, as well as wears out. Nothing remains as good as new, even if unused.

There are two principal causes which promote saving and the increase of Produced Wealth. The first is the desire for a provision for the future. One lays by for a rainy day, for the time of sickness, for a year of failure of crops, for old age. This desire to save varies greatly with different people and different nations. Where it is strong, the stock of the productions of industry is certain to be large, because people will live in some way, and save a portion of what they get. Opportunities for saving, such as building and loan associations, a postal savings-bank, the purchase of a piece of property to be paid for in the future— all promote habits of saving on the part of the people. It is sometimes said that certain men did not begin to grow rich until they ran in debt; the reason being that they saved what before they spent on themselves or families.

The second cause of saving is the need of some form of capital. A workman or a manufacturer sees that he could succeed better by the aid of new machinery, and saves to buy it or to pay for it.

While it is true that Produced Wealth is always the result of saving, it would be equally true to say that it is usually the result of extra labor. An easy-going settler in the West, living in a sod house or dug-out, finds himself just able to make both ends meet in providing for himself and family. If, now, himself and boys were to work more hours a day, and in the extra hours mold and burn brick from the clay on his farm, and afterward lay them in the walls of a house with their own hands, they might have a better dwelling as a result of extra labor. It would, of course, be savings, since they might have used this extra labor to produce some luxury to eat or to wear. But it is directly the result of additional labor. This is probably true of the greater part of all accumulations of the productions of human industry. Most men naturally consume all they produce, or get possession of. When they realize the necessity of saving something, of some capital or machinery to use, or of a house to live in, they get it rather by additional labor than by saving out of present products.

CHAPTER IV.

POPULATION AND SOCIETY.

Society, like labor, is embodied in population. The number of people in whom one can be personally interested is very limited. A traveling man once stated that he knew twenty-five hundred physicians, whom he could call by name. Few individuals have the capacity to remember so much about so many people. An acquaintance with a few hundred is all that most persons care for, or are able to keep up. There is, however, a desire for the presence of a much larger number than one can become personally acquainted with. We like to see a crowd on the street or at a place of entertainment. Part of the pleasure of a lecture comes from the hundreds, or thousands, who may be in the same room, in sympathy with each other so far as the common object of the evening is concerned. There is a satisfaction in numbers, in the consciousness that thousands are enjoying the same magazine, or book, that we are reading. Even without a personal acquaintance, we may have a general knowledge of men, and may be in sympathy with vast numbers. The world would not be as satisfactory as it is, if the number of people were limited to those we could personally know.

It has also been said, in an earlier chapter, that a large number of people is necessary in order that production may be carried on to the best advantage, and wants satisfied in the most economical way. It is impossible, with all the resources at the world's command, to satisfy wants without a division of labor. Undoubtedly a very considerable division of labor could be had in a community of a few thousand people. There would be farmers, carpenters, blacksmiths, physicians, teachers, merchants, etc., and the division might be carried far enough to give more than half the advantage enjoyed at present. By means of foreign commerce the division of labor may include all the world, so that even a small nation may reap the advantages of it.

It should be understood that, in this respect, numbers satisfy wants by their *presence*, not by their efforts. This is the distinction between Society and Labor. Looked at as laborers, people satisfy their own wants, and aid in the satisfaction of the wants of others. Looked at as society, others unite with us in desiring the same goods, and creating a demand for large quantities. A thousand people need a thousand times as much as one, and the supply for the thousand may be produced at one-tenth the cost to each individual. In many instances the saving is even greater. The cost of a certain weekly newspaper exceeds five hundred dollars a week before a single copy is printed. If such a paper were produced for one man, a wealthy prince, it would cost him at least twenty-five thousand dollars a year. It is furnished to its subscribers at four dollars. Its publication is possible only because thousands of people want it; but this means a population of millions. One could hardly afford to cultivate his voice for a lifetime to sing to one person; but if he is to sing to thousands, each listener may enjoy the pleasure, and the cost for all not greatly exceed that for an audience of one. Most of the common comforts and luxuries of life are furnished as cheap as they are, because produced in large quantities.

It is the *wants*, and not the *number* of people, that make a demand for large quantities of goods, and their cheap production possible. If only one person in every hundred thousand desired a particular book, there would scarcely be a demand for seven hundred copies in the United States, not enough to pay for publication. If one person in every hundred wishes the book, it would require a nation of only a hundred thousand people to take a thousand copies. The presence of Italian " dagoes " does not add at all to the demand for the rarer articles. For the common productions, such as sugar, shoes and cotton, the demand of a single million people is enough to make production economical. It is the number and character of the *wants*, and not the number and character of the people, we are taking into account in estimating the advantage of Society. A large variety of wants embodied in few people (provided we have the means of production) are just as advantageous in affording a large market as the same number of wants with a larger population. To make this clear, suppose two countries, one with a million people, the other with ten millions. Let us suppose that by reason of superior intelligence, knowledge and self-control, the labor power of the one million is as great as that of the ten millions. This is no unreasonable supposition. A million picked men of the United States would have as great labor power as fifty million native Africans. Let us also suppose that the wants of our nation of one million are as numerous, and as great, as those of the ten millions. This, also, is no unreasonable supposition. They can not eat ten times as great a quantity of food, but they will desire a greater variety of food, which may require as much labor power to produce. They may actually wish ten times as much clothing. They will wish many things, such as pianos, that the savages do not care for. We assume that they are homogeneous, of comparatively like tastes, so that a considerable portion of the people desire the same class of goods. Now, by our supposition, the labor power of the two nations is equally great, the sum of the wants is equally great; hence goods can be produced in as large quantities in the one nation as in the other. The advantage, indeed, is on the side of the civilized nation. It does not take a very large number of people to cause a demand for the common necessaries of life, since every person wants the same thing in nearly the same quantities. Every person uses sugar, shoes and wheat. Ten thousand families are enough to give employment to several men in raising wheat, even with improved machinery; and it could be produced, if there were only ten thousand families in the world, without very much more labor, per bushel, than at present. A very small and thinly settled country has people enough to make possible the production on a large scale of the common necessities of life. When it comes to the more costly comforts and luxuries, the demand is from a very small percentage of the people. The higher the civilization, the larger the proportion of the population which wants them. We may imagine a nation so well educated that every family will desire the best books, and the highest class of magazines, with all the comforts of a well-to-do family of the United States. With such a civilization, there may be in a country of fifty thousand people as large a demand for the rarer kinds of goods as would exist among five million Poles with a few American overseers. Many persons want these things who can not get them, but they will never be produced until people desire them. Compare the wants of a tribe of African savages, or of an Indian tribe, with those of a merchant or mechanic in the United States!

While, therefore, the presence of a considerable number of people is desirable, there is a limit to the number required by the need for Society. A hundred million persons may afford no better opportunity for the economical satisfaction of wants than ten million. Indeed, there is reason to believe that a population of one million highly cultured people would afford opportunity for carrying the division of labor as far as is for the advantage of the race, and give, practically, all the economic advantages to be had from large numbers. Both their wants and their labor power would be from ten to fifty times as great as those of an equal number of savages. They would gain greatly by exchange with other nations, in articles which could be better produced elsewhere. There will always be some things in the production of which some one nation will have a decided advantage. But in the satisfaction of most of the wants of its people, it is probable that, leaving out advantages of climate and soil, a nation of one million people of the highest intelligence and knowledge, would be able to reap so nearly all the advantages of a division of labor that the rest can be safely disregarded. The difference between one family providing for all its wants, and a division of labor among a million people, is almost beyond the power of imagination. Most of the advantages will have been gained before we reach the million limit, and the gain from further additions will be barely perceptible. In this, we have assumed an educated and cultured population, equal to the best and most intelligent in the United States; let us say the best million of the sixty-five. It will be readily seen how the presence of this million people would give us nearly all the advantages we now enjoy. The demand for very many goods does not now extend much further. It is the number of wants, combined with labor power to satisfy them, that creates the demand and makes the division of labor possible; the *character*, rather than the number of the people.

In satisfying the wants that grow out of the need of Society, then, as well as those which come from our need of the other resources, we find that a considerable population is an advantage, but that there is a limit beyond which this advantage ceases.

We have thus far said nothing about the agreeableness or disagreeableness of neighbors as a part of Society. After it has increased to a few dozen people, the social advantage of a larger number depends altogether on their character. When there come to us cultured and Christian Englishmen, our society is enriched by so much. When we receive a shipload of the lowest Poles, Italians or Chinamen, we have more people, but society is so much the worse. We have them to govern, or rather (to our shame be it said) to help govern us. We come in contact with their vices. Their filth is a source of sanitary danger. Socially, they are so much rubbish, which we could well afford to pay something to get rid of. Whatever advantage is gained from their labor is more than lost by their presence. The gain from their labor accrues to a few wealthy manufacturers. The loss is the loss of the entire people. It is unfortunate for us to add to our population a single person who has not already a desirable standard of living, and labor power enough to maintain it.

VALUE OF SOCIETY.—The value of the society of one class of people is very different from that of another class. To have value, Society must first have utility. The presence of a highway robber has no utility to a traveler. The presence of a friend during the journey might be very useful. The society of Chinese has no utility for Americans, even when their labor is desired. The society of families of intelligence, good morals and agreeable disposition is of very high utility. In the satisfaction of wants indirectly, the society of a thousand Hottentots, who consumed no goods, would add very little to the opportunity of increase in economic production through the division of labor. The society of a thousand average American families would add materially to the wants to be satisfied and to the demand for goods.

Granting that the society of any particular persons or class has utility for us, its value, like the value of all resources, depends on its scarcity. The man who has all the agreeable acquaintances he can meet, does not greatly care for more. The presence of his man Friday had great value to Robinson Crusoe. The presence of another man would have been desirable, but not worth so much to him.

So in satisfying wants indirectly. A single family can divide the necessary labor between its members, to great advantage. A thousand families can carry the division of labor to an extent which will gain the major part of all that is possible to be gained by this means. The value of the society of another thousand would not be anything like that of the first thousand. The value of the society of a tenth million would be very little. As in most other instances, value decreases very rapidly as the want becomes partially satisfied. A little of anything desired is a hundred times the value of the same quantity after the want is nearly satisfied. Our object is to satisfy wants. The quantity of anything which man desires is limited. Value is what a given quantity is worth to him. After he has all he wants, an additional quantity is worth nothing. Long before one's wants are fully satisfied, the value of the article decreases. The value of Society a hundred years ago, in the United States, found expression in the desire to get more men of a *good class* from Europe. Now it has no value at all, and the instincts of the people have led to a realization of the fact. The country now has all the people it needs.

In all this it must not be forgotten we are considering Value in Use, and not Value in Exchange.

We may sum up the last four chapters as follows:

1. The Resources of Nature can not be increased; but are very abundant, and will satisfy the wants of a certain number of people better than when population is less dense. When the number exceeds a certain limit, in a given state of civilization and progress, there is less of the Resources of Nature for each one; this limit is the point of diminishing returns to *labor* bestowed on land. The discovery of new Natural Resources opens the way for satisfying the wants of a larger population, but discovery is not creation, and nothing can be discovered which does not exist.

2. The labor power of nations is seldom in proportion to their population; the labor power of any nation may be multiplied many times with no increase in the population; and there may be a great increase in population with very little increase in labor power. The labor power of a nation depends on the *kind* of people rather than on their number. With no immigration, however, there is no reason why increase of labor power should not keep pace with population; and, with education and proper training, the power of

the people to labor should increase faster than their number.

3. The accumulated Resources Produced by Human Industry bear no fixed relation to the number of people.

4. The advantage of Society depends on the character, and not on the number of people.

There is an almost inestimable advantage in a population large enough for the purposes previously described; but this number is comparatively small, and there is only slight gain in further increase.

It is evident, then, that the wants of each person can be satisfied much more easily and fully by an increase of population up to a certain limit. When that limit is passed, there will at first be a slight gain in some ways and a loss in others; and it is probable that the population might be doubled, and, it may be, multiplied by ten, without greatly affecting the welfare of each individual; but with continued increase in the number of people there is certain to come a time when the satisfaction of the wants of each individual will be far more difficult than if the population were smaller. Not more difficult than it was a half century ago, but more difficult than it would be now, were there fewer people. This condition of things has been reached in England. England suffers from many traditions, the presence of privileged classes, and misgovernment. No doubt the average welfare of each individual might be far greater than it is, but it is impossible that each should have as much as if there were fewer people on the island. The condition of affairs is disguised by importations from foreign countries, so that the English people use not only the land of England, but the wheat fields of the Dakotas and Southern Russia. Were the English people shut up in England, the impossibility of each having as much as if there were fewer would be plainly seen. Her statesmen realize this, and are sending colonies to all the world. She is seeking, not for more lands to conquer, but for more lands to colonize.

In this country, the question is not one of emigration, but of immigration. Ideas penetrate the masses of the people slowly, and when once accepted retain their hold long after changed conditions have made them dangerous. At the close of the Revolutionary War, we were a small people with a great country, and little of the land was in actual use. There was room for millions more; and our fathers rightly judged that the nation would be better able to defend itself against foreign powers if it had more men. There is also a pride in numbers. We like to brag of how great we are, and how many we are. The fathers were right in holding that an addition of a few more millions of men *like themselves* would be of great advantage. The men who came were of a good class. They expected hardships in the New World, and they were men of the temper and ability to meet them. The idea that immigration is an advantage remained in the minds of the people after immigration became one of our greatest dangers. The early immigrants were not objectionable as society. They were English, Scotch, Irish and German—people like ourselves, whose children and grandchildren are to-day among the best of American citizens.

All this is now changed. This country, if not full, is so nearly filled that land and other Natural Resources should be saved for the children of those now here. It is to be remembered that when there is land enough and room enough, population increases very rapidly, without immigration. We should soon be a hundred million if no other emigrants came to our shores. Were there land enough without crowding, a generation thereafter would see two hundred millions. The majority of the people we are now receiving from abroad are no longer desirable. We have long since passed the point where increase of numbers is of any advantage. We have more than enough to use the Resources of Nature beyond the limit of diminishing returns; more than enough for society and to afford the widest opportunity for the division of labor. There is still room for the cultured Englishman and German. They add diversity to our society, and their continued coming will be a gain. But they are only a fraction of one per cent. of the immigrants we get. Most of those who come to us are not the best, but the worst, of the nation which sends them. The Italians are here in large force, and they are the class of Italians which Italy is glad to spare. We have narrowly escaped being overwhelmed by a flood from China. It illustrates the strength of old terms and sentences from which the idea has departed, to see how many good men of New England were horrified at the thought of restricting Chinese immigration. They appeared utterly heartless and brutal in regard to their own countrymen. They were not so in reality; it was merely the strength of old methods of thought, and the habit of saying: "America is to be an asylum for all nations." As if the splendid civilization of America is to be buried under the rubbish cast off from all nations in the world! Many of these men were Christians and firm believers in the Scriptures. When the Lord saw that the race of men was so wicked that nothing could be made out of them, he destroyed them with a flood, in order that the world might be filled of the descendants of one family, better than the others. It is a mistake to suppose that the teaching or the spirit of the Bible requires us to open this civilization to the influence of the lowest classes of every nation in the world. The United States was originally settled by men of splendid stock. They brought with them the most advanced ideas of their time. The doctrines of religious liberty, of moral and religious training, of general education, of political liberty restrained by firm government, of the development of the individual — these and many others have helped to make the nation what it is. To permit it to be buried under a flood of Chinese, Italians, Poles, and the lowest people of every nation in the world, would seem to be the thought of a demon determined to arrest the progress of the race. Our duty to send missionaries to teach the gospel in heathen lands is clear. Our duty to protect our homes and our land against the incoming flood of ignorance and vice, is no less clear.

CHAPTER V.

THE LAW OF THE INCREASE OF POPULATION.

Malthus occupies the same relation to the subject of Population as Adam Smith to that of Labor. Perhaps no man has been more misrepresented, not because of any lack of clearness in his writing, but because what he wrote is seldom read, except by special students of the subject; and flippant writers have found it convenient to use his name for almost anything they pleased. Malthus was an English clergyman, the father of eleven children, a Christian who desired to alleviate human misery, and to do all that lay in his power toward the development of the race in its highest character. His " Essay on Population," published a hundred years ago, was mainly devoted to an historical investigation of the causes which have kept population down to its present limit. He was a keen logician, a careful investigator, and the world owes him a great debt. John Stuart Mill pressed the same views somewhat farther than did Malthus; yet so has the name of Malthus been identified with the subject of population, that no one thinks of any other name in connection with it.

One who writes to-day has the advantage, not only of Malthus' investigation, but of all criticism that has been made upon it, and of the new truth evolved through the discussions of a hundred years. I have sought neither to avoid nor to follow the methods of statement of Adam Smith on Labor, or of Malthus on Population. My only purpose is to present what seems the truth on each subject, in as direct and simple a manner as I am able.

Men, like plants and animals, tend to fill any country in a period which is very brief compared with human history. Clear off the forest, and a crop of weeds springs up the first season. They were not there before, because there was not room enough for them to grow. If the ground is kept clear of other growths, the seeds of a single plant will soon cover a large area with luxuriant vegetation. Nature is very prolific, and there is no limit to the possible increase of any species of plant or animal, except the lack of room, subsistence, or conditions of life favorable to it. Were every other species of vegetation kept down, a single bushel of wheat could cover all that portion of the earth in which the climate is fitted to its growth, in a period of twelve years. A few horses left in South America filled all the plains. There are but few animals which would not fill the whole earth with their kind in a hundred years if there were no other animals to interfere with them. Man is no exception to the law of rapid increase where there is room for him. To find that room we must take a new country, where there is work for all, with a living, respectable in the eyes of one's neighbors, for all who are willing to work; and where there is no reason for delay in marriage. An approach to such a condition of things was found in this country a few generations ago. People had a poorer living than at present, but there was more equality. Young people were expected to marry at an early age, and it was generally believed that the married man made as good a living as the single man. The conditions for the rapid increase of population were far from the most favorable; but from 1790, the time when the first census was taken, the population of the entire United States doubled, by natural increase, in twenty-three years; and doubled again in about the same period. There was very little immigration. The census of 1790 showed a population of less than 4,000,000; fifty years later, in 1840, there were more than 17,000,000. Malthus assumed a tendency of population to double, in round numbers, as often as once every twenty-five years; but under favorable circumstances, with plenty of room, and no doubt of a livelihood for each one and his family, it is evident that population would increase much more rapidly, probably doubling every eighteen or twenty years. The precise period is, however, of little importance compared with the fact that the increase is in geometrical progression. Geometrical progression is familiar to most persons, in the story of the horse-shoe nails; yet we are all astonished at the results, the moment we make the calculation. The number of people on the earth at present is estimated at 1,500,000,000. If the population of the United States were only 60,000,000, and were to double every twenty-five years, in twenty-five years there would be 120,000,000; in fifty years, 240,000,000; in seventy-five years, 480,000,000; in one hundred years, 960,000,000; in one hun-

THE LAW OF THE INCREASE OF POPULATION. 119

dred and twenty-five years, 1,920,000,000, nearly one-fourth more than the present population of the globe. Either the United States, England or Germany would re-people the earth in less than a hundred and fifty years, if the inhabitants of every other land were swept off by a pestilence. A single million people would fill the United States with 64,000,000, its present population, in less than a hundred and fifty years. The question of the future is whether the people of the United States in the next century shall be descended from the best element of American citizens, or from Chinese, Italians, and other immigrants. India is full of people—240,000,000; China's population could overrun the entire earth in less than a century if it had the opportunity.

For a hundred years, every possible effort has been made to break the force of these statements, which one would suppose must be almost self-evident. It is difficult to see how any one can doubt their truth the moment his attention is called to them, but some strange ideas have been advanced.

The most common objection is that these statements can not possibly be true, because, as a matter of fact, population has not usually increased at the rate mentioned. But no one said that it had. Such an increase for a thousand years would be an impossibility, because the earth would not support the people. It is only affirmed that it is the *tendency* of population to increase at this rate, that it will do so where there is room for it—where the people feel reasonably sure of a living, and where the increase is not checked by external causes, such as war or pestilence. Mr. J. E. Cairnes has illustrated the truth by centrifugal and centripetal forces: the tendency of the attraction of gravitation is to draw a planet to the sun, while the tendency of its momentum is to fly off in a straight line; the result of the combined action is to cause the planet to move in an ellipse around the attracting body. We should make little progress in science if we did not understand and measure both these forces; when we say the tendency of the attraction of gravitation is to draw a planet to the sun, we mean that it would draw it there were there no opposing forces. The tendency is a real force, which must be taken account of, though the actual result can not be ascertained except by estimating the combined effect of all the forces.

The final check to the increase of population is lack of subsistence, not for all, but for the poor. But there are other checks which diminish the rate of increase, and in most civilized countries prevent its reaching the point where any considerable portion of the people suffer from lack of food.

War.—War has always been one means by which population has been kept down. As the animals have been hunted by man, so men have been hunted by each other. A Scotch laird said he did not care how hard-shot his estate might be, by one who leased it for hunting, since there were always enough animals left to replenish it. But for the natural power of men to multiply rapidly, the race of men might have become extinct in the barbarous wars of savage tribes.

Such civilized nations as the Greeks and Romans, and Eastern nations before them, carried death where they carried their arms. The number of people may be no less to-day than if there had been no wars; the destruction of war has given room for more rapid increase in time of peace, and the limit of subsistence has not been so quickly reached. There is reason to hope that the slaughter of men by each other will, in time, be abandoned, and this check to the increase of population will then be removed.

Cruelty.—Closely allied to war is simple cruelty. Human life has often been held very cheap. Slavery, oppression, and cruelty of all kinds, have destroyed life recklessly all through the world's history. Savage tribes have put to death all that came in their way, women and children as well as men; and some of the highest civilizations of the ancient world have shown more cruelty than the savage. The history of the world is red with blood. Unfortunately, it has often been the best men whose lives were lost. Could the earth have been peopled by their descendants, instead of their slayers, civilization might have made more rapid progress. Suppose the Huguenots had not been slaughtered, there might have been no more people in France to-day, but a considerable portion of the French population would now be descended from those Huguenots. Suppose the Christian martyrs could have peopled the earth instead of their slayers!

Pestilence.—Pestilence is sometimes only a part of the destruction caused by famine; but, aside from this, the loss of lives from such raging diseases as cholera, and even smallpox before the principle of vaccination was discovered, has contributed greatly to the keeping down of population. Such pestilences as the Black Death of the fourteenth century have contributed their share. All pestilences, not the result of famine, are filth diseases; not so often caused by filthy habits in the immediate sufferers, or even in the nations where they work their greatest destruction, as by those of other people and other lands in which they originate. The filth of the East has been the cause of cholera in Western nations. With the spread of medical and sanitary science, a pestilence will soon be a thing of the past. Smallpox is practically under control, and the present generation can scarcely understand the ravages it made a century ago. There is very little to fear from cholera in this country, notwithstanding the certainty that it will be occasionally brought to our shores. The lower nations will in time learn more of sanitary science, and pestilences will become less frequent in the East. These great checks to the increase of population are certain to act with less power in the future, and may in time be entirely removed.

With the history of the past before us, it seems peculiarly fortunate that this tendency to rapid increase of population exists. It has enabled man to fill the earth, to repeople localities almost depopulated by war and pestilence, and has provided a powerful force which almost immediately closes up any gap in the number of people, when there are fewer than the land will comfortably support.

THE LAW OF THE INCREASE OF POPULATION. 123

Overcrowding.—Where the population has not been kept down by war and pestilence, the simple crowding of people in narrow quarters itself tends to prevent a rapid increase in their number, through an increased death rate. It is true that the death rate in great cities of the present is less than in many parts of the country, because of the excellence of modern sanitary arrangements; but this is only true of the city as a whole. In the localities which are the more closely crowded with the poor, the death rate, especially among children, is far greater than in the city at large, or in the country. It is not possible to obtain accurate statistics of ancient times, but; from what is known of the methods of living, there can scarcely be a doubt that the mortality caused by the huddling together of people in cities has been a powerful check on the increase of the population. The sanitary arrangements where people are few, may be even worse than in crowded cities, but the isolation and wide space of country are themselves among the best sanitary measures. A family of ten people may occupy a house of two small rooms in the country, but this is a very different thing from two rooms in a tenement house in a city, with other families over and under and around them, and no ground to step upon but the crowded street. As with war and pestilence, this check is also rapidly disappearing, or rather, in consequence of sanitary arrangements, population will bear much greater crowding than before. In such cities as Glasgow, the provision, even for the poor, is so good that we must expect a rapidly diminishing death rate; and the most crowded portions of the largest cities in the world may be made more healthful than some country villages. All this, however, is accomplished at a rapidly increasing cost as population becomes more dense.

Famine.—When the natural tendency of population to increase is not overcome by other methods, it soon presses upon subsistence. We do not mean by this that the earth is not able to produce ten times more than it does at present; but that in the state of civilization at any given period, population will press upon the subsistence which is actually produced by the methods of the period. Shortage is first shown in frequently recurring famines. In good years there is sufficient, but there is only a small reserve accumulated for bad years; and a series of bad years, or a year in which the product is greatly reduced, means a famine. It is, of course, the poor who suffer. There will always be enough for a large portion of the population, and those who have most wealth will be able to secure abundance; but though a few may have more than they need, and may waste in carelessness, there is not enough for all, even if it were equally divided. This is true of all recent famines—in Russia, India and China. A few years ago, in northern China, the people had eaten the green earth bare, and were dying of hunger; the tales of the famine in Russia in 1891-92 made little impression on our ears, for we accepted the fact that the suffering must be great, and cared to hear as little about it as we might. In some provinces, the people ate everything that could be eaten, and then lay down to die. Comparatively few people die of actual starvation, even in a famine. Insufficiency of food brings disease. A general state of unhealthfulness prevails, and those who die of diseases caused by insufficient food, and from other effects of the famine, are many more than those who actually starve. If no other cause acts to prevent the increase of population in accordance with its natural tendency, we may be sure we shall always find its growth checked here.

It is easy to say that with better methods of production, better government, and more equal distribution of products, the present population of every province of Russia could easily be supported; but it is certain that in the present condition of Russian society these improvements will not be made, even with the certainty of a famine in some province every few years. Population has reached the limit of subsistence in the present state of society in that country. The time will come when it will support twice as many in greater comfort; but twice as many people at present would mean more deaths from starvation, and greater suffering to all. Neither has the pressure of population upon subsistence anywhere in the world's history, of itself, tended to improved methods of cultivation, or to a provision for the support of a larger number. The greatest progress has been made in countries like the United States, which have not been overpopulated, and where the opportunities for each one to improve his condition are, therefore, so much the greater. The improvement of the individual leads to practical improvement in methods of production. Progress in overcrowded countries is due to other causes, and is in spite of the pressure of population on subsistence, rather than in consequence of it.

Deferred Marriages.—The checks which tend to prevent the increase of population thus far noticed may all be reduced to misery, vice or crime. They are such as we are seeking to avoid. The population has been kept down by starvation, overcrowding and pestilence, and by wars, murders and other crimes. There is an entirely different class of influences, which in civilized countries operate to counteract the tendency of population to increase with its natural rapidity. The most important of these is the delay of marriage through one's inability to support a family in the manner he desires or considers respectable. In a new country, where we suppose population to increase with less restraint, people marry at an early age. It is evident that early marriages mean larger families. It is not simply that each family has a larger number of children; they have them earlier in life, and the second and third generations begin sooner. Many a man now marries at thirty who would have married at twenty-five or earlier had he been able to support a wife. All causes which tend to delay marriage act as a check on the increase of population. These causes increase as population presses harder upon subsistence. In a new country such restraints are little felt. It is the popular opinion that a man gets along better after marriage than before. As the country grows older and more densely populated, he sees that he can not provide for a family in the way he regards necessary, and defers marriage until he has learned a trade, or accumulated a little money, or finished his studies and established himself in his profession, or got a start in business, or secured a position which will enable him to support a wife and family. All this may take ten years. The unfortunate feature of this influence is that it acts to prevent the increase of the better classes of the people, and leaves the gap to be filled by the descendants of the worthless and the ignorant. Those who are satisfied to live and bring up a family in squalor marry young, so that the great increase in population in every country comes from them. It would be better for the future if the conditions could be reversed; if it were the intelligent, the enterprising, and the best element among the people which marries young, and if the greater portion of the next generation could be their descendants instead of those of the reckless, the shiftless, and the ignorant. If there were no pressure of population upon subsistence, it would be so. If every man felt able to bring up his family in what he regards as a condition of decency, early marriages would be the rule. This was the condition of affairs seventy-five or a hundred years ago. The energetic young man believed in his ability to make a living which his neighbors would regard as respectable, and marriages among the better class of people were as early, and families as large, as among the others.

The opening of new employments to women has had a very decided effect in preventing or delaying marriages among the better classes. Many a woman now supports herself who a hundred years ago would have married before she was eighteen, because marriage was the only avenue open to her. If unmarried, she remained at her father's, or with relatives, in a position thought inferior to the married state. If she were compelled to earn her own living, domestic service was almost the only employment open to her. All this has been changed. Women have almost a monopoly of teaching in the common schools. They have become telegraph operators, stenographers, typewriters, clerks and saleswomen, and are practicing law and medicine. A still larger number are at work in factories, and nearly every employment which woman chooses to enter is now open to her. This must have an influence on marriage. Fewer women are likely to marry merely for a home. Women who are able to support themselves with the respect of society are not likely to marry except from choice. The effect is rather to defer marriage for a few years than to prevent it, although fewer marriages take place than would occur under other conditions.

Public opinion has much to do with the number of marriages. In many instances this has been thrown on the side of early marriages, and men were led to feel that he who brought up a family rendered a service to his country. Such a public opinion must lead to somewhat earlier marriages, on the average, since one will take more risks of being able to provide for the future. Where public opinion is on the other side, and says that one has no right to marry and burden society with a family which he will not be able to support, it must tend to make even the reckless more prudent. The less intelligent members of the community, those who would never read a book on Political Economy, are more likely to be reached by this influence than by any other. In fact, public opinion is almost the only force which acts to defer marriages among the ignorant and the lower classes of society. Their death rate, however, owing to unsanitary surroundings, is abnormally high.

An attempt has been made in some countries to regulate marriages by law, and to refuse permission to marry unless some satisfactory evidence of ability to support a family is given. The effect of such laws, as might have been expected, has always been an increase of the number of illegitimate births, and of immorality. Such laws do, however, act as a check on the increase of population.

Other legal prohibitions and regulations have often had a very decided effect on the increase of population. The requirement that one must serve in the army until a certain age tends to defer marriage.

Poor Laws, especially laws where relief is given outside of almshouses, have the opposite effect of increasing the population. We have seen that the fear of want and starvation is almost as powerful a check as starvation itself; but where one knows that neither he nor his children will be allowed to starve, he trusts to luck and the poor laws. It is true there is an independence which prefers starvation to charity; but this independence is not possessed by all, and is very easily weakened. Once let a man be driven by distress to accept aid, and his independence is broken; he soon comes to seek for aid, and to prefer charity to labor. It is in the cities and old countries, where population is dense, that we find so many sad instances of this kind.

How much crime has to do as a check to the increase of population can not well be determined. In China population is almost held stationary by the murder of infants, especially females; and the exposure and murder of infants was common among many nations of ancient times. Crime, including the murder of infants, and lesser crimes and vices, has undoubtedly been a powerful check to the increase of population; but the extent of its effect can be only guessed.

Enough has certainly been said to explain the meaning of the statement, "*tendency* of population to increase, and to double as often as once in every twenty-five years." Enough of the causes which check this natural increase—war, pestilence, famine, overcrowding, crime, and the delay of marriage—have been enumerated to show the power of the influences which have tended to prevent the increase of population in the past. If these causes had not acted, we may be sure that starvation would have effected the same result. It would seem that no one could argue that, because population has not increased at a certain rate since the beginning of history, it has no *tendency* to increase at that rate. Had there been no checks to their increase, a single thousand people would have become 1,000,000,000,000,000 in a thousand years. We know that population will not increase at the rate of a favorable new country, because, even with all the improvements and discoveries that can be made, there will be no room for it.

The law of the rapid increase of population is in harmony with all other laws of nature. Nature is very prolific, and provides abundantly for the increase of all living things. If the law of population were different, man would be an exception to every other living thing upon the earth. With the world's history of war and crime and cruelty, if there had not been this tendency of population to increase with startling rapidity, whenever it had the opportunity, the race might have become extinct.

The fact that population increases in geometrical progression has been the occasion for many attacks on Malthus. It is not probable that he himself attached much importance to this particular form of statement, and many modern political economists have been inclined to state the truth in some other way. But the fact that every increase in population becomes the basis for further increase makes it geometrical progression. This is what distinguishes geometrical progression from arithmetical. The rate of increase may change; and the tendency to increase has been limited in the past by the various checks described; some of the most cruel we may hope will soon cease to act.

The natural rate of increase of population would doubtless be found to be somewhat different among different races and peoples; but there is probably no civilized race which would not double in twenty-five years, or less, were all checks, such as war, cruelty, pestilence, etc., removed; and were there abundant room in the country, with sanitary surroundings, and opportunity for every honest laborer to support a family in respectability.

It is not probable, however, that Malthus meant to lay any particular stress on any assumed rate of increase. He selected twenty-five years for illustration because it is a round number, and he believed that history had shown that the tendency is to double in shorter periods. It would certainly be unfortunate for us to lay much stress on any particular rate of increase. The important fact is the tendency of any people to fill rapidly any country where there is room for them. There can be no doubt that, if other inhabitants were swept away, a thousand people of any civilized nation would very soon fill the whole earth. This tendency is fortunate, though it often entails suffering. But it forces on us the question, What people are to be the ancestors of the people of the future—the intelligent or the ignorant? the moral or the degraded?

There has been another attempt to break the force of the law of the increase of population, which should be treated with more respect. It has been assumed that the tendency of population to increase decreases with the age of the world, or of any nation or people, and with the advance of civilization; so that it approaches the point where the death rate and the birth rate will be equal. This assumption—for it is a pure assumption—has naturally arisen from the fact that the rate of increase in some countries has diminished through the action of deferred marriages, and other checks, which do not show any weakening of the natural tendency of population to increase as rapidly as ever, under favorable circumstances. The best example of a population nearly stationary is that of France. It is stated that in the provinces, where the land is divided into small holdings, young people as a rule do not marry until there is a place for a new family. They wait until a holding is vacated by death, or some place filled by people in their station in life is opened; so that the population is practically kept stationary through deferred marriages. How much crime, especially in the cities of France, has to do with keeping the population within its present limits, it is impossible to say. As it becomes more dense than can be supported with the greatest comfort to all, a great variety of checks come into play to prevent its increase. The fear of starvation, or of want, or insufficiency, or even inability to live in the manner which one's acquaintances will regard as respectable, is often as potent an influence as starvation itself. But this does not go to show that the natural tendency is weakened in any degree, only that other influences have come into play. The French people would certainly fill this earth in less than two hundred years, were all other nations suddenly destroyed by a flood.

That the tendency of population to increase is not weakened is shown by the knowledge we all have of society and history. Who can doubt that if a thousand Englishmen, Germans or Frenchmen were placed in an unoccupied country, where more men are as desirable as they were in the early days of this republic, where the position of each is not far from equal, and there is no doubt of satisfactory provision for all, the increase of population would be as rapid as in the first fifty years of the United States? Imagine society in a state of socialism, and the state to agree to provide for all, and the children of all, does any one doubt that the population would increase as fast as in the early days of this republic?

CHAPTER VI.

APPLICATIONS OF THE LAW OF THE INCREASE OF POPULATION.

1. EMIGRATION.—The most natural remedy for an overpopulated country is emigration. It is by this means that the whole earth has been peopled. Men go West, where land is more abundant, where there is more room for new families. England has sent her colonies all over the world; she laid the foundation of the United States, and is now filling Australia and New Zealand. So long as there is unoccupied land, or land occupied by savages, it may be peopled from the older nations of the world. The new country is fortunate if the emigration is of the best blood of the old, as happened with this country before the Revolution. Yet when even the worst class of people are selected, they seem to do better than at home. New surroundings, more room, the encouragement to exertion which more room brings, appear to build up the strength and character of a majority of the emigrants; and their descendants are likely to show a still greater advance. We can not expect them to equal those from better stock, but they appear to make more progress than in the country whence they came.

Countries suitable for settlement are, however, filling rapidly. Europe and Asia have as many people as they can support to the best advantage in the present state of the world's progress. England is now endeavoring to settle the country north of the United States; but the cold northern regions can support only a sparse population. South America is largely peopled by men of lower civilization, many of them descended from Indians. With the methods employed by modern European nations and the United States, that country would give room for a vast population. The greater portion of South America lies in the torrid zone, which is not so suitable for settlement. The southern portion, especially that occupied by the Argentine Republic, appears to offer the best opportunity of any country in the world, for the surplus population of other nations, but even this land is limited. Australia, by reason of the climate, offers little land for settlement except the coast line and the northern portions. Only a very few, except the original inhabitants, can live in the interior. There are three million Englishmen on the island — about the population of the United States before the Revolutionary War — and they will fill it with people in a short time. Of Africa, the northern part, except a narrow strip on the sea, is a barren desert; Egypt is full; the southern portion of the continent is in the possession of the English and Dutch; the central portion has recently been opened by explorers, but whether the intense heat will permit any considerable immigration, is still an open question. Civilization will result in a great increase of the native population, but it is doubtful if Africa offers a place for any extensive emigration from Europe.

A survey of the world shows very little land available for emigration from other countries. Most nations are rapidly coming to understand that all room will soon be filled by their own people, and prefer to keep it for their descendants rather than for foreigners. Every great country in the Old World is seeking for a place to plant colonies. China would be glad to take Australia, but the people, backed by English ironclads, absolutely refuse them admission. They understand that they have no more land than they need for their own children. European countries have been sending their people to the United States, but it is not to be supposed that public opinion here will tolerate this much longer. Each nation must soon come to take care of its own people; and emigration as a check on the rapid increase of population will soon be a thing of the past.

REFUSAL TO PERMIT IMMIGRATION.—Understanding the power of any people to fill its own country in a comparatively short space of time, it would seem that the instinct of self-preservation would cause an absolute prohibition of immigration long before the point of diminishing returns is reached. It is not strange that a new country, such as the United States a hundred years ago, or Australia at the present time, with land unoccupied, should desire the immigration of people *like themselves* from the country from which they came. But that they should desire this after they have become numerous enough to reap all the advantages of a large population, is something to excite wonder. It is partly accounted for by the slowness with which ideas permeate the mass of the people in ordinary times, and partly by the fact that a few persons can make a great deal of money out of such immigration at the expense of the entire nation. It is through these men, and their friends and supporters, that ideas favorable to the admission of immigrants are industriously circulated.

WHO SHALL PEOPLE THIS LAND?—The most important deduction from the law of the last chapter is that, since the descendants of a very few thousand people are able to fill any country in a comparatively short period, the future of the world depends on the nations or classes of people from which posterity is to come. It is particularly fortunate that England rather than China has been the colony-planting nation, pressing into new lands and filling them with the English rather than the Chinese race. It was also fortunate for this nation that our early immigration came from the English, the German and the Irish races, rather than from Asia. The present immigration is one of the most unfortunate that could exist. With a few desirable immigrants, we are receiving the scum of Europe — criminals, paupers, and diseased persons, which the older nations are willing to pay something to get rid of. There is a large emigration from Italy, Austria and Russia. The persecution of the Russian Jews has driven numbers of them to our shores—a very undesirable class—not so much because they are Jews, as because of their ignorance and habits of life. It is not even the addition of this half million people annually to our population that is our greatest danger; it is the fact that it will be their children, rather than the children of those who have made the United States what it is, that will people this land in the future.

That there may be no doubt about this, let us see what "room for population to increase" implies. In the struggle for existence it is not the best plants, the most desirable, that succeed; it is usually the weeds that overrun the ground. The more desirable plants need external help. They do not survive on the *laissez faire*, or let alone, principle. The farmer has a continual fight, all the long summer, to raise his crop. Weeds crowd out the corn. The farmer uproots them, fights them, keeps them out of his field, to give his corn a chance to take possession of the ground. The question is whether the weeds or the corn shall have the land. Free competition always gives it to the weeds. Every farmer knows this, and keeps the weeds out. When Darwin said "the survival of the fittest" he had no reference to the morally fittest, but to plants and animals which could best live in the conditions about them. The pest of the Canada thistle survives, because it is better fitted to the conditions than is useful grain. Let the field alone, and it will soon be covered with Canada thistles, with no grain to be seen; and the seeds of the weeds will be borne by the wind to stock other fields, and crowd out other grain. Vermin multiply, because fitted to the conditions around them. Some plants can stand the cold; others, perhaps more desirable, are killed by it. The Chinaman can live on less than an American, and therefore fits the conditions of a crowded population. When the American comes in competition with him, he must either starve or live as these Chinese live; assuming that there are Chinese enough to make the competition real. Many of us have unconsciously transferred Darwin's phrase, "survival of the fittest," to the morally fittest, using it in a sense in which it is utterly false, and which he never intended.

The number of people which a land will sustain depends on how they live, as well as on how much they are able to produce. Take the American mechanic, farmer or merchant; he desires to live decently and with what he regards as necessary comforts. He thinks it would have been better not to have been born than to live on a lower scale. He wants a house for his family, or, if in a city, room enough for privacy. He wants sanitary surroundings, conditions for a fair degree of cleanliness, comfortable clothing, schools for his children, and some intellectual entertainment. Let one see what the New England factory girls demanded, and how they used the little money received as wages! Compare such lives with the Chinese quarter of California, with Italian dagoes, and with the quarters occupied chiefly by the poorer immigrants in New York and Chicago. It costs something to live on the American plan. The poorest of our people live in a way that is princely compared to many of the poor of the Old World. Now, when it comes to a struggle for existence, those who can live the cheapest, and at the same time do the work, crowd out those who must live on a better plan, if they live at all. Especially is this true of a country as well settled as the United States has come to be, where the Resources of Nature, and especially the land of the country, are in the hands of private owners; and where the great mass of the people are more and more compelled to work for wages. It is not a question of how much can be produced; it is rather a question of what one can get the work done for. The Chinaman, living as he does, regards the wages of an ordinary American workman as princely, and can afford to accept pay on which a self-respecting American family would actually starve. We would think that it would be better for him and his children to starve than to adopt the Chinese method of life. Let Chinese immigration be free, and enough of the three hundred and fifty millions come over to take the place of the American workman, and what is he to do? It is easy to see what the best of them will do. They will not marry, for one thing. Even now such a man defers marriage until he sees a prospect of being able to support a family. As a single man he may compete with Chinamen, but the children of Americans (except of the wealthy class) will become fewer each year. The Chinese have hardly begun to bring their families here as yet, but if they had a real footing they could support a family with the wages that would scarce keep an unmarried American in decency. The numerous descendants of the Chinaman would promptly fill the gap caused by the lack of children of Americans. With free immigration from China, it would be but a few generations before we should see the great mass of the people of this land descendants of Chinese or other immigrants. Good men lament the small increase of the old American population, and think there is something wrong in the fact that men of American descent do not marry earlier, and that there are so few children of the old American stock; but their lamentations will not alter the fact. There *is* something wrong, and it is that there is no room for the increase of Americans; that ignorant and foolish people have invited the degraded of every nation under the sun to come and fill up the land, instead of preserving it for the descendants of those who founded and made this nation.

What has been said of the Chinese is true of nearly all of our present immigration, which, it is to be remembered, is of an entirely different character from what it was twenty years ago. In some respects Russian, Italian, and immigration from some other parts of Europe, is even worse than that of the Chinese. They are near akin to us in race, and if not too numerous are more likely to assimilate with us; but the danger of the crowding out of the old American population is still greater than from an equal number of Chinese. The European immigrants bring their families with them; their children are numerous, and although they expect better wages than the Chinese, their competition tends to degrade the American laborer. He can not live as they do. He ought not to live in that way. The only chance he has in competition with them is in the fact they have so much larger families to support than he; and this means that they are crowding his descendants out, and that their large families are to take the land. There is no room for the American population to increase; there is room for that of the European immigrant. This tendency is somewhat affected by the higher death rate of the foreigner, but nevertheless the rate of his increase is even now far greater than that of the American people. The very rich are exempted from these conditions, because the question of providing for a family need not trouble them. It is the great bulk of the sturdy American people, the best material to make a nation out of that the world has ever seen, who are slowly being replaced by the lowest people of Europe and their descendants. The foreigner can live in harder conditions, on poorer food, and in more filthy surroundings.

There is no doubt that the people of any nation will rapidly increase where there is room for them, but room is a relative term. There is room only for a certain number of hills of corn to an acre, if the crop is brought to its greatest perfection. The farmer will perhaps plant the hills not less than four feet apart, each way. This may seem to be a waste of land, but it is all the corn there is really room for. There is plenty of room for weeds, however, between the rows; they will grow close together. Let them alone, and they will kill the corn. Families, like corn, need a little space between. The highest state of civilization and of manhood requires nourishing food, comfortable clothing, and many things which can be had only where population is not too dense. But when there are all the people who can subsist in the manner in which it is desirable that the race should live, there is plenty of room for Chinese, the Italian and the Russian. He can live between the rows of corn, and pack his children into a Chinese quarter, or an Italian tenement house. Let him alone, and his descendants will crowd out the American. There is room for a hundred of him where there is room for one American family.

The most important application of the law of the increase of population, then, is that, so far as we are able to control the matter, room should be given the best nations to expand, that the earth may be peopled by the best rather than the poorest. The people of Australia and New Zealand understand this better than we. While there is at present room for more people there, they propose to save the land for their own descendants. The same course should be at once adopted by the United States. Independent of the character of the immigrants, the people of this nation have an interest in preserving the United States for their children, and children's children. There is no people in the world from whom a race of high social order is so likely to come as from us. To abandon this land to the people whom Europe is anxious to get rid of, is a crime against the human race.

But what about the increase of population within a nation itself? In China, India and Russia, population is kept within its present limits partly by starvation; not by starvation each year in every part of the country, but by frequently recurring famines in extensive districts. In India, population was formerly kept within its old limits largely by wars and the cruelty of the upper classes. With the settled government of the English this cause has been removed, and population presses harder on subsistence, notwithstanding the great increase in the productiveness of the country under English rule. People seldom die of actual hunger. Insufficient food leads to disease and death from other causes.

In the United States there has been a very decided check to the increase of the better classes through a deferring of marriage, because of the unwillingness of men to marry until they can support a family, and because of the opening of employments to women. If this check could reach the criminal, the drunken, and the ignorant classes, it would be to the advantage of the future. If we could select out the worthless and semi-worthless, and induce them to defer marriage, society would be the gainer. Unfortunately, this check acts on precisely the people whose posterity should fill the land. It is the intelligent, the prudent, the men and women who wish to live in decency, whose children are the hope of the country, that are now deferring marriage. Every Bible reader knows how much honor was put on marriage, and a family, among the Israelites. The Lord had chosen a race and nation for a peculiar purpose, and that they might become numerous, peculiar honor was given to a numerous family. The fact that it is the tendency of population to increase so rapidly, that the descendants of those who are a curse to society tend to increase in geometrical progression, makes it all the more necessary that the moral and the intelligent should hold the world against them. There may be too many people in some parts of the world, but they are not of the right sort. If the Bible account of the flood means anything, it means that the Lord destroyed a race because unworthy to people the world of the future. The future of this nation depends on the number of the descendants of the intelligent and moral classes.

It is not easy to do anything to secure the possession of the future by the descendants of the better classes. Any suggestion of the deferring of marriage reaches precisely the class who ought to marry as young as possible, and from whose children the world has the most to hope. No one who ought to defer marriage reads a book on Political Economy. It has been found, in England, that the indiscriminate giving of outdoor relief to paupers has had the effect of supporting large families, whose children continued to be a burden on the state after they were grown up. Paupers of the permanent class, that is, those who require more than temporary relief, should be provided for in public institutions, where, of course, marriage should not be permitted.

Outside of actual paupers there seems to be very little that can be done toward controlling the increase of population within a nation itself, unless it be to encourage early marriages and consequent larger families among the well-to-do and the intelligent and educated classes, that from them may come a larger portion of the people of the future. Any attempt to suppress the increase of population is sure to act, if it acts at all, on the more intelligent and prudent people, whose descendants the world greatly needs. The attempt to prevent the marriage of those unable to support, or unfitted to care for, a family, has been tried to some extent in various countries; but, as might have been expected, results in illegitimate births, and lowering the morals of the people, though it undoubtedly has had some effect in diminishing the rate of increase of this class of the population.

By the education of the children of the masses in the common schools, we make them more fit to be the fathers and mothers of families. The natural check of deferring marriage will also reach them sooner; so that instead of marriage being deferred by the best class of citizens, it will be more likely to be put off a year or two longer by all. It is only a question of what families shall fill the land. Shall it be the most intelligent, those from a long line of good, honest, hardworking, intelligent ancestry, the educated, the well-to-do; or the ignorant, the vicious, and those with weak characters, or unable to support themselves?

BOOK III.

OWNERSHIP AND CONTROL OF THE RESOURCES.

BOOK III.

OWNERSHIP AND CONTROL OF THE RESOURCES FOR THE SATISFACTION OF WANTS.

CHAPTER I.	PRIVATE PROPERTY OR SOCIALISM,	151
CHAPTER II.	THE OWNERSHIP AND CONTROL OF LABOR,	160
CHAPTER III.	THE OWNERSHIP AND CONTROL OF THE RESOURCES OF NATURE,	165
CHAPTER IV.	THE OWNERSHIP AND CONTROL OF THE RESOURCES PRODUCED BY HUMAN INDUSTRY,	181
CHAPTER V.	CONTROL OF SOCIETY,	189
	Individualism and Socialism.	

BOOK III.

OWNERSHIP AND CONTROL
OF THE RESOURCES FOR THE SATISFACTION OF WANTS.

CHAPTER I.

PRIVATE PROPERTY OR SOCIALISM?

Who shall control the vast resources for the satisfaction of human wants? The first question that meets us to-day is, Private Property or Socialism? It would not be easy to give a definition of Socialism which would be accepted by all Socialists; but in all of its forms Socialism is antagonistic to private property. The popular form at present is State Socialism, which has been defined as "The ownership by the State of all instruments of production and distribution." The instruments of production and distribution embrace the greater part of what is now private property, and under State Socialism at least these must be owned in common. Putting the control of them in the State is a method of communism. Instead of providing for some new way of managing the goods held in common, State Socialists would use our present election machinery, and call the managers by the familiar names of our present government officers. State Socialism is the holding of *all* the instruments of production and distribution, usually including dwellings, in common. State Socialists do not demand a division of goods, but that the State shall take possession of all the farms, and the factories, and everything by which civilized man gains a livelihood, and work them on the common account. The State is to conduct all branches of business. This leaves no room for private enterprise, or for the private ownership of anything, except personal articles of the nature of clothing, books, household furniture, etc. Every man must be employed by the State, and work for it or starve.

Perhaps the most popular presentation of Socialism in this country is Bellamy's "Looking Backward." In it he assumes that the division of the product of the nation's labor is to be equal; that it is to be "share and share alike." Each person is to receive precisely the same, without regard to merit or labor performed. This is the practical abolition of private property. It is not the division of property among a people, but its absorption by the government, so that no man owns anything and the State owns everything, with absolute equality for all. No Socialist objects to a practical ownership of some articles for personal use, such as clothing and household furniture; though some would, in theory, regard these as belonging to the State, and assigned to the use of individuals, as a railroad company may assign a locomotive to an engineer in its employ. This is a matter of no consequence, however, for, under

Socialism, even the fullest right of private property in such articles can have a very limited application. All the means of production, including stores and warehouses, Socialism insists must be in the hands of the State. All business of every kind, all production of goods, is to be conducted by the State.

There are many Socialists, the followers of Rodbertus for instance, who do not advocate equal incomes for all. They would have every man paid in labor tickets, using common labor as a basis, and estimate other forms as being worth so many times as much as common labor, hour for hour. Such a system would probably present even greater difficulties than the other; but in either would practically destroy private property, except in the few articles mentioned. The varieties of Socialism are numerous, but all are practically antagonistic to private property; so that we may set the principle of private property on the one hand, and the various forms of Socialism on the other.

Few Socialists at the present day hope to gain their end by violence, or by any sudden confiscation of goods. Many talk of full compensation for property as fast as absorbed by the State; but they then proceed to show how useless such compensation will be, except for the personal gratification of the former owner during his lifetime. As the State absorbs all property, the owner can not invest it, and can only receive an annuity in the shape of a larger share of goods which he may consume during his lifetime.

THE NATURAL RIGHT OF PROPERTY.—Is there any natural or moral right of property, or is it a mere question of expediency? For there are those who deny the *right* of property, who nevertheless hold to its *expediency*. Not all men who deny a natural right of property are Socialists. Some hold that it is better for the majority of the people that property should be recognized. Most of us believe, however, that in questions like this it is best to see if there is any natural right or moral principle, which is firmer ground than our opinions of expediency, because the results of social experiments are very uncertain.

The *right of individual property* is found in the innate conviction that a man is entitled to the result of his own labor. However closely we are related, and mutually dependent, each person is nevertheless a unit by himself. He is conscious of the freedom of his will to do as he pleases. He has a sense of responsibility to others and to higher powers. There is an innate conviction that he owns what he has made—that the bow he has shaped from the sapling is his. He may exchange it for flint arrowheads, with one who has learned to chip them into shape. He may exchange his labor with an employer, for money or for goods, but he feels and knows that his labor is his own. The house that he has built with his own hands is his, provided what he has gained from others has been with their consent. This ownership of himself is not inconsistent with his duty to others; with his duty to aid his tribe or his nation in mutual defense; with the duty of a parent to take care of the child until it is able to take care of itself; with the control of minor children, or with other duties instinctively recognized

PRIVATE PROPERTY OR SOCIALISM? 155

in Society. These duties may be a very considerable tax upon him, and require a large portion of his labor or its results; but they do not change the fact that he owns himself, and owns the article he makes without the aid of others.

When two or more people unite in production, the product belongs to them as a body; and the question of its division must be settled by agreement made beforehand, and will be governed by natural laws to be considered hereafter. Where a thousand men unite in a factory, the distribution of the product of their combined labor is a complicated affair. Where one man agrees to accept a specified sum from an employer, in exchange for his labor, the result belongs to the employer; but all this recognizes, and is based upon, the fact that man is naturally a freeman; that he owns himself; that he is entitled to the results of his own labor, and has the right to dispose of its product, or to dispose of the labor itself, as he pleases. He must not be held to unreasonable contracts which he has made without understanding them. He can not sell his labor for a length of time that involves slavery. Every bargain must be based on the fact of self-ownership.

This fact—that, of right, a man owns himself and is entitled to the results of his labor—is the natural Declaration of Independence of humanity,—independence of slavery, and independence of Socialism. He will call no man owner, and he will not sink his independence and himself into a slave of the majority, which he may find a tyranny worse than that of an individual.

The right of private property goes down to the foundation of things. It is like the axioms in geometry, or the fundamental principles of morals. Regardless of all questions of expediency, it is the natural belief of man that there is a " mine " and a " thine "— that there is such a thing as a moral right to property.

It would be easy to show the *expediency* of permitting property to be held. With men as they are, Socialism would be most disastrous to the welfare of the honest and industrious, and would arrest the progress of others. Socialism is not a means of reforming the wicked or elevating the indolent. Not only would it be terribly unjust and cruel to put the intelligent, hardworking business man on a level with the laziest and most degraded negro of the South, but it would be a great economic loss. The negro would not be benefited, while the man of higher civilization and character would be injured. Generations of civilization are required to make a man, and the differences between men are great gulfs which can not be bridged by Socialism. If Socialism could succeed anywhere, it would be in an organization of the most intelligent and honest. But such experiments as have been made give no more encouragement than we should naturally expect. The question of expediency, however, while not a difficult one to work out, would require more pages for its elucidation than can at present be spared. It would be necessary to compare thousands of details of the two opposed plans for the organization of society. John Stuart Mill held that the decision rested upon the control which each method might exert over the increase of population. The danger which he feared was that there would be more people than could be provided for under any system, and he held that Socialism would exercise less restraint on the increase of the lower orders of people than Individualism.

Any advantage which Socialism might have in any one respect would be more than overbalanced by the destruction of individual independence, by the denial of the right of one to the result of his own labor, and of his right to act for himself in business undertakings. Socialism strikes at the highest principles of manhood, and would tend to give us a lower grade of men. It would be as intolerable to men of a certain stamp of character as would slavery. It is probably true that some negroes had better food, medical attendance and care when slaves than after they became freemen. It was better for them to work on a well-regulated plantation than loaf in idleness. Nevertheless, freedom is better than slavery—better even for the negro. And Socialism is the slavery of the individual, with the majority for his master. It would be a system so intolerable that the relative economic advantages of the two systems are hardly worth considering. Whatever economic advantages Socialism claims must be secured without the abolition of individualism, individual rights, and the rights of private property.

WHAT RESOURCES MAY BECOME PRIVATE PROPERTY.—The right of private property does not mean that everything may become property. Neither does it determine what goods belong to particular individuals. We first determine that there is such a thing as property. The means by which it is acquired, the terms on which it is held, and the discussion of what resources are the subjects of property, are subordinate, though most important questions. The right of property does not include the right to steal property,—by which we mean the taking possession of what belongs to another individual. It does not imply the right of one man to appropriate what belongs to all men in general, any more than the right to take from one in particular. It is always in order to inquire how one got his money. The fundamental fact is that there is such a thing as a natural right of property in distinction from Socialism. This natural right rests solely on one's ownership of himself and the thing which he makes. Each man owns himself and his labor. Thus the only natural right of property is that of each one to what he has produced, or has obtained by honest exchange. Enormous wealth may result from the proceeds of one's own labor. Joseph Jefferson has obtained the power (by a lifetime of painstaking labor) to act in a theater in such a way that thousands desire to see him. They are willing to pay a dollar or two, each, for the entertainment he can furnish in a single evening. Jefferson has thus received a great fortune in exchange for his own labor. No right of property can be higher. The ability of a railway superintendent may save his company a hundred thousand dollars a year, by better management than that of any other man whom they could employ. This great power of labor belongs to himself, and whatever he can obtain for it in an honest bargain is his. A well-informed merchant may do a great service to both buyer and seller by bringing goods from distant points, paying more for them than the producer would otherwise receive, and selling them cheaper than the purchaser could otherwise buy. The profits of the transaction are the sole result of his labor, and as he has a moral right to his labor, so he has a moral right to the profits. We have seen in a former chapter that the power of labor varies, and there is no doubt that the services of some men to society are worth a thousand times as much as those of others.

The moral right of property does not extend beyond the results of one's own labor. If property is conceded by society for any other reason, it is because of expediency, and by mutual consent. Right is right, and one is entitled to the right, even though in the smallest minority. On the ground of expediency, he may claim only what the general consent of his nation allows.

CHAPTER II.

THE OWNERSHIP AND CONTROL OF LABOR.

In considering the ownership and control of the four great classes of Resources, we shall not follow our usual order, but begin with Labor. Since this is the foundation of all right of property, it naturally comes first in this connection.

It is a self-evident truth that, with a few exceptions which only illustrate the principle, the power of labor belongs to the man in whom it is embodied. The ownership of himself carries with it the ownership of all his powers. He must be free to exert those powers as he pleases, so long as he does not interfere with the rights of others, or compel them to provide for his wants. Not only moral right, but also the principle of expediency, demands freedom and recognition of the fact that one's labor power is his own.

1. It is demanded by the desire for liberty. The whole object of our science is the satisfaction of wants. One of the desires common to all men, though stronger in some than in others, is liberty, and the control of one's own labor. Whatever other wants may be satisfied with the subversion of this principle, this one remains unsatisfied. The most perfect organization of communism would fail to satisfy this most important want. It may be said that with private property men are obliged to put themselves under the control of

others; but one may change employers, or turn to other forms of labor. If land is free, as in new countries, he can withdraw entirely from the wages system. Thousands of the best men of the Eastern States have gone West and taken up farms for themselves. Under Socialism, there is no escape.

2. The best power of labor is not called out except by freedom. If one consents to work under compulsion, or the lash of the slave-driver, it is only the lower powers that are engaged. It is instructive to compare the Southern States, as they existed before the war, with the Northern. Under slavery there was little invention, little use of labor-saving machinery, and everything was done in the hardest way. Where one is assured of the results of his own labor, or even a considerable part of it, labor power is increased many fold. The power of invention and labor-saving is called into exercise. Intelligence takes the place of muscle, and the wants that can be satisfied are vastly greater.

APPARENT EXCEPTIONS.—The apparent exceptions to the right of each person to the control of himself and his labor are:

1. *Children.*—This is simply because they are not yet men, but men in the process of growth. The infant is utterly helpless, and incapable of properly directing his efforts. The period of childhood is temporary, and every child, if he lives, will come to the age when he ought to be free. It is impossible for parents or others to give him the proper care and education,

except with considerable power of control. The child is a debtor to his parents and others for this support during earlier years; and this also forms one of the grounds of his obligations to Society, whose protection is sometimes more important than that of the parent. At just what age he should come into the full control of his own labor can be determined only in each case. The control of the child before he is able to take care of himself forms no real exception to the rule that a *man* should control his own labor.

2. *Idiots and Insane.*—The control of these is justified by the fact that they are not in their right mind, not men in the enjoyment of the ordinary powers of manhood. Such control is sometimes necessary for the protection of the equal rights of others with equal rights with themselves.

3. *Paupers.*—If one is unable to provide for his own wants, and throws the burden on Society, it is entitled to the control of his labor as compensation therefor. Even if it made a profit, it would be entitled to the profit in return for its supervision; but in most cases Society hopes at the best only that the labor of such persons will pay the expense of their care. It seldom does as much as this.

4. *Criminals.*—Society must protect itself from these, and the most humane form of protection is their imprisonment at hard labor, which is also better for them than idleness. The labor seldom pays the expenses of maintenance. If it did, the excess would be a just fine as punishment for crime. A criminal, of course, forfeits some, *not all*, of the rights of a freeman.

5. *Rights of Others.*—One's freedom is also limited by the freedom of others. He has no more right to infringe on their privileges than they on his. Living in society requires limitations which must be the same for all, that all may have equal rights. One's control of his own labor is thus limited. He may justly be forbidden to engage in a business which is offensive to his neighbors, but there must be the same rule for all. If one man is forbidden to erect an offensive factory within a certain district, no one else must be allowed to create the same nuisance. That is, Society may prescribe the terms on which manufacturing must be carried on, and require all to conform to them. Every man is thus on an equality. There is a limitation of one's control of his labor, but it is a limitation imposed on all.

6. *Taxes.*—Society is justly entitled to a part of the proceeds of one's labor in return for the protection it gives and the benefits it bestows. These benefits make all the difference between civilization and barbarism, so that no man is ever asked in highly civilized countries to pay the full value for what he receives. The proper view is that government is carried on as a co-operative organization, or a great partnership. Those who manage its details are bound to conduct the business of the government as cheaply as possible, and the cost must be paid by the members under some one of many systems of taxation. To take any more than is necessary, is robbery of the people. One can not withdraw from Society, because there may be no place to go; but he may not make the excuse that he does

not desire any government, to avoid paying his share of its cost. It would be impossible to take its benefits away from him, unless he were declared an outlaw, and public proclamation were to be made that no one would be punished for seizing his property, or for personal assault on himself and family. The supposed case shows what Society does for one under a high civilization. At the same time, the measure of the benefit received is not the measure of the payment to be made, because he is a part of Society, and no one has a better right than himself to the advantages of the Society of which he forms a part. The measure of his obligation is only the cost of the most economical maintenance of the government.

These are only seeming exceptions to the truth that one owns his own labor as a matter of right, or they are rather the limitations which properly define and strengthen it.

CHAPTER III.

THE OWNERSHIP AND CONTROL OF THE RESOURCES OF NATURE.

Since no man has created these, there can be no natural right of property in them. Any qualified right must be granted by Society solely on the ground of expediency. There is no clear thinker who takes any other view. Many argue that private ownership is the best system for all concerned; but no one can find any natural right of property in the Resources of Nature, which no man has made. Two self-evident statements are necessary to clear the ground:

1. We must put aside any personal interest. One who is thinking how any possible conclusion may affect himself is in no condition to reach the truth. Scientific investigation is intellectual and cold. It seeks the truth, though the truth should be distasteful. One difficulty with all studies in Economics is that the results touch the personal interests and prejudice of every man. If conclusions run contrary to a dogma of one's political party, he will have none of them. If there is danger that in practice they would lead to personal loss, he indignantly affirms that they can not possibly be true. Hence we can hope for correct results only from one who has the scientific spirit, which puts truth above everything else, and searches for facts regardless of consequences.

2. Our investigation will not lead us to any form of confiscation. All present rights must be respected. We may properly take from one the goods he has acquired by fraud, and restore them to their rightful owner; but where Society has guaranteed property in any form, it must not confiscate what it has recognized. If any loss is to be borne, it must be by Society as a whole, and shared among all, on some such principle as governs the raising of taxes.

3. We must separate the Resources of Nature from those produced by human industry; land from the improvements. With the atmosphere as a resource of nature, complicated questions seldom arise. Very seldom is human labor combined with it. The same is true in a less degree of water. But land is seldom used without improvements. The fences, the drains, the buildings of a farm, are all products of human industry. The commercial value of a farm must always be separated into two parts: First, what the land would be worth if a natural prairie with neither fence nor drain nor timber on it; second, what the improvements are worth, and the commercial value of the improvements may be greater than that of the land. The separation is more easily made in a city. We understand that a building-lot is worth so much, and the building so much. Frequently the two have different owners. The proprietor of the building pays ground rent to the owner of the land. Many buildings are erected in cities on leased ground, and the ground rent is sometimes a variable sum. As no one knows what land will be worth in the future, it is agreed that the

builder shall pay a fixed ground rent for a period of five or ten years, and that there shall be a revaluation of the land by arbitrators every five or ten years thereafter. The owner of the building thus agrees to pay whatever the annual use of the land may be worth. Unless this distinction between land and improvements is clearly seen, and firmly fixed in the mind, all further discussion will be useless. Land is a resource of nature; improvements are the products of human labor. The distinction is as fundamental and as important as any that can be made in the science of Economics. It is the distinction between the gift of nature and the work of man.

It is precisely because the Resources of Nature are the gifts of nature, or the gifts of God, that there can be no natural right of individual property in them. For one man's right to nature's resources can be no higher than that of another. They are given by the Creator to all men. The discussion of the control of Natural Resources centers in land, although the same principles are applicable throughout the list. Socialism would settle the difficulty by working land by the State on the common account. Individualism sees the necessity of some means whereby possession can be given to individuals, who will improve and work land on their own account. It also recognizes the natural desire of most men for a home of their own—a piece of ground from which they can exclude others, and which they can improve after their own fashion. A natural suggestion is therefore made that, since land is the gift of nature to the human race, a nation like the

United States divide it equally among its people, giving to each his due share; or sell the public domain on the common account. The injustice of this plan arises from ignoring the rights of the *next generation*. The earth was created for the human race, to be used by each generation in turn. Men of Washington's day had no better right to land than we, and if this generation seize on the territory of the nation and divide it among themselves, what is the next generation to do? What will the man who is born to-morrow do? If it be said that the land naturally descends from parents to children, the reply is, that if we profess to give one a title to his share of the land forever, he may exchange it for whisky, and have no land to leave his children, whereas their natural right to a share in the earth's surface is as good as was their father's. A nation might properly divide its land among those now living, if it gave each one only a *life interest* therein. The earth was made for man to be used, but no one's natural title can extend beyond his lifetime; otherwise he would trench on the rights of the next generation.

THE LAND LAWS OF MOSES.—The land laws laid down by Moses are admirable in their practical application of these principles. It was fully recognized that the land belonged to Jehovah, and that Palestine had been set apart for the use of the Israelites. It was divided among them—first among the tribes, and then among the families of each tribe. The fact that individuals had only a temporary interest was recognized by making the land inalienable in each family. It could not be sold for a longer term than fifty years, and seldom for so long a period. At the year of Jubilee the land of each family was to revert to the seller or his descendants, and as the Jubilee occurred once in fifty years, the average period for which land could be sold was only a quarter of a century, or less than the ordinary life of one generation. If sold immediately after a year of Jubilee, it was still for a period of less than an ordinary lifetime. By this provision, one could dispose, roughly speaking, of not much more than his own life interest. Had Moses' law been carried out, there would have been no landless families in Israel. The plan was adapted only to an agricultural people, and would not be the best to-day. Its interest consists in the fact that Moses, under Jehovah's direction, recognized the principles here laid down—that the use of land belongs to all the people alike, and that there can be no absolute ownership by any one.

The right of each generation to the use of the earth extends only through the lifetime of its members. The man born a thousand years hence will have the same right to a share of the earth's surface as those now living. No laws we can make can affect the right of a future generation, or any member thereof. A man can not rightfully sell the life interest of his grandchildren.

VALUE OF LAND.—Value is given to a particular piece of land, not by the improvements its owner has made, but by those which others have made on other land around it. A city lot lies vacant for years, possibly in the possession of minor heirs. Its original owner bought it for a trifle, and has paid nothing but the taxes. Five and ten story buildings have been erected about it, and it is now worth a million dollars an acre. This enormous fortune is not the result of his labor, or of any service he has rendered in Society. It is the result of other men's effort and enterprise. The increased value belongs, of right, to those who have made the city and given his lot all the value it possesses.

The value of the land in the city depends on the country around it—the trade which it can draw, the markets it can find for its manufactures. In short, the value of all land depends on the people who live on and around it, or have relations with it. Not on their number alone, but on their habits, tastes, the number of wants they have to satisfy, their ability to labor, and their moral character. What would an acre of land be worth in Chicago, were there no people west of Lake Michigan? Since the value of land is due entirely to the people, it follows that the value belongs to them as the result of their efforts and character.

The perpetual ownership of farming land in a country like the United States is not a matter of great importance, because of its abundance. We could not allow one man to monopolize a large portion for a private park, but the absolute ownership of an ordinary farm, under the condition that it is kept in cultivation, would not give the owner so much advantage over others. The real land question is the land of cities and favored localities. It is absolutely necessary that there be centers of population, and that the combined efforts of all people shall go to increasing the value of a little land in those centers. The simplest instance is a western county. Let us suppose the land to be equally fertile and useful, equally desirable so far as the work of nature is concerned. County lines must run somewhere, and the county must have a county seat—one place where the public offices are located and the courts are held. Suppose its location is determined by the convenience of the entire population, and is in the geographic center. The fact that the county business must be done here makes it a better location for all lines of business; and the county seat is certain to be something of a place. If its lots are worth twenty dollars a front foot when farms are worth twenty dollars an acre, the added value is given by the population of the entire county—by those ten miles distant as well as by the residents of the village. If added value comes from natural advantages, such as a water power or a natural location for a railroad, these natural advantages belong to all the people—to one man as well as to another. Everything, therefore, that goes to make land worth more in this county seat is the property of the people.

So far as the value is created by the presence of a civilized and intelligent population, it is justly shared among all. So far as it depends on natural advantages, it belongs to one man as well as another. From either point of view, it is plain that all the land and its value belong to Society—equally to all men in the nation—and that this property right holds through all changes of value, since all increase is due to Society. It can not be said too often that land must be distinguished from its improvements; and that the latter are the property of the maker, by the highest of rights. When one builds a house, it is his because he made it. The fence is his, by the right of his labor. The improvements can not always be removed from the land; but this is not the only instance where people have an undivided interest, and where two people or corporations own shares in the same thing. The chief value of land is in favored spots or localities. The least desirable land is usually worth nothing.

On the assumption that all the value of land is created by Society, it belongs equally to all members. It is not a question of how much of the land of a nation has value. More than half may still be unoccupied. Whatever value is found in the more favored portions has been given by Society.

PRACTICAL METHODS.— There being no natural right of individual property in land, or in any of nature's resources, those who defend such property do so on the ground of expediency. The importance of individual possession is well understood. The necessity for some security in possession is equally apparent. Improvements can seldom be removed, since from their nature they are attached to the land. It is the supposed impossibility of making the best use of land, of satisfying the want of families for homes, and of securing one in making permanent improvements that has led so many to reject the truth of the natural ownership by the people. Without permitting himself to answer the question, Can there be any right of private ownership in the Resources of Nature? one naturally jumps to the other question, How will it work? If we can see any way by which all the advantages of private ownership of land can be had, it will disarm prejudice, and make us more willing to admit the truths of the preceding pages, from which there is no logical escape.

IN A NEW COUNTRY.—If no private titles to land had been given, and we were at the beginning of a new nation, when all the land is "government land," the proper method would be simple. The natural way of managing the land of the people is to rent it under a perpetual lease, with a revaluation of the rent every few years. It is the system under which some of the best buildings of Chicago have been erected, except that the rent is there paid to private owners, instead of to the people.

Land can be cultivated by the *government* only under some form of State Socialism. It can not be absolutely sold, since the rights of future generations are the same as those of the present. To lease for a short period, or to sell a life interest, prevents proper improvements; no one will erect a brick block on land which he expects to forfeit, and the expectation of permanent possession is needed to satisfy the wishes of most holders. There is, however, not the slightest difficulty in leasing land with a *permanent tenure*, the rent to be precisely what the use of the land is worth, and to vary as its value varies. While we can not bind future generations, they would recognize the right of the holder to improvements; and would certainly permit him to continue to hold the same piece of land on payment of what they estimate the annual value to be.

If we were at the beginning, in a new country, all would be easy; and it is easy enough, now, in the United States, with the government land still unsold in the West. Let us start right. This land belongs to all the people—to those now living, for their lives, and to the people who come after them. Its use is not worth much, if anything, at first. We do not know what its use will be worth in the future. We want some honest, practical plan by which men can go to work on a quarter section and improve it, with a reasonable assurance of permanent possession on terms which will insure them the results of their own labor. So we say to every man who desires, " Take a piece of land and improve it; build on it. It is worth nothing now, and you need pay nothing for its use the first year. After a year or two, you shall pay precisely what the use of the land, *aside from your improvements*, is worth. Markets will come with society. The land you live on will gain value from the people who settle around you and beyond you, and from the progress of every part of the great nation. We do not know, nobody knows, what the use of this land will be worth in twenty years. It may be in the heart of a city. What it is worth each year will be determined by an assessor. Every year, or few years, there shall be a revaluation; and what that piece of land, apart from the improvements, is worth, you shall pay, whether it is ten cents an acre in the country, or a hundred dollars a front foot in a city. You pay nothing for ownership; the actual title is in the government; but the possession is yours so long as you pay what the rent of such land is worth; and you pay only for its annual use." The estimate of this value of the annual use would not be more difficult than assessing taxes at present. The standard is unimproved land. A lot with a ten-story building would pay no more rent than the lot beside it with a one-story building. The farm with a five-thousand-dollar house and the best improvements, in the highest state of cultivation, would pay no more rent than the farm with no buildings. Each pays what the use of the *land* is worth, and no one pays taxes on buildings or improvements. Improvements are to be encouraged, and the best farmer gets the benefit of all he makes.

It is not likely that an assessor, or board of assessors, would estimate the average rent of land at more than half its real annual value. There would be no danger that any man would be required to pay more than the true economic rent. The fact that he paid less, would give land a selling price; but that selling price would represent only that part of the annual rent which Society is unable to collect, through undervaluation in giving the holder the benefit of the doubt. The right of Society to take full rent would be undoubted. If, for any reason, the government desired to take a piece of ground for public use, as a park or street, it would pay the holder the value of the *improvements* thereon, but nothing for the land. That always belonged to Society, and has only been rented.

The next generation would not be embarrassed by such a contract. Its ownership of the land is fully recognized. It will see, as we do, the natural right of the holder to the improvements. The government will not want the land. If it takes it, it will have the improvements to pay for. If the holder pays the annual rent, he will be left in possession. This rent the future will fix; that is, each year's rent of the land will be determined—increased when a particular piece becomes more valuable, diminished when it is worth less to use. It is strict justice, not benevolence. Society takes what belongs to it. The holder pays each year what the use of the land is worth. If he fails to pay, his improvements—not the land—are sold, and the money paid to him; possession of the land is given to the one who buys the improvements, for so long as he pays the rent.

The collection of ground rent would do away with the necessity of taxes. There would be some farms where the rent would be even less than the taxes the farmer now pays on his land and its costly improvements. There would be many property-holders in villages who would pay less in rent for the ground their houses stand on, than they now pay in taxes on the land and buildings combined. There would be no taxes on personal property. There need be no indirect taxes. The largest increase of rents would be in cities, where land is so valuable.

There is no doubt that this system should be immediately adopted with all government land yet unsold. There would be no question of present ownership, since the government is still the owner. It would at once stop the taking of government land for speculation. No one would go on such land unless he intended to make use of it. It would be of no advantage to any corporation to get possession of large tracts to sell at a higher price. Land would not be pre-empted until it was needed. Settlements would extend by bringing into cultivation land adjoining that already occupied. Settlers would not need to go far into the wilderness to get beyond the land already taken, but not occupied. If a new Indian reservation were opened, we should see no such scramble as now; because every settler would understand that he would have the rent to pay on all the land he got, and that the rent on the choice pieces, and the town sites, would be as much as they were worth. The ownership remains in the people. We violate no principle of right or justice; and no one knows what the public heritage may be worth in the future.

The plan of leasing land at a variable rent, to be fixed from time to time, is not only the natural method for the use of all government land, but it is the only escape from State Socialism, on the one hand, and gross injustice, on the other. The ground for its advocacy is right and justice, not expediency. It would confer on a nation the greatest blessing of any economic reform, but this is secondary to the fact that it is the only just method of permanent possession of land by an individual.

IN OLDER COUNTRIES.—In older countries land is not in the hands of the original takers. It has been sold again and again, and the government has guaranteed the title, and is as much bound to protect the holder as to pay the national debt. We are in a position where justice to all parties is impossible. The government, which attempted to give a perpetual title to land, sold what it did not own; but the purchasers were innocent, and must bear no greater loss than those who have invested their money in other ways. It would be as unjust to take the thousand dollars which one man has paid for a vacant city lot under the encouragement of the laws, as to take the thousand dollars another man had invested in machinery. Here is the mistake of Henry George. He assumes that because the government had no right to sell land in the first place, the people may take it from the present owners. He argues that if an innocent purchaser has bought stolen property, the law requires him to give it up to the original owner; the owner can take his property wherever he finds it. So, he argues, the people, as the original and rightful owners, may retake their land; and the private holder is in the position of a man who has paid money for personal property to which the seller had no title. The two suppositions are not parallel. He who buys a horse, buys it knowing that he takes the risk of its having been stolen. The land is taken under the forms of law, transferred from purchaser to purchaser in accordance with law, and its title *guaranteed by the government.*

John Stuart Mill, who clearly saw the relation of landholders to Society, writing for England where almost all land is rented, proposed that the present rent of all lands be recorded; and that the government take any natural increase in the future. He recognized the right of the holder to the present land values, but demanded that the private absorption of increase of land values be stopped at once.

The principle of private ownership has received a severe shock by the action of the British Government in Ireland. Land was there held on the same terms as in the United States. An Irish landlord had no power which is not possessed by every American farmer. The latter is permitted to manage his land himself, or rent it for all he can get. If the tenant fails to pay, he can put him off. Yet the English Government has changed this tenure, unquestioned in law for a century, into a mere right to such rent as may be fixed by the court. The owner is actually prohibited from taking possession of land which was his by the law of one of the strongest governments in the world. It is a more violent change than would be the taking of all landed property by our government. The cause was the pressure of the people of Ireland.

The right of Society to take possession of any and all land *on payment of its present value* is unquestioned; and this right is freely exercised by condemnation for public uses, or for such semi-public purposes as railways.

The only practical step which presents no difficulties is to stop the sale of public lands. Not another acre should go into private ownership. No matter how poor or worthless at present, it belongs to the people; and there is no excuse for deeding away the people's heritage. The Adirondack Mountains were once thought to be worthless, and they went into private ownership. Now the people want a great park in this wilderness, and they will pay roundly for it. The reservation of such great parks as the Yellowstone is a step in the right direction; and, although privileges are given to private parties, the fact that the government ownership of the land is recognized will be a basis for their correction in the future. All *public* land should, hereafter, be leased on the condition that the occupant pays whatever it is worth each year, forever; and that if the people need to retake possession of their own, they pay only the value of the improvements. Prompt legislation of this kind would save to the people millions of acres of land yet unappropriated, much of which lies among mountains and about the headwaters of rivers, and should never be cultivated. It should be reserved and protected for the benefit of more fertile land below.

For this generation, at least, the great body of land will be held as private property. What the next generation will do, it is impossible to foretell. We have no right to bind them if we could, and no power to bind them if we would.

CHAPTER IV.

OWNERSHIP OF THE RESOURCES PRODUCED BY HUMAN INDUSTRY.

It is self-evident that Produced Wealth, being the result of labor, is a proper subject of property. The idea of property adheres to it. The question is rather, To what person does a specified article belong? It will be easier to begin with the simplest cases, and proceed to the more difficult.

1. We have seen that there is an innate belief that the Indian owns the bow which he has made. Whenever we find a man making an article without aid from others, we instinctively admit that it belongs to him. The most practical application of the truth that one owns the result of his own labor is the unexpected one of copyright. The Indian takes the sapling for his bow from nature's resources. If he did not use it, some one else might; yet we all agree that the bow belongs to him. The result of the author's labor is an arrangement of words. There can be no property in ideas, because the ideas of one man may be those of a thousand others. If the thinker had not worked out his thoughts to-day, another might have discovered the same mental truth to-morrow. To give him property in his idea is giving him a monopoly of what others have the same right to discover as himself. But the arrangement of the words of a book is purely the re-

sult of an author's labor. What is more, no other man would ever write with the same arrangement of words. A book is therefore purely the result of an author's labor *which conflicts with the rights and privileges of no one else.* There can be no higher right of property. The facts that there has been so much difficulty in recognizing it—that the laws do not protect one in his possession, at least for life, that there is so great a difficulty in securing international copyright—all go to show how much we still depend on force, rather than right, for our ideas of property. The freebooter, the robber, the swindler, who gets possession of goods and holds them by killing anybody who interferes with him, is, even yet, the popular ideal. Every attempt to defend property on the ground of force leads to Socialism. The many are stronger than the one. It is no worse for the people to plunder the wealthy man than for individuals to gain wealth by the plunder of society. Unless we can find some moral right of property, we may as well abandon it. The right of an author is one where force does not come into play, and is therefore one of the best tests of a nation's honesty. Let the farmer or the capitalist who refuses to support the *moral* right of property expect to see his own earnings taken by organized Socialism. The proper answer to his complaint would be: "Your theory used to be that *might* makes property. We have the might; hence we have what was formerly yours." The many are stronger than the few, and organization will give Socialists a power that no individual ever had.

2. In this day of organized production, almost all goods are made in factories, and hundreds of men are often engaged in the production of a single article. This can not affect the truth that the article belongs to the men who have made it; but the question of its *division*, or the division of the money it sells for, opens up the whole subject of Distribution, now one of the most important in Political Economy. By Distribution we mean only the distribution of Produced Wealth—that is of the Productions of Human Industry among the parties to whom they belong. This subject will be considered hereafter. We touch it here only so far as is necessary to show the right of property in general, without attempting to settle the share which comes to each. If each receives the share to which the results of his labor entitle him, the shares will be very different.

3. The total product of a factory does not go to labor. A part is paid to capital, and it is necessary to investigate the claim of the capitalist to a share. A lone fisherman builds a boat, with extra hours of labor. The day's catch, he knows, is due in part to the possession of the boat. Two men who are fishing on the rocks propose to go with him in the boat and unite in catching fish. Will they divide the catch into three equal parts? By no means. All will recognize that the owner should have something for the use of his boat, since they are enabled to catch more fish by means of it, and he owns the boat because he made it. If he prefers to stay on shore, the other two will give him something for the use of his boat, rather

than fish without it or stop to make one. The boat is the product of his labor, and if we recognize the right of property we must see that the owner is entitled to something for the use of it. This division was common in the catch of whaling-ships. The proceeds were divided—a certain share for the owners, and the remainder among the men who had done the work; the largest share for the captain, and a fixed share for each man, as previously agreed upon.

4. The right to the proceeds of one's industry carries with it the right to exchange this product for other goods. But exchange gives rise to opportunities for fraud, and it is sometimes against the interests of Society. The right of exchange is limited by the general interests of Society, and title to property acquired in this way is always open to investigation. To acquire any moral right to property by exchange, it is necessary that the exchange be between equals. If not, it is not really an exchange, but a persuading of an inferior to make a gift. William Penn showed good management in giving the Indians a few trinkets for their land: it saved him trouble and prevented bloodshed; but to say the trade gave him any moral title is nonsense. It would be as correct to say that a confidence man was entitled to the fortune which a child had inherited because the child had agreed to give it to him for sugarplums. Moral title passes only when exchanges are fairly made between equals, and when some proportional value is given on both sides.

The right to property acquired by exchange is not so certain as to that produced directly by the owner, since there is always a chance that the exchange is only another name for fraud. A shrewd horse-trader starts with a broken-down beast, and ends a series of trades with a fine, sound animal; but his moral right to the horse is not quite that of a farmer who has raised a horse from a colt. Nevertheless, property would be almost worthless without the right of exchange; and as a matter of expediency, if for no other reason, Society must protect property acquired under certain regulations, except in cases of fraud. There is very little of the Produced Wealth of the country which has not changed hands, and the title to nearly all property rests in the fact that one has got it by trade from another.

Property is not robbery, as the Socialists would have us believe, but a good deal of what passes for exchange is little better than robbery. No one claims that all great fortunes made by buying and selling stocks and bonds are made honestly. The dealer sometimes so manipulates prices as to make the matter simply robbery. It becomes one of the highest duties of government to throw all possible guards about such transactions, to punish fraud, and to give opportunities for losers thereby to obtain compensation.

DISPOSITION OF PROPERTY AFTER DEATH. — The control of one over his own labor and all property acquired thereby naturally ceases with his death. Any further disposition of it which he desired during his lifetime must be enforced for him. The right of one to dispose of his property after death is not so self-evident as it may at first seem, and has not been so generally acknowledged as the right or property during one's lifetime. In many countries, the disposition of one's property after death has been carefully fixed by law, so that he had very little control over it. The right of bequest has been more fully recognized in recent periods. It would seem that any full right of property carries with it the right to give it to whom one pleases, *subject to such conditions as the welfare of Society makes it necessary to impose.* As the right of one man is not higher than that of another, so any use of property which is an evil to Society may justly be forbidden. That is, the right of property is a right of possession, but the right of its use is limited by the rights of others. If there is any reason for forbidding one to give large amounts of money to a particular person, Society is evidently justified in prohibiting such gift, and in limiting one's power in using or disposing of his property to avenues not injurious to Society.

The right to give away property during lifetime, or by bequest at death, does not imply the right to follow the property longer, or to control it forever. The laws very properly impose restrictions intended to limit one's control to a comparatively brief period. All together, the right of disposal of property after death is now greatly limited in all civilized countries, and there is reason to believe that a still further limitation would be for the interest of all, by which any one person should not take by bequest more than a given sum. This proposition was first advanced by John Stuart Mill, who made a distinction between the privilege of disposing of property by will and of the right to receive property by bequest. He was the first to place the limit on the receiving. As countries grow wealthy, the danger of the accumulation of enormous fortunes greatly increases. By permitting one to make what disposition of his property he pleases, except that he can leave only a certain amount to any one person, he would still have great freedom in its bestowal; but the danger of great inherited fortunes would no longer exist. Such laws would often be evaded, and the limit imposed exceeded, but they would have something to do in forming public opinion, and would usually be effective. One would prefer to make a disposition of his property within the limits allowed by law, rather than run the risk of forfeiting a part to the State.

The right of persons to receive property which they have not produced, and for which they have given no equivalent, but have obtained from others by gift or bequest, is a right strictly limited by the general welfare of Society. If it is agreed that large fortunes are an injury, it is certainly proper for Society to limit the fortune one may receive without labor, leaving him free to add to it to any extent by means of his own exertion. To be effective, the total amount which he should be allowed to receive during his lifetime should come within the limit of a given sum, so that he may not take two or three fortunes through different persons, or evade the law by any means. If such a sum were to be fixed, it should be liberal, and in a country like this a million dollars would be the round sum most likely to be named—a sum large enough to enable one to make a liberal provision for his descendants and those in whom he is interested, and yet small enough to break up unusual fortunes as often as they may be accumulated.

The right of property in Produced Wealth then rests—

(1) On one's right to the results of his own labor.

(2) His right to a share in what he produces in co-operation with others.

(3) His right to a share in the proceeds of any enterprise in return for the use of capital which he has saved, and which is used in the enterprise.

(4) His right to what he gets by exchange, without fraud, and within limits which Society can permit without injury to itself.

(5) His right to what others may freely give him, or what he may obtain by bequest or inheritance from deceased persons, such right being subject to the limitations which the general interests of Society may impose.

CHAPTER V.

CONTROL OF SOCIETY.

Resources, Population, Who shall control the Resources—this is the order. The question of who shall control the world's resources seems naturally to precede that of the best or most economical method of their use. The control of Labor, Natural and Produced Wealth, is largely one of ownership. We saw that a man owns his own labor, and discussed the ownership of Natural and Produced Wealth. The control of Society does not involve the question of ownership, since Society is not the subject of property. The question of who shall control it is, however, as important as that of the control of the other three resources.

The control of Society is its government. The question now before us is simply, Who shall govern? not, What shall the government undertake? In discussing Labor and Wealth we did not undertake to show how these should be used, but who should control their use; or rather who should own them, since ownership implies control. The question of how these resources can best be used will come up hereafter. So, now, we are to consider merely *who* shall control Society; the question of what those who control the social organization should undertake will come afterward.

The majority of men do not care so much how they are governed as that they are well governed. There is no natural right entitling each person to take part in the government, such as the natural right of each one to his own labor. There is a natural right of liberty; that is, of each one to govern himself and do as he pleases, so far as he does not interfere with the equal liberty of others. There is no natural right to take part in this ruling of Society. Nothing is involved but the question of expediency. How can we get the best government—not the one which will promote the greatest good of the greatest number; but the one that will protect the weakest in his rights, insure justice to all, afford the best opportunities for progress to all, and do the best for Society as a social organization? It is not necessary here to consider all the possible forms of government; all that need to be noticed are included under the various forms of a republic, or a constitutional monarchy, in which a large part of the people take part by their votes. It is evident that every man who votes is an actual ruler. To confer the privilege of suffrage upon any individual is to make him one of the rulers of the nation, one of those who control Society. The two requisites for a governing power are intelligence and honesty, and it is very difficult to unite the two in a ruler. One man like George Washington, with absolute control, might be able to give a nation a better government than with universal suffrage. But few men can be found who would use such power for the benefit of the people and the enforcement of strict justice. The chances of getting such a man for a king are small indeed.

The difficulty with universal suffrage is the lack of

intelligence and knowledge. The vote of the most ignorant counts as much as that of the competent ruler. The people as a whole, however low the moral character of individuals, or even a majority of individuals, are more likely to try to do right than any narrower governing power—than a king or an aristocracy. The mass of the people is more honest than the individuals which compose it. The danger lies rather in ignorance. It used to be thought that the ballot would be a great educator, but with the power of the modern demagogue its benefit is more than doubtful. The object of the leader is to get into power. By the vehemence of public speech, the most dangerous ideas are fastened on the people, which are not shaken off in a generation. If any limitation is to be imposed on the privilege of suffrage, it should be that of education. A class which can have no hope of ever taking part in public affairs may be dangerous to the State, and the situation of its members is an unspeakably cruel one. But an educational qualification, not so high as to forever bar out any man of sound mind who chooses to prepare himself for it, would be no hardship, and would act as a powerful stimulant to the voter's real ability to help rule. Suppose the requirement to be a knowledge of the branches usually taught in the common schools. There is no one who could not master them some time in his life, if he chose to exert himself. Such a rule, in the United States, might at first disfranchise half the voters; but who can doubt that it would give us a government far better for all those who were disfranchised as well as the others? The moral standard would be no lower, and the average intelligence of the voting population would be vastly increased. An entirely different set of men would be chosen as representatives. So far as those who were disfranchised are concerned, they can be divided into two classes: first, those who feel it something of a disgrace to be deprived of the privilege of voting; and, second, those who care nothing about it. The first class would comply with the educational requirement within a few years. The prize of the suffrage would do more to make education universal and popular than any other possible influence. As regards those who do not care enough for the suffrage to obtain the requisite knowledge, it is safe to say that they will not be deeply concerned over the loss of the right to vote. The chief care should be that no impossible standard is set up, and no man deprived of the suffrage who has the will to obtain it.

So far as the experience of the world has taught us, we may believe that among civilized nations the best form of government attainable will be one where the power resides in the votes of a very large body of the people; and that the only requirements of the suffrage should be intelligence, common morality, and such education as is in the power of each to obtain, at some period of his life, if not at the earliest age fixed for the casting of a vote. The question of the advisability of inviting woman to take part in the government need not be discussed here. It probably depends on the answers to two questions: First, would it give us a better government? Second, would it be best for woman?

Having noticed the more important principles connected with the ownership and control of each of the four classes of resources, we should in this chapter return for a moment to the question of Socialism, since it has as much to do with the control of Society as with the ownership of property.

Socialism is government action which practically prohibits every individual from engaging in Production or Exchange on his own account. The difference between government management of all the business of the country, or only certain lines of it, is radical. In the one case the government enters a field occupied by thousands of others, leaving them as free as before; in the other, it drives all private enterprise out, and takes the whole field to itself. The mere management of a few public interests by the government does not shut out private enterprise. Schools, to be sure, stand on a somewhat different footing from Production and Exchange, but the public schools of the United States do not prevent great numbers of private schools. The post-office does not prevent the express companies from carrying matter that might go by mail. It is always well to have the possibility of competition of private parties with government business. But even if the government has a monopoly in certain enterprises, it leaves all the other business free to the citizen. The burden of proof is on those who advocate government control of any specified business. The lines of business which may properly come under the direct control of the government are comparatively few, and are likely to involve large interests. They are precisely those which would otherwise be carried on by great corporations, and probably by monopolies. All other lines of business remain, and are so numerous that they form in the aggregate by far the greater part of all the productive business of the country. Suppose that all *natural monopolies* were turned over to public management—that street-car lines, and even railways, were run by government officials, as they are in many countries in Europe. How much would this interfere with the opportunity of the ordinary citizen? He would probably have a better chance than before, since the government must treat all alike, and large corporations would not be able to crush out the smaller by reason of discrimination in freight rates. People may well say that when a business gets so large as to number thousands of stockholders, managed by officers elected by their votes, especially if it is of such a nature that there can be no competition, it would better be managed by the government. It may, or may not, be wise for the government to extend its business operations: that is another question. What we wish to emphasize here is the radical difference between shutting the citizen out of all business and the admission of the government as another business firm—a business firm which competes only with the large corporations, likely to become monopolies; and which in any case leaves the field as free to the ordinary citizen as before. Socialism is distinguished from all other organizations of society. Its characteristic is that it *shuts out* the citizen from production, not that it admits the government to some departments. Socialism demands that *all* the instruments of production shall be owned by the State. It is here that it is irreconcilably opposed to Individualism. It allows within certain limits, it is true, the use by each one of his income in his own way; but in Production and Exchange it permits no independent action, and here absolutely destroys Individualism.

There are, indeed, three well-marked schools of thought: first, the *laissez faire*, composed of those who would make the government merely a police force; second, those who would have it undertake such lines of business as experience shows can be much better managed by public than by private enterprise, and, under general regulations, compel all private business to be conducted in a way that will not interfere with the highest interests of the whole people; and third, the Socialists, who destroy all individual enterprise, prohibit the individual from engaging in business, and have *everything* done by the State. The difference between the last two schools is a hundred times as great as between the second and the first. It would be as great a mistake to call the second Socialists as to class them with the *laissez faire* school.

As in other instances, extremes meet. Socialists and men of the *laissez faire* school unite in the claim that everything which is not *laissez faire* is Socialism. The former wish to gain adherents by representing that the difference is only one of degree. The *laissez faire* school hope to prevent any further extention of government powers by crying "Socialism!" The cry was for a time effective. It was easier to make people believe that the management of a street-car line by a city "is only a step toward Socialism," which, if taken, "other steps are sure to follow," than to discuss the question on its merits. But the cry has now come to have the reverse effect from that intended, and has done immeasurable injury. People have reasoned, "If municipal control of gas-works is Socialism, Socialism must be a good thing." This indiscriminate attack by the *laissez faire* school on enterprises which the people are coming to approve, is one of the causes for the remarkable increase in the number of good men who call themselves Socialists. Now the great mass of common-sense men, who are neither Socialists nor in favor of letting everything alone until it goes to destruction, need to define their position. They must not allow themselves to be classed with Socialists, Christian or any other kind. They are to say that, while we do not believe in unnecessary interference with private business, we do not intend to let employers alone who work children under ten years of age in factories. We do not intend to let the father alone who is breaking down the health of his child, to throw it, when a man, a burden on society. We do not intend to let a corporation alone that is unduly oppressive to the people. We propose to move carefully, but we have no hesitation in giving the control of any business, like the post-office, to the government when there is good reason to believe it will be for the best interests of the people. We should show that none of these things are in any way related to Socialism; that the management of natural monopolies by the government is not Socialism; that the government of Germany, which owns the railroads, is not Socialism; and that the city of Paris, as now governed, is not a socialistic organization. They should indignantly refuse to be classed with Socialists, because Socialism is utterly opposed to their spirit.

There can be nothing more unfortunate than for the people to suppose that control of some *natural monopolies* by the government, means that all private enterprise shall be abandoned. It is only the intellectually weak man who fears that the doing of some things involves the doing of everything.

There is no doubt that the minds of the people have been somewhat confused on this subject; and that many advocates of government control of such public undertakings as seem necessary, fear that they are Socialists. They are nothing of the kind. Neither is a government which engages in necessary public undertakings, in as much danger of becoming socialistic as one managed on the "let alone" principle. One extreme tends to drive people to the other. When the mass of the people understand that the highest Individualism does not prevent the government from undertaking anything which is shown to be for the best interests of the public, does not prevent regulations for the humane treatment of children, or designed to secure their education, the converts to Socialism can never become numerous enough to enslave society. Socialism is to be fought on the ground of its tyranny, its proposal to enslave the minority by the power of the majority, and its attempt to prevent the individual from engaging in Production or Exchange.

BOOK IV.
ECONOMICAL USE OF THE RESOURCES.

BOOK IV.

ECONOMICAL USE OF THE RESOURCES.

INTRODUCTION,	. . . .	201

CHAPTER	I.	THE ECONOMICAL USE OF LABOR, . .	203
	PART I.	The Constant Employment of Labor, . .	203
	PART II.	The Irksomeness of Labor, ...	209
	PART III.	The Division of Labor, ...	214
	PART IV.	The Development of Labor Power, and the Prohibition of Certain Forms of Labor,	221
CHAPTER	II.	ECONOMICAL USE OF THE RESOURCES OF NATURE, ...	225
	PART I.	Permanent Natural Resources, ...	225
	PART II.	Consumable Natural Resources, . . .	231
	PART III.	Public and Private Use of the Resources of Nature, ...	234
CHAPTER	III.	ECONOMICAL USE OF PRODUCED WEALTH,	242
CHAPTER	IV.	THE USE OF THE RESOURCE OF SOCIETY,	252
CHAPTER	V.	THE PURPOSES FOR WHICH THE RESOURCES SHALL BE USED, ...	256

BOOK IV.
ECONOMICAL USE OF THE RESOURCES.

This subject is not the same as "Production" in the older books on Political Economy, but includes it. Our point of view is entirely different from that of the older political economists. They treated of the "Production of Wealth," its Distribution and Exchange; we are treating of the Satisfaction of Human Wants. Many of these wants are satisfied, directly, by labor without the intervention of wealth at all. The teacher, singer, preacher, as well as most persons engaged in personal service, satisfy wants directly, instead of by the roundabout way of producing something which shall afterward be used in their satisfaction.

The economical use of the Resources is of even more importance than their extent. Our Resources are greater than in former times. We have discovered many Resources of Nature unknown to the past; the power of labor is greater in proportion to the population; and the accumulations of Produced Wealth are vastly larger, but the better satisfaction of wants is due as much to modern methods of using the Resources as to their increase. Not only are wants better satisfied, but the world is able to provide for far larger numbers of people. Methods of using the Resources also determine to some extent whose wants shall be satisfied, irrespective of the question of the ownership of property. In Book I. we saw what Resources a nation has for the satisfaction of the wants of its people; in Book II. we considered the number of people whose wants are to be satisfied; in Book III., the ownership or control of these Resources; and we now come to the question of their practical use in satisfying the wants of the people of a nation.

We shall find that the simplest plan is to treat of the use of each Resource separately. Such treatment can be only of general principles. The detailed use of the Resources must be determined, each one for himself; and skill in details brings fortunes to many. We can not pursue the subject so as to determine how a farm or a factory should be carried on. This requires a knowledge of business, of thousands of minor matters. Few men can learn more than one line of production. But there are certain fundamental principles, such as a statesman should understand, which underlie all business, all methods of production, and all methods of satisfying wants.

We may take up the four great classes of Resources in any order, but it will be more convenient, as in the last book, to begin with Labor.

CHAPTER I.

THE ECONOMICAL USE OF LABOR.

Part I.—The Constant Employment of Labor.

The first requirement for the economical use of labor is to use it—to provide for the constant employment of all the labor of a country. No waste is so great as that of idleness. The chief misfortune of financial panics, and of a change in the value of money, is that multitudes of men are thrown out of employment, and fill the country with an army of idlers or tramps. The work that these men might have done is so much loss. The loss from the idleness of a thousand men is just as real as that from the destruction of a million dollars' worth of property by fire. This explains, in part, why a country sometimes seems to recover so quickly from disasters. Let us suppose a part of a city to be burned. Here is a real loss of Produced Wealth. The city must be built up again, and the burned structures may be replaced by new which are even better than the old. Here is a call for additional labor. If there are thousands of idle men all over the country willing to work for pay, they may be at once employed. Some will be put at work in the city where the loss occurred; others will be added to the working force of mills in other parts of the country, for the production of building material, builders' hardware, glass—every one of the thousands of articles which go to replace the buildings destroyed. The additional work will not all be done by new men. Factories which were running on short time may now increase their hours of labor. When the city is rebuilt, if we could trace the processes, we might find that it was all *extra* work; that is, hours of labor which would not have been put in had there been no fire. The balance sheet of the country may show as well at the end of the rebuilding as before the fire. There has been a great loss; but there has been an equal gain in additional labor performed. The loss has been replaced by men who would otherwise have been idle, or worked fewer hours. There has been a shifting of property. The owners of the buildings have lost, and the workmen of the country have gained.

We have assumed that there was a large body of men out of employment, or of men who would work more hours. On the contrary, if all men were at work before the fire, and the city is rebuilt by labor taken from some other form of production, the country is so much the poorer. The single truth now before us is, the misfortune of the idleness of large numbers of men. Labor is a Resource for the Satisfaction of Wants which, if not used to-day, is lost; since the work that would have been done to-day can not be done to-morrow. Every month of enforced idleness is so much loss to the country.

For it must be remembered that one must live whether he works or not; if he has nothing saved, he must borrow; if he can not borrow, he must live on the charity of others. The view of some of the English political economists has been too much that of the manufacturer, who counts only the wages he pays; if he shuts down his factory, he saves the wages. When we stop a steam-engine we, at least, save the coal, but when a man ceases work he does not save the necessity of food. Practically, it costs the same for him to live whether he works or not. It is true that men do live on less; but that is because one never knows on how little he can live until he is obliged to make the experiment. He might live in the same way when he is at work, and save the difference between the lowest cost of living and his wages. He requires a little more food when at work, but the increased cost is not enough to be taken into account. It is also true that many men when they lose employment at one kind of labor do not actually cease to work, but earn a smaller sum in some other way, or by labor at home reduce their family expenses. But the cost of living depends very slightly on whether one is at work or not; hence if he is doing nothing, the present available resources for the satisfaction of wants are so much less. The first requirement for the use of labor power, then, is that it be constantly employed. As a practical country merchant observed, "I have always noticed that where all the people worked, and were economical, they got rich or well-to-do." The steady power of continuous labor, year after year, tells.

It is of the utmost importance, then, that every man has a chance to work when he desires, under conditions which will give him at least the greater part of the results of his own labor. Society has in some way to keep all persons from starving, whether they work or not. A few are supported by charity, and a few live by robbery; but it would be better if all were employed in useful labor.

The people are the purchasers. The fact that great numbers are out of employment prevents their purchasing, and leaves stocks of goods on hand. Producing must be stopped until the stocks are worked off. It is like a row of bricks. Each set of men is knocked down one after another, and there is no market for anything, because nobody is producing anything, and has nothing to buy with. So long as human wants are unsatisfied, there should be opportunity for the employment of men. Suppose, in a panic when thousands of men can find nothing to do, we should send to each one and ask him what he would buy if he had the money! Now suppose we put this army of the unemployed to producing just those commodities—to satisfying their own wants! These men would be at work, and these wants would be supplied. The workmen are the consumers; they are their own market. It costs them no more to live when at work than when idle, and proper statistics should show where labor is most needed. We may be sure that it is needed somewhere so long as any wants remain unsatisfied.

The direction of production is now mainly determined by the demand for goods at certain prices; but the falling off in the demand does not show itself until production has been carried too far in one direction. It sometimes seems as though there is no demand for any goods, that the market in every line is overstocked; yet we have at the same time idle men who want these very goods, but have nothing to buy with. There is capital enough; the men must have food and clothing in any case, but no business man sees his way, from the demand and supply of the market, to undertake to set them at work at anything. The ordinary facts of demand and supply at certain prices need to be supplemented by public statistics which will help to show where these men can be put to work with profit. They should be producing something to exchange for the surplus stocks of goods which burden the shelves of the merchant. The difficulty is not in a lack of desire for the goods, but in the fact that idle men are unable to exchange their labor for them.

Financial panics are the means of throwing large numbers of men out of employment, and panics are frequently due to a change in the value of money. Even if there is no panic, when the value of money is steadily increasing and the prices of goods falling, men hesitate to engage in business. An increase in the value of money is the same as a fall in the price of goods. Now, when the prices of all goods are falling, men are afraid to manufacture. By the time the returns are to be expected the goods will be worth less, and a fall in price will absorb the profits. No one knows how great the fall will be. Everybody is cautious. Employers try to keep on the safe side, but while they are on the safe side thousands of men are idle because they can find nothing to do. Business men are on the safe side because they fear a change in the value of money.

Labor unions and strikes are a cause of idleness. Let us suppose that a strike succeeds: the country has nevertheless lost so much by the long period of idleness on the part of the men. Suppose that the strikers are maintained by the contributions of other men of their class; and that, by reason of the labor unions, these contributing members *do* get higher wages, so that the limited number of men at work actually receive as much in wages as would the entire body of workmen, strikers included. Nevertheless, the country has lost the labor of the idle men, and they have gained nothing. They are no better off under the anxiety of the strike than if they had been constantly employed. The people have lost by the strike, and the workmen have gained nothing. Idleness is waste, and unfortunate, whether it comes by commercial panics, when employers are compelled to shut down their mills, or by strikes in good times, when men refuse to work.

The opportunity for more constant employment of labor may be found in co-operation, in which the workmen own the business; and perhaps a large part, if not all, the capital with which it is carried on. If they owned the land, the building, the machinery, and other capital necessary, they would come as near being independent as is possible. In dull times the returns to their labor would be less, but they would at least have something to do, and get all they make. I realize the difficulties of co-operation as fully as any of those who think it impracticable, but the security of employment counts for much.

Labor should also be used without waste of strength. Some men will expend twice as much energy as others in accomplishing the same result. This is as true of mental labor as of physical. There are a few who have learned to think directly about the subject in hand, and about nothing unnecessary to it. Other persons are obliged to settle many preparatory and incidental questions before they come to the real one. Such men must cut down a whole forest, and examine each tree, to get the one piece of timber they want.

WASTED LABOR.—It is assumed that labor is to be economically employed for the satisfaction of wants. Labor may, however, be wasted, when the loss is as great as that of idleness. One may work hard all day in carrying stones across the road and back again, but the world is no better off, and no more wants are satisfied than if he sat still by the roadside. There is undoubtedly a great deal of wasted labor in consequence of misdirected effort. Goods are produced which nobody wants, or are made so poorly from lack of skill and knowledge that they are useless.

We have little conception of the wasted labor in the world. The employer who turns it in the direction where it is all of use, has saved to the world all that would otherwise have been wasted, which may be half of all the labor he employs. All that has been said about the importance of the constant employment of labor has no force except with the implied assumption that the labor is to be used for practical purposes, and shall aid in satisfying wants.

PART II.—THE IRKSOMENESS OF LABOR.

The desire for leisure is as real as any want we have to satisfy. Most men dislike to work, and are looking forward to more leisure, and would be glad of shorter hours. Thus far we have considered labor power simply as any other force which can be used. If all men preferred labor to leisure, we should have only to consider how to get the most accomplished by the members of a given society. But the workman embodies in himself both the labor power and the wants to be satisfied. All through the world's history there has been an effort to have one class work, and another class eat, thus completing the circle of Political Economy. The smaller class which ate, was indifferent to the larger class which worked. The modern conception is of a people nearly all of whom are engaged in some economic labor; that is, in an effort to satisfy wants by the use of muscle or mind, or both. Where all the people work, we have no wants except the wants of the laborers; and one of these wants is more leisure — shorter hours, longer vacations, less labor. The question is, how far we shall ever be able to satisfy this general desire for leisure, and at the same time satisfy the numerous other wants; and how this desire for leisure compares in importance with other wants. When it is a question of food and raiment for one's self or family, the common opinion of Americans holds up to scorn the man who is unwilling to work for them to the extreme of his ability without physical injury. But there are many who hold that the provision of the common comforts of life ought, in the present stage of civilization, to leave some leisure to the workman.

We observe that most labor becomes more disagreeable as the hours per day are increased. There is indeed a very general conviction that a certain amount of work is for one's benefit. Although one may desire leisure for the time being, his judgment tells him that for most men, and probably for himself, continuous employment for say five hours a day, six days in the week and forty weeks in the year, would be better than idleness. Eight hours is more than twice as irksome as four, and twelve more than twice as irksome as eight. So far as mere results are concerned, it is now the opinion of those who have collected the fullest statistics on the subject that, in the average of mechanical trades and shopwork, the maximum result is accomplished by about eleven hours of labor per day. A farmer with a great variety of duties in the open air, including the care of his stock and what are called "chores," may perhaps accomplish more in sixteen hours than in less. But with the intense strain of the factory, nearly all men will do more in twelve hours than in sixteen, and in many instances more in ten than in twelve. There are a few employments in which one can accomplish more in less than ten hours, but not many. So far as the *results* of labor are concerned, the present hours of labor in most employments probably enable the workman to accomplish the maximum amount. A further reduction in the hours must be for the purpose of satisfying the desire for leisure— as real a want as any beyond the mere necessities of life.

Many workmen claim that as four sets of men tending a machine for four hours each, can now accomplish a hundred times as much work as the same number of men working sixteen hours a day a hundred years ago, they ought to be able to secure a living with fewer hours of labor. On the other side, it should be said: (1) The saving of machinery is as great as this in only a few employments. On the farm, for example, while much machinery has been introduced, there is much that must be done at which one can accomplish little more than was effected fifty years ago. The amount of hand labor yet required is very large, and the average saving of machinery is by no means so great as at first appears. (2) A large part of the gain from machinery is absorbed by an increased population. Without labor-saving machinery the present population could not be supported with anything like the degree of comfort of fifty years ago. (3) The saving of machinery is shown in the better satisfaction of wants. With all the present hardships, the condition of the workingman, and of the entire people, is far better than before. (4) There has been an average shortening of the hours of labor. But there is no doubt that the wants of the people, where population is not too dense, could be fairly well provided for with a further reduction in the hours of labor, especially if our industrial system was so perfect that employment could always be found by all persons willing to work.

For the highest satisfaction of wants laboring men should demand that the hours and days of labor be reduced, at least to the point of the greatest return; that is, to the point where as much can be accomplished, year by year, as with longer days. More labor than this is waste. The employer for a month or year may gain by it, but the people, in the long run, gain nothing, and the laborer has lost the satisfaction and advantage which he might have had with shorter days. The most important regulation is that of one rest-day in seven. There can be no doubt that the average man will accomplish more by working six days a week than seven. Sunday work is therefore waste work. To say nothing of the fact, that one will receive no more wages in the end for seven days' work than for six, it is also true that he can not earn any more. In a few cases where Sunday work is a necessity, the workman should insist on another day for rest at some time during the week. The Sunday force should have Saturday or Monday. One entire day out of every seven is worth more for rest than the same number of hours scattered through the week. Ten hours a day with a Sunday rest is better for any person than seven days' work with only eight and a half hours per day for seven days. The continued monotony of daily labor needs to be broken up. So, a week or two, "out of work," at some time during the year is not time lost. If the workman does not accomplish more during the year, he at least gains something in increased advantage to himself. After a Sunday rest has been provided for, every shortening of hours is an advantage (except to the few who spend the leisure time in dissipation), and with the increased use of machinery and improved social organization, a very considerable shortening of the labor day may take place.

Part III.—The Division of Labor.

Adam Smith made the term "Division of Labor" classical, and, if the name is not the best, it is almost universally understood. It is the dividing of labor among different men in such a way that each shall do only one thing, or at most attend to a class of similar things. So far has the division of labor been carried in factories that in the manufacture of mowing and reaping machines one man does nothing but drill holes in a frame. He learns only the smallest piece of a trade, but becomes very expert. Practice shows that the gain from this minute division of labor is far greater than Adam Smith imagined, or than would have been expected from theoretical reasoning. The secret of the enormous increase, which seems to have escaped most writers, is the automatic action of the human body. To put forth a conscious effort at every movement is very wearisome; but after we have done the same thing a certain number of times, the nervous organism takes care of the necessary movements without conscious effort. Where one performs an act for the first time, he is compelled to give mental attention to it; but continued repetition establishes an automatic action, by which the nervous system continues to repeat the motion. In walking we do not think of the steps we are taking. Many a philosopher strolls through the country thinking as he walks, hardly conscious that he is walking. It is so with every kind of labor. By continually doing one thing, we come to do it automatically, as we walk, with no more fatigue than the necessary muscular exertion. One may be able to do for ten hours what, if attempted for the first time, would weary him in one hour. In addition to this automatic action we gain all the skill that comes from constant repetition. It is not only the "learning how" to do a thing; it is the doing it until it is done automatically, which increases one's labor power.

The actual gain from the division of labor is beyond what is easily realized. It would be impossible to satisfy a hundredth part of the wants of the present day if each man were to do everything for himself. Adam Smith's famous example of pin-making in his day, showed that in a small factory ten men, with indifferent machinery, could make forty-eight thousand pins a day, or four thousand eight hundred to each man; whereas a man working independently could not make twenty; that is, the result of his work was increased two hundred and forty times by the division and recombination of labor. Pins are now made by a machine with a far greater saving of labor than in Adam Smith's day.

The division of labor makes machinery possible, and the use of machinery renders a division of labor necessary. A valuable machine can not always be trusted to unskilled labor; one must learn its management, and the man and the machine go together. Historically, the division of labor was introduced by reason of the economy of one man's devoting his time to a particular trade; but it has been carried to its present minute subdivisions by the introduction of machinery, and the setting of one man to tending a machine.

The division of labor has been as productive of increased results in the highest employments as in the more simple operations, and as much gain has been made in the division of mental labor as in muscular. No man now expects to learn everything. He who hopes to add to the sum of human knowledge must have his specialty. One man gives his entire attention to chemistry; another, to some department of natural history. By devoting so much time to a narrow field, one becomes very proficient. His work, if well done, may not need to be done over again, or may be reviewed with comparatively little effort. In economic science, he who would add anything to that already known must not only know what has been done, but must give a great deal of time to original investigation. The number of men now devoting their lives to specialties is very large, and it is because of the division of the field of knowledge into so many parts that the exploration is proceeding so rapidly. It should also be noticed that one person may spend many years in preparing to investigate a specialty, and so make himself a very competent investigator. If he were to attempt the whole field of knowledge, he could make no such preparation.

An extended division of labor is not practical except where there is a considerable number of people. It does not require a very large community to need the service of a shoemaker, but when we come to a factory which employs at least a hundred men in the manufacture of a particular kind of shoe, it is evident that there must be a large population to keep these hundred men at work. So, a large population is required to support the business of piano-making. Theoretically, it might seem that a population of a few thousand people would afford opportunity for a very great division of labor; but, practically, the division of labor to its present extent is impossible except with a population of a great many thousand people. It is not necessary that these people all reside in the same city, or even in the same nation.

How Far Should the Division of Labor be Carried?—The only question concerning the division of labor at present is the extent to which it should be carried, and here we have to take into account the wants and welfare of the laborers as well as their increase in labor power; for we shall make a mistake wherever we lose sight of the fact that the laborers embody in themselves both labor power and the wants we have to satisfy. One of these wants, as we have seen before, is leisure. Another, is individual development, both physical and mental; and another is agreeableness of the labor performed.

The division of labor must be supplemented by a combination of the scattered parts of the work. Each man must be matched against others of a set. If one man is to spend his entire time in drilling holes in a frame, there must be many others engaged in making the frame. If a thousand men are at work in this machine shop, there must be hundreds of thousands at other employments. The difficulty in this division and recombination of labor is to keep just the right number of men at each part all of the time. If one class of workmen strike, they stop the set with which they are connected. If too many people are engaged in one employment, there is soon an overproduction in that particular line. More shoes are made than can be worn, and enforced idleness is the result. The enforced idleness of one set of laborers reduces their income and power to purchase the productions of other sets, and throws some of them out of employment. Eventually things will adjust themselves by a change of employment on the part of a portion of the laborers, but this adjustment comes only after a panic and hard times. Thus, where each man does only a very simple thing, and has not learned the other parts of his trade, the adjustments must be very close. Then there are likely to be too many men of one class in proportion to those of others, and some of these must be idle. Where each man understands an entire trade, instead of a part of the trade, he may do any portion of it for which laborers are needed. He may take the place of those who fail, or go where there is the greatest need. If a young man learns only a part of the trade, in later life he is liable to be thrown out of work through changes in the methods of production, or through the excess of laborers in his department; and it is not easy for him to pick up the other parts of the trade. Where one has learned to do a considerable variety of things in his youth, and mastered at least the whole of one trade, he is able to continue at work in places where the division of labor is not carried very far; and in large factories he can fill any one of several places, thus insuring constant employment for himself. The extreme division of labor tends, therefore, to throw large numbers of laborers out of employment whenever anything unusual occurs in the methods of production. It is a question whether the division of labor at the present day, considering the loss from necessary idleness, is not carried farther than is profitable, even when we take into account only the results accomplished. Nevertheless, the enormous gain from a division and recombination of labor is so great that it is likely to be still further extended; and we need better means for distributing the laborers among different trades, so that fewer will be out of employment.

TENDS TO BELITTLE THE LABORER.—It is evident that an extreme division of labor tends to belittle the laborer. The man who does one simple thing day after day, which he comes to do automatically, will not develop himself as did the traditional Yankee, who could do anything. The fact that one is able to do a considerable variety of things, and does do very many things in the course of a year, tends to make him alert, to increase his inventive power, and is undoubtedly one of the causes of the unusual skill of American workmen. When we take the welfare of the laborer into account, we can not afford to have men reduced to mere machines. The scope of their work must be broad enough to give them the skill and general ability of the traditional American mechanic.

The injury to the laborer by the excessive division of labor may be partly overcome by working fewer hours in the day. His development then depends upon how he spends his leisure time. It may be wasted, or may be used in study which will make him more of a man than would even a great variety of work. But, for the average workman, nothing will more conduce to the development of his powers than a variety of work, or a range of work wide enough to occupy his mind and develop his inventive genius. We could well afford to sacrifice something in the amount of labor which can be accomplished, for the sake of the character of the laborer.

It should also be noticed that the gain from the division of labor *decreases* very rapidly the farther it is carried. There is enormous gain in dividing the work of the world into different trades; and, frequently, in a very much more extended subdivision. But after the division of labor has been carried as far as is for the advantage of the laborer, the subsequent gain from more minute divisions is very much less. We might almost say that the advantage from the extension of the division of labor decreases in geometrical progression. And the philanthropist will never desire to see it carried farther than is for the benefit of the workman.

Closely connected with the division of labor is the advantage of each man doing what he can do best. This is not the same thing as the division of labor. There would be great gain from the latter if we deliberately put each man to doing what he is least fitted for. A few years' practice at the work at which he was set would make him far more efficient than the best natural untrained hand. Nevertheless, much more would be accomplished by apportioning the work with regard to natural ability. It is true there may not be work enough of a certain kind for all the men who are better fitted for it than for anything else, but the poorest must take something for which he is not so well fitted, though there is always a second and third choice.

PART IV. THE DEVELOPMENT OF LABOR POWER AND THE PROHIBITION OF CERTAIN FORMS OF LABOR.

Labor power, unlike Natural Resources, does not live forever; but is developed and dies with each generation. The education and training of men has reference both to their power to do something, and also to their character and personal well-being; but, considered only with reference to their power of labor, their education and training are of the utmost importance. More will be accomplished in a generation by devoting the first twenty years of the child's life to education. This education might include the learning a trade. A little development of skill may double the laborer's power for forty years. A slight increase in intelligence may make the laborer ten times more effective. It is undoubtedly for the interest of society that the early years of life be given to preparing for labor thereafter. Child labor, aside from that in the home, is particularly wasteful. It is unfortunate that a child under twenty years of age should be compelled to support his parents. Society can not afford to have the youth of the rising generation wasted in this way.

The labor of children to a moderate extent on a farm or at home is often the best part of an education. So, also, the learning of a good trade by a boy who can not go to school, is the next best thing to school training; assuming, in both cases, that labor is not carried to excess. But child labor in factories, and in many other conditions, is a different matter. Seldom is any trade learned; the child is deprived of school education; and there is the danger of permanent physical injury. When we come to child labor in mines, and under circumstances which work physical injury, it is not only abominable, but economically unprofitable. That is, the child will accomplish less during his lifetime than if he had not been injured in childhood. The reports of the labor of children in the sulphur mines of Sicily. show a complete ruin of the child before he comes to manhood. The labor of children in English coal mines a century ago was not much better. The breaking down of the physical constitution of the child not only affects his own life, but that of future generations. This much, so far as the mere amount of work accomplished is concerned. When we take the wants of the child into consideration, the case is far stronger. The welfare of the child for his entire life depends largely on his childhood.

All unhealthful conditions of labor, such as badly ventilated factories, not only decrease the power of the laborer, and reduce the amount of labor he will be able to perform thereafter, but also detract from the satisfaction of his own wants. Life is much harder for him on this account, and his satisfactions are fewer.

More attention will doubtless be given in the future to the healthful conditions of the laborer, and to agreeable surroundings during the hours of labor.

PROHIBITION OF CERTAIN FORMS OF LABOR.— 1. *Prohibition of child labor in mines and factories.* In all that is said about the right of a man to control himself, we understand one who has reached the ordinary age of judgment. A child is not a man, and does not know what he himself will want as he grows older. Society is the natural protector of all children. They are to become men, to be voters, and their influence on other people will be felt all their lives. Society has an interest in their labor power, and can not afford to have a child ruined before he becomes of age. There is seldom any necessity for State interference with child labor at home. The boy on a farm is in the open air, and works under conditions which have given us some of the ablest men in the nation. But when the child is compelled to work for others than his parents, or to work under the conditions of factory life, it is time for the State to interfere. A child in a town where there is a factory ought to be in school. A farm boy should be in school also, but the loss is not so great when he gets the Yankee education that comes from farm life. The labor of children under fourteen in mines and factories should be absolutely prohibited. For a few years after that period, it should be tolerated only under certain conditions, such as a half-day in school, or the learning of a trade, and even then the State should see that the conditions are healthful, both physically and morally.

2. *The prohibition of the labor of women in certain employments.* The welfare of woman is so important to Society that her degradation can not be permitted. She must not be allowed to work in coal mines, as in England years ago, or at certain other kinds of labor; and, if in a factory, the State should require the conditions to be healthful.

3. *The prohibition of the labor of men under certain conditions.* Men can be found who will destroy their health for wages. Society can not afford to have its labor power broken down unnecessarily, nor to have the population deteriorate. Hence every factory should be inspected, and the conditions of life therein be made as healthful as the nature of the employment will allow.

CHAPTER II.

ECONOMICAL USE OF THE RESOURCES OF NATURE.

The Resources of Nature, it will be remembered, are either *permanent* or *consumable*. The first includes land, the atmosphere, water, etc., and is by far the larger and more important portion. The second consists of coal and other materials, the natural fertility of the soil, timber, wild animals, fish, etc. The economic requirements for the use of the two classes differ because the one is not destroyed in the using, but continues from age to age; while the other class is consumed as used. Some of the Consumable Natural Wealth will be replaced in time by Nature, and other portions can be replaced by man, while still other varieties, when once used, are destroyed forever.

PART I.—PERMANENT NATURAL RESOURCES.

The Best First.—It is economy to use the best of the Permanent Natural Resources first, and hold the rest in reserve. The best satisfy more wants with less labor than the poorer, and as they are not destroyed in the using nothing is lost. The very best may give a few people a fair living almost without work; while from the poorest it would be impossible to obtain the most meager subsistence for the laborers. It is very unfortunate for any nation to be compelled to use the poorest of its Natural Resources, and perhaps no nation has ever brought into use every known Resource of Nature in order to support its people; there is always a poorer reserve out of which intense labor might still wring a scanty return, though not enough to support itself.

As population crowds a country, it is often necessary to bring into use the inferior Resources of Nature by which wants are much more poorly satisfied. The owner of a good farm can provide a much better living for his family than the owner of inferior land. A city located on a good harbor has the advantage over one on a poor harbor, or one with no harbor at all. The people with pure air and pure water have a great advantage over those breathing the miasma of a swamp, and using water that is polluted by vegetable decay or otherwise. So, the people with abundance of room have an advantage over those who must breathe the air of the crowded tenement districts. It is an advantage to use the best air and the best water. The best Resources of Nature are not always used first, because they are not always the easiest to get at in the beginning. The early immigrants to New England came upon the rocky and poor land. The Western prairies were reached later, with great difficulty. We hear a great deal of late about the abandoned farms of New England—abandoned because there is better land for agricultural purposes in the West, and we are coming to use the best Resources of Nature. With the dense population of the Eastern cities, these abandoned farms are often much more desirable for summer residences than the crowded city or the Western prairie;

and hence are being rapidly changed from agricultural to residence land. For residence land they are the best, and follow the law enunciated.

This economic requirement is violated by land speculators in new countries, who often hold the best land out of the market for a higher price; also, in cities where private owners hold the land best fitted for building purposes out of the market for an increase in value. Enterprising builders are compelled to go beyond them, to travel a greater distance or to use less desirable building-sites, while the use of these best locations is lost for many years. Indeed, one of the strongest arguments which those who favor the nationalization of land make, is the claim that the best land and the best locations would be used first, and only the poorer, and the more distant, brought into use as required. The proper way to build a city is, beginning at a center, to extend business blocks, continually; and residences one after the other as closely as the sizes of lots makes desirable. There should be no vacant blocks or spaces, and no unnecessary distance to travel. So in the settlement of a new country, it is not best to run over the whole land at first, and to open a new farm miles distant from other habitations. When the new farm is needed, the land adjoining one already cultivated should be taken, and so the farms on the prairie should extend toward the west, one joining the other with no uncultivated space between. This would give the advantage of compact society and of a sufficiently dense population. When we say the best land, we do not always mean that which will produce the largest crops; but that which, all things considered, is best fitted to satisfy wants. The *location* of the land may be more important, even for agricultural purposes, than its quality. In cities the location is everything.

It would undoubtedly be proper for the government to require that all land be brought into use as fast as needed, notwithstanding private ownership. Should the owner be unwilling, or unable, to use it for the best interests of society, it might be proper to order that it be condemned and sold at a fair price to one who would so use it. Land in cities, very necessary for building sites, has long been held out of the market through the action of the law in regard to minor or insane heirs. Because no title could be given to those who would use it for the interests of Society, it has been covered with unsightly buildings and used for immoral purposes. Some provision for the use of all such Natural Wealth should be made. The first rule in regard to Natural Wealth is to use the best of it first, and to leave the poorest as a reserve.

It is not always possible to use the best Resources of Nature first, because more time is required to put them in condition for use than the people at the beginning are able to bestow.

Many of the Natural Resources, especially the forces of nature, are discovered late in the world's history. They were not used earlier because not known, but as soon as discovered they add greatly to the satisfaction of wants. What was the best, years ago, may become the poorest through the discovery of something better.

For years men were largely dependent on the force of the wind to sail their ships. With the discovery of the method of using steam, and of the beds of coal to produce it, it is found more economical to use coal and steam to some extent than to depend entirely on wind and sails. We have recently discovered practical methods of separating the metal aluminum from the clay combinations which hold it. How much man gained when he found that he could melt a red ore, and produce an iron which could be hammered into shape! Stone then became useless for cutting purposes. More recently we have discovered the reservoirs of petroleum beneath the surface of the earth, and the rock gas which, so long as it may last, takes the place of coal. The rich swamps may be brought into use late in a country's settlement. This may sometimes happen through ignorance of their utility when drained; but more often because the new settler has not time to drain them, or to wait for the sour land to be sweetened by the sunlight and air. It is economy to use the best of Nature's Resources first, but time, frequently more than a year, is required before results are secured. The new settler, even if he knows the utility of the swamp, has not a great store of Produced Wealth on hand, perhaps but little machinery, and he must live. If he is poor, he is quite likely to take the land he can work the easiest, and get results from quickest, even though they be small. After he has accumulated a supply of food for a year, provided some machinery, and can spare some labor from the present needs of his family, he will drain the swamp, adding Produced Wealth to Natural Wealth—drains to the swamp—and may find the latter so much better that he will abandon the poorest of his old land.

Use to the Point of Diminishing Returns, but Not Beyond. — Natural Resources should be used to the point of diminishing returns, and not too far beyond. The meaning of the phrase, "diminishing returns," was explained in Book II., but unless the reader has a very clear conception of it, it would be well to turn back and re-read what is there said, for this is one of the most important principles in Political Economy. By diminishing returns we mean the returns to a given amount of labor employed on land. It pays to work a farm well. The good farmer gets a larger return for each day's work than the poor farmer. The poor farmer can frequently double the labor expended upon his land and more than double the crop, but there is a limit to such increase. After a certain amount of labor has been expended upon land, additional work will produce better crops, *but not better in proportion to the labor bestowed.* If ten days' labor produces twenty bushels of wheat, an additional ten days' labor will produce only ten bushels, and consequently the returns to labor have diminished. In the first instance we have two bushels of wheat for each day's work, in the second only one and a half. It is very important that land be worked to the point of diminishing returns; because it pays better than when the cultivation is poorer, and because it gives opportunity for a more dense population, and the advantages of society. It is clearly unfortunate to be compelled to work land be-

ECONOMICAL USE OF NATURAL WEALTH. 231

yond the point of diminishing returns, because the reward of labor is so much less. A dense population in an agricultural country is compelled to work land far beyond this point, unless food is imported from abroad.

Something analogous to this occurs in the erection of a building. There is economy in building a business block of several stories; but a height is soon reached where every additional story costs more in proportion, either in the cost of building or in the cutting off of light and air from other buildings. Tall buildings are erected only because of the great value of the land on which they stand. If an adjoining lot could be had for nothing, the buildings would be lower. It is an advantage to have population dense enough to require buildings of as great height as can be economically erected, but when we go beyond this, the cost of room is increased.

PART II.—THE USE OF THE CONSUMABLE RESOURCES OF NATURE.

1. *These should be used without waste*, since they are destroyed in the using, and are limited in quantity. Of the minerals, such as coal and iron, it is certain that there is enough for the next hundred years, but a hundred years is a very short period in the world's history; the coal was produced by the growth of forests for thousands of years; and the interests of the people five hundred years hence should be considered as well as our own. To be sure, some substitute for coal may

be discovered, but no one knows that it will be discovered. The only certain method for the production of a substitute which we could now put in practice is the devoting of large tracts of land to forests, and by the slow growth of timber supply fuel for heat and power. All this is no reason for suffering the coal to remain unused—our interests are just as important as those of the people who shall come after us—but it is a reason for insisting that all such Resources of Nature should be used without waste, and the prevention of waste should be enforced by government authority.

Timber. — There is another class of Consumable Natural Resources which can be replaced by human effort, and some of which nature will replace unaided. Of these are timber, wild animals and fish. Timber can be grown, but it requires the use of land for many years. The time will perhaps come in the United States when we shall grow timber as a regular crop, as we now do wheat; but the great expense connected with such production is a reason for insisting on the protection of our present timber lands. For the effect on climate, the forests should doubtless be maintained in many mountain regions; and if these lands of little value for agriculture were kept in the possession of the government and protected from depredations, timber could be sold from them each year. The question of forestry has received more attention in Europe than in the United States. It will be fortunate for us if we refuse to sell the land still in the national possession which is suitable for public parks and forests. The forests will be a protection for river sources, and exert a favorable influence on climate. Once sold for a pittance, the national possession of this land can not be regained except at more than ten times the price. Steps should also be immediately taken to regain possession of land which ought never to have been sold.

Fish.—Fish, as one of the Resources of Nature, are a very important food supply, both for the savage and the civilized man. When the catch is not too great, the supply is maintained without human effort or supervision; but as population increases it is very easy to diminish, and perhaps exterminate, some of the most desirable varieties. Hence, supervision of the fishing interests is a very proper part of the work of any government. Although all fishermen may know that reckless fishing is ruinous in the end, even to their own interests, the quantity which any one fisherman may take can not be large enough to make any perceptible difference, and his course will have no influence on that of others. The fisherman whose operations will be limited by the law may, therefore, be perfectly satisfied with the law which compels others as well as himself to observe certain rules. The United States Fish Commission is now exercising a very general supervision over this class of Natural Wealth; and is studying the habits of the fishes with a view of making this resource of more use to the people. New waters are stocked with new varieties, and protection given to the finny tribes where they are in danger of extermination. Excellent State laws have also been enacted, and the future of this form of Natural Wealth is very hopeful. Like all the Resources of

Nature, fish are, of right, the property of the whole people; and, fortunately, the difficulty of fencing them in has made their appropriation by private parties difficult. Such appropriation has been attempted, and to some extent carried out. The public ownership of all the fish in our waters is the ground of the right and duty of the governments, both State and national, to encourage fish production, and to regulate the manner in which fish shall be taken.

Any reader will understand that where fishing is free, competition will reduce the selling price to the cost of taking, so that the people really get their own fish for nothing, paying only the competitive price of catching and handling by wholesale and retail dealers.

Part III.—Public and Private Use of the Resources of Nature.

The greater part of land is now held as private property, and its use controlled by him who has the title in fee. If all land were still in the hands of the government, the first question would be whether it should work the land on public account or lease it to private parties. To work all land on government account would mean Socialism, since it would necessitate State ownership of most other instruments of production. The State would be compelled to improve the land, build houses for its employes upon it, own teams and farming implements, and erect the buildings in cities. The objections already urged against Socialism condemn this plan. The fact that Society owns the

ECONOMICAL USE OF NATURAL WEALTH. 235

Resources of Nature no more implies that government should work them on public account than the ownership of English acres, or an Irish estate, implies that the proprietor works the land with his own hands. As a matter of fact, he rents it. A government can lease land as easily as an Irish landlord. Neither is there any difficulty in giving the occupant permanent possession, so that he may be sure of living in the house he builds, and leaving it to his children after him.

The natural, indeed the only, course for the government to pursue, if it retains possession of its land as a trustee for the people, is to give a perpetual lease at a variable rent—rent which shall be increased or diminished, annually, as the value of the land changes.

In any case, therefore, we may expect the great bulk of the Natural Resources to be *used* by private parties, and not by the State. Under the private ownership of land, as it exists among us, this is the case; and with recognition of State ownership, the land would still be leased to private parties who would use it in individual enterprise precisely as at present. All the instruments of production would, of course, be in the hands of private persons. Private parties would make the improvements, erect the buildings, and control all the machinery for carrying on production. Society would go on as at present, with the exception that the rent of the Resources of Nature would be paid to the government as trustee for the people.

Neither ownership of land in fee, nor a perpetual lease to private persons at a variable rent, should prevent the *general* control of the Resources of Nature by Society. Usually he who has possession of the land may be trusted to make the best use of it, or at least some use which will be for the interests of Society. If he cultivate it, he provides food for the multitude; if he covers it with buildings, these are for rent to the people, or for use in the production of goods. But there are some exceptions. Where land is scarce the people may very properly forbid the fencing in of a large portion of it for a private park, even by the owner. If it is a public park, all can enjoy it; but land for a private park is withdrawn from public use for the gratification of a very few people. Where land is sown with wheat it does not make so much difference to Society about the ownership, because the wheat will be produced, and is certain to come on the market; but a private park is practically taken out of use for the satisfaction of the world's wants, except for those of a single family. Where land is abundant, so that every family can have a park if able and willing to pay the price, there is no objection to such a use. The general right of the public to control the Resources of Nature must not at any time be lost sight of. If land is wanted for public uses, it must be taken, with compensation for improvements. If the use made of land by its holder is inconsistent with public policy, or if it is not used for the satisfaction of wants, the public have the right to interfere.

PUBLIC USE OF THE RESOURCES OF NATURE.—Not all of the Resources of Nature should be managed by private enterprise. In some few instances the government may properly attempt their improvement for the general good of the people. The most common instances are roads, harbors, and public parks. Any Natural Resource which can be used by the people in common is better in the hands of the government. The harbors on the coast are improved by national authority in order that they may be used by the ships of all nations. So natural water-ways, such as lakes and rivers, are properly improved by the government. It would be very unfortunate if they should ever become private property. On the same principle, governments have frequently constructed canals; and the Erie Canal in New York is an example of an artificial water-way, built and maintained at the public expense, and free to all who wish to use it. This principle of free public water-ways should be extended as far as possible.

The difference between a canal and a railway is that it is easy to use the former in common, while the latter must almost of necessity be managed by a single company. Each boat may be owned by a different person, who runs it, under simple regulations, to suit himself.

Country wagon roads and city streets are also used in common, and are properly made and maintained by public authority.

Within the last few years more attention has been paid to public parks, which the government undertakes to improve and maintain for the benefit of all users. The famous Yellowstone Park is a credit to our nation. All land not fitted for private use; all land about the head-waters of rivers, and in mountains, where a forest should be maintained, as well as such striking pieces of natural scenery as the Yellowstone Park, should forever remain in the possession of the government. A considerable part of the public land now unsold might well be retained for park purposes, and such land as that of the Adirondack Mountains may well be purchased for the maintenance of forests.

The public park principle is liable to abuse for the reason of our unfamiliarity with land under national control. Special privileges have been granted in many instances, which amount almost to private ownership. It must be insisted that any privilege, such as that of erecting a building, is for only a limited period, and that a *variable* rent shall be paid, which shall be increased each year as the value of the privilege increases. On the island of Mackinac, in Michigan, there is a national park which is practically the private park of a few summer residents, and maintained by the government mainly for their pleasure. Building leases have been given without proper restrictions. All leases, and all park privileges, should be granted only on the principle before mentioned, viz.: that of the payment of the full value of the use of the land each year, and an increase of the rent as the value of the privilege increases.

There will be, altogether, a very considerable portion of the Natural Resources which ought to remain under the control of the government, to be used by all the people in common. The atmosphere is, of course, to be used in common. The waters of lakes and rivers are also to be navigated in common; and harbors must be maintained at the public expense. The extension of the canal system, with roads and streets, will retain a considerable portion of the land for public use; and the wide extension of the park system will bring a large acreage of land into public use. Parks in cities are the common land of the people. All Natural Resources that can be properly devoted to public use should be improved and maintained by the State.

We have a good deal to learn in the way of forestry from Europe. In many localities—such as the Adirondack Mountains—land should be condemned and purchased by the government. It was a terrible blunder to sell it, but it had better be re-purchased before the price is carried higher by the increase of population. Narrow strips of land on great lakes and the ocean should be reserved or secured for public use. It is an outrage that one may fence the people off from the sea. Yet all along the Atlantic coast the choicest portions of the land are being occupied by private residents who control to the water, and virtually own the sea. A narrow strip, like a public highway, should always intervene between the private residence and the water. In cities on the coast, land has become too valuable to purchase for public use. The large government forests, often about the head-waters of rivers, under intelligent management would produce a great deal of timber which could be cut so as not to destroy the forest nature of the land. The sale of the timber should be a source of revenue. The acreage of land in highways, public parks, and government forest should, in the older States, be vastly greater than it is.

Special provision should be made for mines. With such placer mines as were worked in the early days of California, nothing is better than to allow each man as many feet of ground as he can work, so long as he works it; but in quartz mining, with costly machinery, the government should retain control of the mines, making some special provision for their working. The leasing of land for agricultural purposes should not carry with it any title to the minerals that may be found beneath its surface.

The fish of the sea are public property, and the waters in which fishing is carried on should forever be the property of the entire people. Where it is necessary to set aside a particular space of water for such industry as oyster fishing, it should be leased by the government to those who use it.

The question of water-rights in irrigation is coming to the front in the West. There are vast tracts of land worthless except with irrigation. He who owns the water controls the land, virtually owns all the land the water supplies, since he can put his own price on it unless restricted by legislation or previous contract. Yet water is one of the Resources of Nature, which used to be cited by the older Political Economists as an example of something without value (exchange value), because so common. All water-works for irrigation purposes should either be owned by the State, or subjected to a strict control. The water should be regarded as belonging to the people, and

ECONOMICAL USE OF NATURAL WEALTH. 241

no one permitted to control it except under the power of the State to fix a price for the service. There is no reason why the water-works should not be held by the owners of the land they supply, and managed by them as a company.

With these exceptions the use of the Natural Resources is best left to private enterprise. Where they have not been sold they should be leased to private parties at a variable rent, as has been described.

If this chapter has appeared to the reader to contain a great deal about government management, it should be remembered that this is because the Resources of Nature are of right public property—the heritage of all the people, of each generation as it comes on the stage of action. Hence, it is impossible to treat of the use of Natural Wealth without more or less discussion regarding government management, since the government is the trustee of the people's property, and their agent for its use.

The greater part of the land will always be under private management, if not under private ownership.

CHAPTER III.

ECONOMICAL USE OF PRODUCED WEALTH.

The older works on Political Economy treated of the "production of wealth" under the heads of land, labor and capital. No term in economic science is more misleading than this same "capital," although its popular use in practical business is unexceptionable. Capital is that part of Produced Wealth which is used in the production of other wealth. Produced Wealth may be used as capital one year, and not the next. The term capital also leads one to imagine either a sum of money or a body of Produced Wealth which can be turned to any form of production the owner desires. This is far from the case. It is better to treat things as they are, and to understand more particularly what we are talking about.

There is no Produced Wealth which can be used for every purpose, and very little that has any great variety of uses. As a general rule, Produced Wealth must be used for its original purpose, or for some other that is closely related. A large part of the Produced Wealth of the world is in the form of dwellings. These can be turned into storerooms, or factories, but when this is done at some cost, they are not found to be as well adapted as buildings erected specially for the purpose. Very little machinery can be used for purposes other than those designed. The vast capital in roads of all kinds can be used for nothing else. The stock of clothing is of no use except to be worn, and even the food supply of the nation serves only one purpose. Whence, then, comes this popular idea that " capital " can be used for any form of production desired? Simply from the fact that the greater portion of Produced Wealth is consumed in the present support of human beings—that it supports labor, and labor can be turned to the production of almost anything we will. The power of the capitalist consists in this: that he, with the houses, and clothing, and food supply at his command, may employ all the laborers he can support; and he can set the laborers at any sort of work he pleases. The producer's capital usually consists of two distinct parts: first, the buildings and machinery; second, command over the food supply and stock of wealth on hand for the immediate satisfaction of wants, with which he employs labor. This labor he sets at work in the line of production for which his machinery is fitted. The use of almost all forms of capital, and all Produced Wealth, is fixed by its nature within very narrow limits. The wealth is rapidly consumed and worn out, and labor can be turned to the production of the same or new forms of Produced Wealth. Instead of talking about capital, then, let us talk of the various forms of Produced Wealth, and the use of each.

The purpose for which permanent Produced Wealth will be used is largely determined by the nature of the wealth. A cotton factory can produce nothing but cotton goods. If there is a lessened demand for the product, the owner in some instances continues to run the factory, turning labor in that direction at a positive loss, rather than have the mill stand idle. He fears either that it may take more injury when idle than when running, or that the scattering of the old hands, and the loss of customers, may be a greater injury than a temporary loss in production at market prices. He submits to the present loss in the hope of some profit in the future; otherwise he would close the mill permanently, and consider the labor invested in the production of the machinery as so much misdirected effort.

Almost all machinery is limited to the use for which it was made. Buildings are limited in their use to the purposes for which they were designed, or others very similar. Roads are of no use except for travel. We may produce almost any kind of wealth in the future; but the wealth now in existence must be used mainly for the purposes for which it was designed.

Produced Wealth is either *permanent* or *consumable*. Nothing made by man has the permanency of the Resources of Nature; and none of our Produced Wealth is more than relatively permanent. Consumable wealth is destroyed, or withdrawn from the public stock, as soon as used, and must be replaced year by year. Hence, it is easier to make any changes in the form of Consumable than of Permanent Wealth, because we can use labor to produce something different as soon as the old is consumed.

ECONOMICAL USE OF PRODUCED WEALTH. 245

It is not expected that the changes in the nature of the Produced Wealth of a nation will be very great from year to year. Although almost the entire food supply is consumed, and we might produce a supply of an entirely different character, yet practically the desires of the people are best satisfied by producing very much the same kinds of food as have been consumed. We need about the same number of bushels of wheat this year as last. Fashions in clothing, and other goods which are consumed in satisfying wants directly, change to a greater extent; but it is rather in the form than the essential nature of the goods. However, the wearing out, and the production of new Consumable Wealth, give opportunity for as wide a variation as the desires of the people demand.

We see, here, the mistake of certain merchants who have held goods year after year in the hopes of selling at the original price. The changes in fashion— the people's desires—make such goods almost worthless. The wise merchant disposes of his goods within a comparatively short time after their purchase, even if it should be necessary to lose something in the sale. He knows the liability of a change in the demand. It is better, indeed, that the wants of the future for consumable goods be supplied by the productions of the future rather than by saving stocks from the present.

Permanent Wealth endures longer, and there may be a very considerable change in the form of that which replaces it. Indeed, improvements in machinery are so rapid that frequently it does not pay to wait for a machine to wear out before replacing it with something better adapted to the purpose.

Permanent Produced Wealth should be Used Continuously. It is seldom that it is greatly injured by use. Most things rust out quicker than they wear out. A dwelling properly taken care of will last longer if used than when standing empty. It is not always possible to use all Permanent Wealth, because such use requires labor, which may be more profitably employed at something else. This shows either that the general course of production has become deranged, or that there has been more of a particular kind of this form of wealth produced than was needed, and its production was therefore waste.

Permanent Produced Wealth should be Used with as little injury as possible. The needless injury to this form of wealth is very great. Every owner of machinery understands the necessity of care. Valuable dwellings are often injured more by a shiftless family than their use is worth. It is true this can occur only with comparatively costly dwellings. It will not cost as much to build a wigwam as its use is worth for a single year. If it be entirely destroyed by a year's use, the gain is still greater than the loss; and there are some families which are fit only to live in a wigwam. A dwelling costing a hundred thousand dollars can easily be injured by a year's use more than the cost of building a moderate house, which would answer the real needs of the family equally well. Sometimes a costly building stands empty for the very reason that the owner can not get enough to pay for the injury to it by such families as offer themselves. One of the difficulties found in attempting to improve the condition of the lower classes in large cities, is in inducing them to take proper care of decent tenement houses. They destroy so much that no owner can afford to provide accommodations of even moderate cost.

SAVINGS.—How much of the wealth produced each year will be applied to the satisfaction of current wants, and how much will be saved for the satisfaction of future wants, or for use as capital in further production ? Usually almost all that is produced is expended in the satisfaction of present wants, and a very small proportion is saved. Yet in some instances men save much more than half, sometimes nearly all, of the share of the total product which falls to them. A great deal depends on accident. A farmer in a new country may find it impossible by any effort to gain more than the most meager living for his family; yet, in order to gain this meager living, he is compelled to improve his farm. He drains a swamp to get a crop for the next year, but the swamp once drained is good land for all time. He builds his fences for this year; he can do nothing without them, but they are accumulated wealth; so that by sheer force of necessity he is compelled to accumulate. Had he lived in a city, he would not have put his family on this short allowance in order to save, and would have saved nothing. The necessity of a tool for present work leads to saving to pay some one for making it. It is in some such way as this that the accumulation of capital begins. At first it is almost always by self-sacrifice, but sometimes the accumulated Produced Wealth returns its cost every year. Many machines have paid a hundred per cent. on the labor employed in their construction. Saving depends on habit, on the custom of one's associates, and on the probable return one is likely to obtain from the use of his savings over and above their preservation.

It should also be noted that saving depends on one's income in comparison with that of those about him, and the style of living adopted by the society he has chosen. With the majority of people nothing can be saved except by the most painful self-denial; it means poorer food, or clothing, or dwellings.

After one has the necessities of life and can live as well as his neighbors, he may easily save. If he go into different surroundings, the expenditure of ten or a hundred times as much may seem necessary, and he may find saving more difficult than with a smaller income among his old acquaintances.

A point is frequently reached in the life of some individuals where saving requires no sacrifice. By various means, millions of dollars of profits have come into the hands of a few individuals. There are three things one can do with it. First, save to control great business interests, taking more pleasure in business than in expenditure after the manner of a European with an inherited fortune. In this case the wealth of the country is increased. Second, he can endow public institutions, or otherwise contribute to the benefit of the people. There is in this country a very general idea that one is under obligation to do something of this sort. It is held that his wealth is the result of the efforts of others as well as his own, that his ownership is not absolute, and that he is in some sense a trustee for the people. Universities and great libraries have been thus endowed. The wealth is here saved, and the interest paid for the use of it goes to satisfy the more important intellectual wants of many people. Great credit is due to men who use a large part of their accumulations in this way. A considerable portion of such wealth is also used in direct contribution for the satisfaction of the wants of others. Schools and churches are maintained, missionaries are sent to other lands, contributions are made to starving peoples. In the third place, one may spend all of his annual income on himself and family.

Although the savings of those with large incomes in this country are great, the total savings of those with small incomes are much larger. We have many millionaires, but very few men with an income of a million a year. Suppose there were a hundred. If they chose, they could save practically all they receive; yet the total annual saving would be only a hundred millions a year. If ten million laborers were to save ten dollars a year, each, the total savings would be the same. The greater part of the savings are the accumulation of men of moderate means who wish capital to do business. Many negroes, since the war, have accumulated comfortable fortunes. Many a poor boy becomes rich, both because he makes money, and because he saves it. Small savings can accumulate only a small fortune; one must make a great deal of money if he is to save a great deal; but the small savings of great numbers of people, continued for a lifetime, amount to vast sums in the end.

Savings must be viewed from two standpoints, that of the individual, and that of the nation at large. Every person would like to save a fortune were it not for the sacrifice of present comfort involved. Viewed from a national standpoint, it is doubtful if this country needs a rapid accumulation of Produced Wealth. We are well supplied with railroads and machinery. With the exception of better dwellings for the mass of the people, a dictator might hold that it were better if nearly all the product of the labor of each year were expended in the satisfaction of the wants of that year. It depends, also, in whose hands the savings are. The accumulation of small fortunes is greatly to the interest of the country. The opportunities which capital gives to active owners, competent to use it, are often worth a hundred times as much as the mere interest on the sum. The great savings of the rich, by decreasing the rate of interest, take away part of the inducement for the poor to save. They are not willing to make the sacrifice necessary to save, when the sum invested at interest would bring so little. Yet many a good business manager, if he had saved a little capital in his youth, would be able to use it to place himself in independent business. Savings depend to a considerable extent on the interest which capital brings. Few men realize how much the mere control of capital may some time be worth to them.

The use of the Resources for the Satisfaction of Wants by individuals, is a matter of practical business, involving endless details and training. The method of use determines one's financial success in life; determines how well he is able to provide for those dependent on him; and how much he is able to do for others, and for the world. Some men become rich by using the resources at their command, even though they be very meager; other men suffer poverty, although they were fortunate in the beginning in having control of far more and better resources than their successful neighbor. A great deal depends on what one has at the beginning, a great deal on luck; but, beyond this, one's material success is due to the skill with which he uses the resources here enumerated. Questions of morals, of course, enter in; and we are not to forget that one sometimes succeeds by dishonest and immoral use of the resources of which he obtains control. The promoters of the Louisiana lottery are supposed to have accumulated enormous fortunes out of money taken from those who gambled with them. The gambling-tables at Monte Carlo are very profitable to their owners, though they have driven many lives to suicide.

CHAPTER IV.

THE USE OF THE RESOURCE OF SOCIETY.

One of the merits claimed for this work, is that it takes account of Society as the means of satisfying human wants, as well as the productions of human industry. We have seen in Book II. how important is the character of the population of any country. Some society is like a heap of waste refuse, not only useless, but unsightly, and in the way. Good society is one of the most important means for the satisfaction of wants, after the simple craving for food has been satisfied. In this book we have to do only with the use of such society as happens to exist in any nation.

There is, first, the necessity of separation. The convicted criminal must be placed in penitentiaries, workhouses or reformatory institutions; otherwise he is a constant menace to society. There is, in addition to this, a criminal class which the future will doubtless deal with. An habitual criminal may be all the more dangerous for having spent a few months in jail or the penitentiary. We shall, perhaps, find it necessary to separate from society every habitual criminal, until there is some reason for believing that he has so far reformed as to be safely trusted at large.

In a perfect society, each individual or family, while tenacious of its own rights, would be equally unwilling to interfere with the rights of others. They also have

USE OF SOCIETY. 253

some conception of what those rights are. With society as at present constituted, even in the United States, it is necessary to insist upon quite strict regulations in order to make it of any value in the satisfaction of wants. The majority of the people have no thought that anything is disagreeable to others which is not disagreeable to themselves. A very large number have no hesitancy in inflicting upon others what is disagreeable even to themselves. The protection of individual rights, where people are massed together as they are in cities, doubtless requires very much stricter regulations than at present exist. The effort of the future will be to make a city a desirable place for all classes to live; and when this is done, wants will be much better satisfied, even with the same income as at present. Unnecessary noises will be abolished. There will be some means of rapid transportation which will not make every house within the vicinity of the line an unfit place to live in. The ringing of bells and blowing of steam whistles between certain hours will be prohibited. Disagreeable street cries will cease. The posting of unsightly advertisements on blank walls, and the disfigurement of natural scenery by advertisements, will be forbidden. The distributing of handbills on the streets, now prohibited in many cities, will then cease everywhere. The model city of the future will be one where a person can walk the streets unmolested, unasked to purchase what he does not want, undisturbed by street cries and unnecessary racket. Beggars and the unfortunate cripples will also be removed to places where they can have proper care; it will be recognized that those who are disfigured and repulsive in appearance are entitled to the support of the community, which will take pleasure in knowing that they are cared for in proper institutions; but they will not be permitted to thrust themselves into the view of every passer-by to work upon his sympathies in order to beg.

For the sake of all persons, sanitary regulations must be enforced against those who have no regard for cleanliness themselves. In short, a city must be made a habitable place to live in, with cleanly and healthful surroundings for the poor as well as the rich. The difference between cities naturally depends on the character of the people who inhabit them, and the way in which they are compelled to live. The securing of advantages described will be worth more to any workingman than a considerable advance of his wages, and will be worth still more to those of larger incomes.

It is said that men can not be made moral by legislation. While this is true in one sense, it is also true that legislation and the enforcement of law have a great deal to do with the morality and the social life of any people. The lowest immoral classes can be prevented from outward acts. The lower social classes can be compelled to live in a way less disagreeable to more respectable neighbors. Vice can be compelled to hide itself from public gaze. The very compelling of the people to live outwardly in a certain way for a generation or two, would most powerfully affect their character, and what is done under compulsion by one generation, may become the habit of the second.

A great deal can, therefore, be done to make society outwardly more respectable; and to make it of far more use in the satisfaction of the wants of all. A great deal can be done in repressing natural outward manifestations of those who occupy the place of social rubbish and disagreeable waste.

A still more important matter is in the development of a better society in the future. We can not do much with a savage unless he is caught young; but under proper influence children of even the most objectionable classes may be less a curse to the body politic than their fathers have been, and may even come to be good citizens. The public schools, the churches, and missionary enterprises, are doing a great deal in this direction, and are our chief dependence.

CHAPTER V.

THE PURPOSES FOR WHICH THE RESOURCES SHALL BE USED.

What goods shall be produced? What wants shall be satisfied? What direction shall the world's production take, and how shall its industry be employed? Shall we dig for diamonds in distant lands? Shall we erect costly State-houses? For what purposes shall these vast resources of nature, of labor, of goods produced by man, of society, be used? It is one thing to use the resources without waste, and so as to accomplish the greatest results; and another to determine what shall be the end of all this use, what sort of wants shall be satisfied.

We have already seen that the purpose for which most Produced Wealth shall be used is limited by the nature of the wealth itself. A paper mill can not well be used for anything except to make paper, yet it may make paper of various grades, as desired. The purposes for which most Produced Wealth may be used is limited, not determined, by the nature of the wealth.

To a less extent this is true of Natural Wealth. All agricultural land is not fitted for wheat or sugar cane, yet most land may produce a considerable variety of crops.

It will be sufficient if we consider the single Resource of Labor. The purpose for which any one Resource is used determines that of the others. If a given acreage of land is to be set aside for the production of wheat, this means that a certain amount of labor and capital must be used in the same production. If a woolen factory is to run continuously, it means that labor must be employed in this mill, and that, somewhere, land must be devoted to sheep-raising. Since land, labor and capital are combined in almost every form of production, when we determine the use of one of them we have practically fixed the use of the others.

It is more convenient to select Labor rather than either of the other resources, because labor is more readily directed. The purposes for which the other resources will be used will need no further consideration than has been given in previous chapters.

THE PURPOSES FOR WHICH LABOR SHALL BE USED.—The purposes for which the Resources are used may be even more important than the manner of their use. We may have a hundred thousand men for a year digging holes in the ground, and at the end we have only holes in the ground. If these men are employed in digging the Nicaragua canal, we have at the end a canal connecting oceans, of great value in satisfying future wants. There is a great deal of misdirected effort and waste of labor.

The class of wants satisfied and the number of people enabled to live in comfort also depend upon the purpose for which labor is used. If a large portion of the labor of a nation is expended in personal services, as in some of the old countries, there is only the satisfaction of the wants of a few people. So, also, if labor is expended in the production of costly wines and expensive luxuries. A thousand men may be employed in the production of some little luxury for the prince or queen. On the other hand, if the greater portion of the labor of a nation is expended in the production of food, clothing, and the common comforts and necessities of life, the very abundance of these makes them cheaper, and brings them within a price that the multitudes can afford to pay. This, however, is only saying that where the entire people are engaged in satisfying their own wants, they will be more generally satisfied than where the majority are laboring to provide something to satisfy the wants of the few.

The direction of labor is usually determined by the employer, rather than by the laborer. The control by the great captains of industry probably brings about far greater results than could be attained if the direction of labor were in the hands of the laborers. The employers are governed, not by the thought of satisfying the wants of as many people as possible, but of providing what the people will pay most for; and where there is great wealth in the hands of a few who are willing to expend it for their personal pleasure, these directors of labor will be sure to turn it to the satisfaction of their wants, rather than to the wants of the people who have nothing to pay with.

It is true that various motives besides profit act to induce one to carry on business, and mistakes are frequently made; but on the whole, the tendency is

WHAT SHALL BE PRODUCED. 259

to produce what the people want most, in proportion as they have the means to purchase it. Let there be a widespread desire on the part of the common laborers of the country for any article for which they are willing to exchange labor, and it is sure to be produced. The desires of the people, in a general way, settle what shall be produced by the labor of the country. The laborer can have bread, beer or clothing produced for him, just as he pleases.

If we could control the wants of the people, we could determine what should be produced. If the desire for beer and whisky could be eliminated, the production of these liquors would cease; the grain would be used for food, and the labor of all the men in distilleries, wholesale liquor stores and saloons would be turned to the satisfaction of other wants.

Let us suppose a man with an income of a million dollars a year. This is equal to commanding the labor of more than a thousand men, including superintendents. The way in which he uses his income decides the direction the labor of these men will take. If he decides to spend it all in building another railroad, there will be a demand for railroad laborers. Suppose he determines to spend all his income on himself and family. A thousand men must now work for him in some way, and he will determine how. He will likely take a considerable number of them for his servants. If he drink costly wines, he will turn labor to their production. If he lives in Europe, such goods as the people of Europe most need will be sent over to pay the bills of exchange he draws. His manner of life in Europe will determine the direction of labor there. If he maintain as many servants as an Englishman of equal income, he turns more labor into personal service. If he loses his money on horse-races, he increases the class of gamblers. If he gives his money to a work like that of General Booth, he sets idle men and semi-criminals to producing food, clothing and shelter for themselves. Whatever he does, whether commendable or otherwise, decides what a thousand men shall do—decides what shall be produced, what direction labor shall take.

What this man with his income of a million dollars a year does on a large scale, other men do on a smaller scale. Every man thus has an influence in directing the labor of the world to honorable or dishonorable employments, to pleasant or disagreeable work, to independent production or to menial service, or to the education and intellectual culture of the age. If he chooses to keep servants to the number of many Southern households in the days before the war, with no better appliances than of that time, he puts more people into personal service; if he adopts all the modern appliances of housekeeping, he sends more men to manufacturing. The whisky drinker puts men to producing whisky; the smoker is the man who directs others to make cigars. These things are produced for one more promptly than if he ordered his slaves to make them.

1. *The Use of Labor in Satisfying Wants Directly.* — A very large portion of all the labor of the nation must be expended in satisfying wants di-

rectly, without the intervention of any material production. The United States census reports show that about one-fourth of those reported as having any employment are engaged in professional and personal services. When we add to this the labor of wives engaged in household duties and the care of the family, which labor is not reported in the census, we see that nearly one-half of all the labor of the nation is expended in satisfying wants directly.

2. *The Production of Consumable Goods to Satisfy Wants.*—Next to satisfying wants by labor directly, comes the producing of something that will satisfy wants. The savage lives largely on the Resources of Nature; civilized man produces goods. For the production of most goods considerable time is required; usually from one to two years elapses from the beginning of the process of production from the soil to the completion of the finished product. A considerable store of consumable goods is, therefore, necessary. We eat last year's wheat; and in the winter wear clothing made in the factories the summer before; the material for the clothing was probably produced more than a year before it was manufactured. Labor is, therefore, directed not so much to producing something for immediate consumption, as to replacing the great stock of consumable wealth as fast as it is consumed. If we are able to increase this stock faster than population increases, there is opportunity for the better satisfaction of wants in the future.

The quantity of Consumable Produced Wealth

which it is profitable to accumulate is decidedly limited. The storage of grain costs something. It is much better to have good wheat land, and skilled farmers able to produce wheat year by year as needed, than to have a great store. Only a prophetic knowledge of the future, such as Joseph had, would justify the accumulation of a seven years' supply. Many varieties of food products must be produced year by year, because they are of a perishable nature. Even clothing depreciates in utility through a change of fashions, and it is far better that the production of each year be worked off as closely as possible. The preservation and storage of all goods is costly. Better far are factories, and skilled workmen able to make the clothing year by year, as it is needed by the people. We need, therefore, only a limited stock of Consumable Produced Wealth; just enough to last until more can be produced, and to tide over any possible failure in production.

Hence, if we are able to direct a larger portion of the labor of a nation to the production of consumable goods, it will result in the better satisfaction of immediate wants. The effect of such increased production might at first be to increase slightly the stocks on hand, but this increase would soon result in greater consumption of these goods by the people. We draw as much out of our reservoir as we put in.

3. *Accumulation of Permanent Wealth which Satisfies Wants Directly.*—By far the larger part of this form of wealth is in dwellings and public buildings. At first, the man in the new country must live

WHAT SHALL BE PRODUCED. 263

in a "dug-out," a cave dug in the hillside which he can fashion in a few days, or in a log house which his neighbors help him to build in a not much longer period. Neither of these shelters is very permanent, though the log house may be an excellent dwelling for several years. If one is able to erect a substantial stone house, it may afford a dwelling-place for him and his children after him, perhaps for centuries. A well-built house, the modern improvements, the water and gas fixtures, the sewerage, the finish, all go to satisfy wants better, not for the present alone, but for a lifetime. If one were compelled to build a house every year, it would necessarily be a cheap affair; because it is permanent, one can afford to give the work of years to its completion.

Public buildings come in the same class as houses. They satisfy the wants of officials, and those of the people for the means of government, and their architectural appearance is a satisfaction of æsthetic wants. Church buildings and schoolhouses belong in the same category. The school buildings satisfy wants directly as well as the teacher. When we have added to buildings for the purposes named above, works of art, we have included most of the Permanent Produced Wealth which satisfies wants directly.

How much of this class of wealth will be produced? How much can be advantageously produced, provided the labor can be spared? Ordinarily one house is sufficient for a single family. Only a few desire two or three. It is the demand for better dwellings that requires so much of the spare labor of the nation. Poor buildings are constantly being torn down to make room for good ones. To provide for all the people as good quarters as they would take care of, would require far more labor than to produce the necessary reserve supply of food and clothing. We hope for progress in erecting better dwellings, with sanitary surroundings. But such buildings are of advantage only so fast as the people learn to use and care for them. One of the difficulties found by philanthropic people of wealth in large cities, is in securing tenants who are fit to use the buildings. The tenants seem to prefer the squalor of the old, filthy tenement houses, and if left to themselves soon reduce the new to the condition of the old. A wigwam is good enough for an Indian, as an Indian; if he becomes civilized, he needs a better home.

The proportion of the labor of the country which will be expended in the production of Permanent Wealth which satisfies wants directly, will depend on how much can be spared from the present support of the people in the way they think necessary to live.

4. *Permanent Wealth which Satisfies Wants Indirectly.*—The types of this are machinery, buildings for manufacturing and commercial purposes, roads and other equipments, and vessels for navigation. Labor will usually be taken from other purposes for the production of machinery whenever the latter is found to be profitable. Machinery which a few men can make in a year may enable ten men thereafter to do the work of a thousand.

Is there any limit to the profitable production of

machinery? It is evident that we may have all the machinery that the laborers can use. The farmer needs only a certain number of plows; one mowing-machine for a small farm is as good as a dozen. One sewing-machine in each family is usually all that is needed. Only about so much cotton cloth would be used in the United States if people had all they desired; and there are probably cotton mills enough in the country, by running full time, to produce that quantity. There is certainly a limit to the number of machines of any one class which it is worth while to build.

Wants, however, develop very rapidly when there is opportunity. Machines are continually invented which will produce something for which a new want can be created, or something that will satisfy wants at a cost which can be afforded by a greater number of people. There is certainly a limit to the machinery that can profitably be provided for any given population, but the limit is far beyond us.

The building of roads, railroads and canals has in the United States required a large portion of the labor which could be spared from the satisfaction of immediate wants. This class of Produced Wealth follows the same law as machinery. It is sometimes said that capital is sunk in railroads; what is sunk is labor, labor which might have been unemployed, or employed in the satisfaction of present wants.

A certain amount of labor is devoted to improvements on land, which yield their return in the future. If the farmer can spare time from making a living for his family, or can put in a little extra labor in the course of a year, he may drain a swamp which will hereafter be the best land he has. This is labor devoted to accumulation as much as in the production of machinery.

Under the last division we have enumerated the principal classes of Permanent Produced Wealth which satisfy wants indirectly. They are the forms by means of which the vast accumulations of wealth in modern times have been rendered possible. For what purposes could labor be used in ancient times beyond the satisfaction of present wants? We have seen there is nothing to be gained by the storing up food and clothing, and other Consumable Wealth, beyond a supply for a year or two. Without machinery, and modern railroads and modern ships, little remained but buildings. Great castles were erected, but there were no forms of wealth known in which it was possible to store up the labor of the present for the future, to the extent it is done at the present. People worked hard enough. Slaves built the great pyramids of Egypt, a useless toil of thousands of men for weary years. Could the same labor have been used in the construction of modern machinery, the production of the future could have been greatly increased. The few persons in control, however, cared nothing for the wants of the people, even if they had been able to produce modern machinery.

All the labor expended in satisfying wants *directly* goes, of course, to the satisfaction of immediate wants, and nothing is accumulated; although the condition of the people may be greatly improved by education.

Future accumulations of Produced Wealth will be in the form of Permanent Wealth, both that which satisfies wants directly — such as dwellings, public buildings, parks, works of art, etc.—and that which satisfies wants indirectly—such as tools and machinery, roads and facilities for communication and transportation, improvements on land, etc. Even now we are talking of expending a hundred million dollars in building the Nicaragua canal. Such an expenditure is equal to the labor of an army of two hundred thousand men for a year, either on the ground or somewhere else.

To one who has the welfare of the race at heart, the question arises whether we have not reached the point where it were better to turn more labor to the satisfaction of immediate wants. The erection of dwellings provides for immediate needs and also for wants in the future. It is doubtful if there is any real need of a rapid addition to the present stock of the machinery of the world's production. There is need of a much better provision for the wants of the great mass of the people at the present time. The philanthropist would probably desire to turn surplus labor, for the next few years at least, to the more comfortable housing of all the people. Such housing, especially in cities, necessarily includes water supply, sewerage, and many sanitary arrangements. He would also direct effort to the securing of pure and wholesome food; which even the rich find it difficult to procure. He would relieve children and persons under sixteen or eighteen years of age from labor outside the family to which they belong; and would turn more labor to the satisfaction of wants directly, in the teaching of these young people in the schools, so as to better fit them for life. If this, and other labor for the immediate wants of each year, prevented the rapid increase of wealth, he would not greatly regret it, believing that there is so much Produced Wealth that its increase, except in the case of dwellings, is of much less importance than formerly.

BOOK V.
EXCHANGE.

BOOK V.

EXCHANGE.

CHAPTER	I.	HOW EXCHANGE SATISFIES WANTS,	271
CHAPTER	II.	THE PRICE OF A DOLLAR,	275
CHAPTER	III.	EXCHANGE VALUES,	280
CHAPTER	IV.	THE LIMITS OF VALUE IN EXCHANGE ARE FIXED BY VALUES IN USE,	285
CHAPTER	V.	SUPPLY AND DEMAND,	289
CHAPTER	VI.	COST OF PRODUCTION,	296
CHAPTER	VII.	MONOPOLY,	306
CHAPTER	VIII.	MONEY,	312
PART	I.	Qualities of a Good Money,	313
PART	II.	What Determines the Value of Money?	325
PART	III.	Efforts to Secure a Money of Uniform Value,	330
CHAPTER	IX.	SUBSTITUTES FOR MONEY,	335

BOOK V.

EXCHANGE.

CHAPTER I.

HOW EXCHANGES SATISFY WANTS.

Extended division of labor is possible only by means of Exchange. Where one man devotes himself to one thing he produces a great deal more of it than his family can use, and he lacks the thousand other things they need. Each one exchanges his personal service, or the goods he produces, for other things which he desires. Exchange makes possible a division of labor, not only between individuals, but also between nations.

The cost of Exchange is sometimes greater than the cost of production; that is, it frequently costs more to sell goods than to make them. The problem is not merely one of transportation. When people want tea, grown in China, the carriage of goods half round the globe is the simplest part of it. The shipload must be distributed among wholesale merchants, and again among retail merchants, who sell it to the customer in single pounds. The merchants must keep on hand a stock of such varieties as may be desired; and the labor of transporting, testing, sorting and distributing is very considerable, to say nothing of the capital employed, and risk involved. A part of this work requires the highest form of skilled labor, which commands the highest price in the market.

Two people can seldom meet, and exchange their products directly; when they do, the seller sometimes finds more labor connected with the selling of his product than with its production. The milkman would perhaps be glad to sell milk to one purchaser at his farm for two cents a quart; he brings it to the city, takes it from place to place, and gets eight cents a quart. Three-fourths of the price is therefore payment for the transportation and exchange, and only one-fourth for the milk. The labor and cost of selling the milk is three times as great as the labor and cost of its production. Of the eight cents a quart, only one-fourth belongs to production, while three-fourths belong to exchange. If the producer sells the milk at his farm for two cents a quart, to a merchant who intends to sell to consumers at eight cents, we have precisely the same division of the returns as before—one-fourth for Production, and three-fourths for Exchange.

These examples are simple wants; more frequently one does not know what he will need, nor have the means to purchase, beforehand. The merchant looks the world over, and sees what people are producing. He finds what the people want, in every nation and hamlet and farmhouse. He purchases goods, and carries them to the people who will give the most for them. He thus encourages the production of some goods and discourages the production of others, according as human wants fluctuate. The capital required for the world's exchange is as great as the world's production. The number of men employed is less, but the risk of loss is greater. Goods are injured, or depreciate in utility. The merchant finds himself mistaken in his opinion of what the people want, and must dispose of some goods at a loss.

It has been common to call it all Production, and to say that the merchant vessel trading with China, the railroad superintendent and the retail merchant are all engaged in Production, since it is just as important that goods be exchanged as that they be produced. But Exchange is not Production, and it confuses our ideas to call it so. To the interests engaged in Production belong all the goods they produce; but if they exchange them themselves they must employ more labor. If one man takes the entire product of a factory, he can not give all he expects to sell it for. One has a right to what he has produced; he sells it on the best terms he can for money to buy other goods, because he prefers exchanging to keeping.

If it be asked, "Since exchanges cost so much, why are they made? Why does not every one produce all he wants himself?" the answer is, first, it would be impossible; and second, the gain from the Division of Labor is many times the cost of exchange. Few people stop to think of the great part which Exchange plays in the satisfaction of wants, and how much better they can be satisfied by its aid than without. It transfers articles from one to whom they have little Value in Use to one to whom they have a higher value; it makes possible the Division of Labor. Without Exchange, only a small fraction of the present population could be sustained, and the wants of these few would be meagerly supplied. We assume its existence, like that of the air about us; and all production, and all efforts for the satisfaction of wants, are made on the assumption that exchanges are to continue.

CHAPTER II.

THE PRICE OF A DOLLAR.

Our first object is to ascertain how much of one commodity will be given for a certain quantity of another. How much for how much? It is more important that one know this beforehand than that he make a good bargain when it comes to a trade. Under the division of labor every man produces more of some one thing than he can use himself, and the excess is worth to him only what he can get for it. But he believes he can get about so much, and produces his goods with this expectation, perhaps employing labor for wages and incurring other expenses. If he does not get about as much as he expected, it means financial ruin. Most failures in production come from miscalculation as to what the product can be sold for. A year is required to raise a crop on a farm, a longer period for some other forms of production; and one must know what he can get for goods, often a year or more in advance. Nothing will enable us to predict this with certainty; yet when the conditions are fairly well known, we may be able to determine within certain limits what the terms of exchange will be.

Optimists sometimes say that every exchange is beneficial to both parties, else it would not be made. Yes; *under the circumstances.* Anything one can not use is worth nothing to him unless he can exchange it for something he can use. If the farmer can never get more than five cents a pound for the wool he produced last year, he would better sell it. However, if he had known that the price of wool would be so low, he would not have raised the sheep. He produced the wool because he had reason to believe that he could exchange it for a larger part of the world's products. A successful manipulator of the market can gather to himself a large part of the value of the world's production, by leading men to suppose they can obtain a certain price for an article, and then so changing the conditions that they can not get half that price. *Under the circumstances*, it is better for one to give up his money to a robber. One never makes an exchange in which he does not believe that he is benefited, under the circumstances, but it is unfortunate that he did not know what the circumstances would be before he began the production of the goods.

It is only in the out-of-the-way lines of production, and under special circumstances, that individuals are able to influence prices, for more than a few days. In the ordinary channels of trade, and in the common lines of production, the terms of exchange are fixed by great natural laws, easily understood. If the producer does not get as much as he expected, it is because he has produced the wrong thing; because production has not gone forward in the way which is most advantageous for the satisfaction of the world's wants. Nevertheless, it is just as important that the producer understand the laws of Exchange, and the principles which govern the terms on which exchanges take place. These principles are equally important where human effort satisfies wants directly, and in exchange of the title to any Resources of Nature.

Exchange Value.—The quantity of goods, or the service, which one will ordinarily receive for an article, is called its *Exchange Value.* When one receives money, the sum is called *price.* Professor Price, of England, called the goods which the money buys, the price of the money; and when lecturing in the United States, nearly twenty years ago, used to ask the question: "If hats are selling for four dollars apiece, what is the price of a dollar?" Of course the answer always came promptly: "One-fourth of a hat." We have been accustomed to say "value of a dollar," rather than "price," meaning the same thing; but there are some advantages in extending the term "price" to both sides of the money transaction. The word "value" is never quite as clear as "price," because we have a value in use as well as in exchange; and only the clearest thinker keeps them strictly separate. The term "price" is definite; and the moment we get used to the strange sound of "the price of a dollar," we know exactly what it means, and the idea can not be confused with anything else.

It is evident that there are as many prices of a dollar as there are goods or services which it will purchase. If the price of a dollar is one-fourth of a hat, it is also one bushel of wheat, twenty pounds of iron, two yards of cloth, twenty pounds of sugar, and so on through the list of everything which money will buy.

Sale and purchase are much simpler than barter.

At first it would seem that they require two transactions instead of one; we sell the goods for money, and buy other things with the money, instead of trading goods directly for goods. But we seldom wish to make such direct trades. The producer wishes to dispose of all his product, and to get a great variety of goods in exchange for it. We want a little of a great many things; and if we attempted to estimate the value of every article in terms of every other article, the task would be endless. It is a great deal easier to refer each to a common unit. It would be impossible to string a wire from the house of every telephone subscriber to that of every other subscriber. To thus connect a hundred subscribers would require 4,950 wires; but by running all the wires to a central office, a hundred are sufficient. Every message goes to the center, and out from the center. There are more than a thousand classes of goods to exchange. To estimate the value of each one of the thousand in that of all the others, would require 499,500 calculations; by means of money it requires only a thousand. So, in seeking for the terms on which exchange will take place—how much for how much—to save the endless combinations we go to a central piece of money, and from that to every article which is desired in exchange. Take the product of a shoe factory. How much can the owners get for it in the things they want? First, how much money can they get for the shoes? This is only half the answer, for they can not eat the money. Second, what are the prices of a dollar? How much will a dollar buy?

How much flour? how much clothing? how many school books? and so on, to the end of hundreds of questions. When we know the price of the product of the shoe factory, and the *prices of a dollar*, we can tell how much the producers will receive. We must know how many dollars they can get for what they have to sell, and what they can buy with a dollar.

In endeavoring to ascertain the terms on which exchanges will take place—how much will be given for how much—we shall assume the exchanges to be made by means of money, because it is so much simpler than barter. Frequently we shall notice only the price of the goods—how much money one can get for an article; but we must always remember that the *price of a dollar* is equally important—that is, the quantity of goods one can get for the dollar.

CHAPTER III.

EXCHANGE VALUES.

An Exchange Value of any article is what one can get for it in the open market. It must be carefully distinguished from Value in Use. Value in Use is what a thing is worth to use; Value in Exchange is what it is worth to sell. The two have some relation, but are often far apart. In fact, Exchange Value is likely to lie between the different Values in Use to different persons. An elephant would have no Value in Use to most people. His Exchange Value is what a showman or park commissioner would give for him. It is sometimes said that a thing is worth only what it will sell for. If by this we mean its Exchange Value is what it will sell for, we are only stating the same thing in different language; but if we mean that its Value in Use is only what it will sell for, the statement is wholly untrue. Value in Use may be a great deal more, or a great deal less, than the Value in Exchange. As has been said before, the first object of this book is to find the terms on which exchanges will be made. Exchange Value is only a shorter name for " the terms on which exchange will be made." We are to rid ourselves of all ideas as to whether exchanges are rightfully or wrongfully made, and of all extraneous circumstances, and remember that Exchange Value is independent of all moral qualities.

It is simply what the article can be exchanged for, in the market.

There will be as many Exchange Values as there are articles for which a commodity can be exchanged. A country shoemaker may be able to trade a pair of boots for a cord of wood, four bushels of wheat, one-half ton of hay, or for certain quantities of various other commodities. The Exchange Values of the boots are the cord of wood, four bushels of wheat, half a ton of hay, or whatever quantity of any other article the shoemaker can get for his goods. It would be easy to compute the Exchange Values of a bushel of wheat in a thousand articles, so that it will have a thousand different Exchange Values.

Price is the Exchange Value of anything in money, and is therefore simply one of the numerous Exchange Values which every article has. For convenience it is usually the only one taken account of. When we say, "the value of an article," we usually think of its value in money, which is its price. The real values, however, to the seller are the values estimated in the goods which he wishes to purchase. The farmer has his wheat crop and desires to use it to purchase goods for himself and family. What he really wants is these goods—groceries, dry goods, clothing, musical instruments, farm machinery, and many other things. Instead of estimating the value of his wheat in these goods, he is anxious about the price, or the value in money. He is likely to forget the values, or the prices, of a dollar, and thinks he gets a high or low value for his wheat according as the price is high or low. An economist looks beyond this. He sees the *values* of a dollar, and estimates the quantities of the goods which the farmer can get in exchange for his wheat crop. If these are more this year than last, the values of his wheat are higher.

The same is true of labor. Many men have nothing to sell but their labor power. What they really want in exchange for labor is their house rent, food and clothing for themselves and family, and numerous comforts and luxuries of life. The laborer exchanges his labor for money, and the money received is the money value, or price, of his labor. But this is only half the exchange. He now has to buy goods with the money, and the values of the money in the thousand different articles he wants—that is, the thousand different prices of a dollar—are what he wants to know. The only way to ascertain whether the real values of a commodity have risen or fallen is to make a computation of the quantities of different goods which it will buy, in the proportion in which the purchaser desires to get them. It is seldom that the value of any article continues the same for any length of time, but it is easy to estimate how much of, say, a hundred staple articles, a bushel of wheat will buy; and to compare these quantities with what it would have bought one, two, three, or four years ago. We thus ascertain whether the value of wheat has risen or fallen. The simplest way to make a computation is to take the prices of each of the articles, at the different dates, then to ascertain how much of each the price of a bushel of wheat would buy on each day specified. We can thus ascertain whether the bushel of wheat has risen or fallen in *values*; as estimated in the goods which the farmer wishes to purchase.

It is in this way that we can ascertain the changes in the values of money. The average value of money is very different to different people, depending on what they wish to buy. The common laborer, whose wages will not be much more than a dollar per day in a town of moderate size, will be somewhat limited in the range of his purchases. After paying house rent, purchasing food and clothing for himself and family, school books for his children, etc., there will not be much left for a wide range of luxuries. The values of the dollar to him must be estimated in the things which he is likely to purchase. A man with an income of five thousand dollars per year will be apt to purchase a greater variety of goods; and his *values of a dollar* will be estimated in a somewhat different and greater variety of objects. The values of a dollar can be got at only by a somewhat general average of wants of the whole people; and we come nearest to the true average value of a dollar by selecting a considerable number, at least a hundred, staple commodities in general use; and taking them in the proportions in which they are called for in the markets of the nation. By selecting a hundred such articles, and taking a proper proportion of each, we are enabled to say whether the average value of a dollar is greater or less this year than last, and to what extent it has changed. Such estimates always show very considerable variation in the values of money, which is far from being the unvarying standard that is popularly supposed.

One should become accustomed to estimating the value of his labor, and of the commodity he has to sell, in all the objects which he proposes to buy—not in money alone, but in the articles for which he wishes finally to exchange it.

It is to be understood that Exchange Values are *not* the cost of the production; are *not* the labor involved in production; are *nothing but the things which one can get in exchange for what he has to sell*. The cost of production, or the labor involved, is often the cause of value, and sometimes determines what the value will be, as we shall see hereafter. But it is not the value, which may depend upon a combination of many causes.

Exchange Value, as we shall see hereafter, has also a relation to Value in Use, but it is not Value in Use, and when we are estimating or thinking of Exchange Value we are to think simply of the price of an article in money, or of the goods that can be had for it in trade. This much is necessary to fix the idea of Exchange Value in our minds before proceeding to inquire what determines it, or what determines the terms on which one article will be exchanged for others.

The reader is urged not to leave this chapter without a clear idea that it is not value, but values, that we are seeking to ascertain. One value of an article may be of little consequence. It has a thousand values, and each one wishes to know the values in the goods he expects finally to get. The advantage of knowing the money value is in the facility with which all other values are deduced from it.

CHAPTER IV.

THE LIMITS OF VALUES IN EXCHANGE ARE FIXED BY VALUES IN USE.

We now come to the question, On what terms will exchange be made? How much of one article will be given for another? The popular statement that every exchange is an advantage to the parties, is true if we add "under the circumstances in which it is made"; that is, no man will make a trade unless he thinks it best for him to make it, *as he is situated*, although the other party may be responsible for the situation. This simply means that one will not give more or take any less for any article than what he supposes to be its Value in Use to himself. But the Value in Use is very different to different individuals. The Value in Use of the elephant to its owner may be nothing. He has no use for him; he can not afford to feed him; he would better give him away than keep him. Consequently, if he gets one dollar in exchange for him, he has gained the dollar. On the other hand, the Value in Use to the showman may be several thousand dollars. He will not give more than this. If he gets him for less, he gains so much.

Let us suppose the Value in Use of the elephant to the showman to be one thousand dollars; to the owner, nothing. The margin here is one thousand dollars, which will be gained by one party in the trade, or divided between both. The limits of the exchange are therefore the Value in Use to the owner and the Value in Use to the showman. We have not stopped to inquire how the owner got the elephant. He may have imported him at a cost of nine hundred dollars, under the belief that he could sell him to the showman for one thousand dollars. If he can not get the nine hundred, of course he meets with a loss. But the loss has *already been incurred*. The labor and the capital have been sunk, and the elephant is worth nothing to him unless he can sell him. If he has only one showman to deal with, he may be compelled to take much less than the beast cost him. On the other hand, if there is no other elephant for sale, and the owner be firm, he may compel the showman to pay his full Value in Use, or one thousand dollars. If there are only two parties to this transaction,—no other elephant in in the market, no other showman desiring to purchase—one can not predict the price beforehand, except to say that it will be between nothing and one thousand dollars. It will depend partly on the firmness of each, or the knowledge which each has of the other's condition, and upon mental traits and accidents which would not be the same with any two parties.

Let us fix, then, in our minds ; first, this principle, that all exchanges are limited by the Value in Use to each party ; but the limits are often far apart, and may mean wealth or poverty to either party. Often there is an element of justice, and one can say that the price *ought* to be so and so, but this will not determine what the price will be.

COMPETITION.—Let us suppose there are two showmen and one elephant. It is not likely that its Value in Use will be the same to both. It will, perhaps, be a thousand dollars to one showman and fifteen hundred to the other. Now, how much will the elephant bring? If these men compete for him, at least one thousand dollars, since either would prefer giving that to losing him. The first bidder will give the thousand rather than to have the other get the animal; and the second will give a little more than a thousand because the Value in Use to him is fifteen hundred. If the full circumstances of the case are known, the owner will get one thousand dollars, or a trifle above that. The second purchaser will not give much more than one thousand, because he knows his competitor can not afford to give more, and that the elephant is worth nothing to its owner. If, however, competition is not open; if the seller can keep the second purchaser in ignorance of the condition of the first, and lead him to believe that the first purchaser would give fifteen hundred, he can obtain something near that price, because the second is willing to give that, if he can not get the beast for less. Open competition, where all circumstances are known, simply narrows the limits of Exchange Value. In the first case, we saw that the price would be somewhere between nothing and a thousand dollars; in the second case, it will be either one thousand or somewhere between one thousand and fifteen hundred.

Let us now suppose other purchasers to whom the elephant is worth eleven hundred, twelve hundred, thirteen hundred, and fourteen hundred, respectively. The owner will now obtain something between fourteen and fifteen hundred dollars for him. He is worth fifteen hundred to one showman and fourteen hundred to another. Competition frequently brings the limits of exchange within a few cents of each other.

COMBINATION.—Combination destroys competition. Let us suppose now that all these showmen combine. They say, "There is only one elephant to be had. He is worth nothing to the owner, and there is no need of giving more than a hundred dollars for him. If, therefore, we agree that one of our number shall offer one hundred dollars, and the others shall refuse to purchase, or offer less than one hundred, the owner will sell at that price, because he will be a hundred dollars better off than to have the animal left on his hands; and we can arrange the gain by dividing it among ourselves." This is combination of many parties against one. Competition is often defeated by combination.

Under either competition or combination, Exchange Value depends on Value in Use. The price can not be less than the Value in Use to the seller, or more than that value to the buyer. If he buys to sell again, he will not pay more than the Value in Use to the final purchaser. Values in Use, therefore, fix the limits of Values in Exchange.

CHAPTER V.

SUPPLY AND DEMAND.

In the last example, we considered the case of but a single animal, although there were several purchasers. Now let us suppose a large number of animals for sale. And we shall not be far out of the way if we assume that in a county in Illinois there are a number of horses awaiting the visit of a dealer. The Values in Use of the horses in this county are very different, according to the circumstances of the owner. Some farmers with a single team could not afford to part with it for a thousand dollars, unless another could be purchased. As they are situated, with their farm and other work, the Value in Use is far greater than this. There are other horses, equally good, for which the owners have no use, which they are feeding in idleness. It would be better for the owners to give them away, if it were certain that they could not be sold at any price within a reasonable time. The habit, however, of considering a horse worth about so much, and the hope of future sale, and possibly of future use, make the owner unwilling to part with him except for some fair proportion of what he thinks he ought to get. We may assume that in this entire county there will be a few average horses for which the owners would take $75.00, each, if they knew that they could get no more. The total supply of horses in this county is all the horses there are; but the Value in Use of some of these is so high that they must be left out of the account. Let us assume that there are a hundred average horses for which the owners would take $150.00, each, if they could get no more. While the total supply is all the horses there are, the supply at $150.00 is one hundred horses.

Demand is desire for any commodity. The *total demand* is the total desire, or all that would be taken by all the people if the price were nothing. The total demand for drinking-water is measured by the amount that is used. For practical purposes we usually have to deal with more limited demands, at fixed prices. The total demand for horses in this county is the number of the horses desired. But there are demands for less numbers at various prices. At $75.00 each, perhaps one thousand horses could be sold. At $150.00 each, not more than ten; hence the demand at $75.00 is for one thousand horses, the demand at $150.00 is for only ten.

We now have the full conditions of Supply and Demand, and assume that we are acting under free competition. The horses for sale constitute Supplies at various prices. The purchasers embody Demands at various prices. How many horses will change hands, and at what price or prices?

We notice, first, that assuming competition to be free, in an open market where each knows what the other pays and receives, horses of the same grade will all sell at the same price. It is true there may be a few men who would sell at $75.00 rather than not sell at all. But they are not numerous enough to supply the demand, and competition among the purchasers will enable them to secure a higher price. So, while there are a few men who would pay $150.00 rather than not buy, the supply of horses at a lower price is so much greater that competition will enable the buyers to purchase cheaper. Each buyer will purchase where he can buy cheapest. Each seller will sell where he can get most. The final result will therefore be to secure the same price for all. What will that price be, and what will be the number sold?

We have supposed ten horses of which the Value in Use to the owners is but $75.00, which will therefore be sold at that price if they can not get more; and there are purchasers who will pay $150.00, each, for ten horses if they can not get them for less. Now, clearly, there must be at least ten horses sold, and the price will be somewhere between $75.00 and $150.00.

But there are other purchasers, and other sellers. While only ten horses would be taken at $150.00, twenty would be taken at $140.00. Let us suppose also that while there are but ten horses for sale at $75.00 there are twenty for sale at $90.00, hence at least twenty horses will change hands, and the price will be between $90.00 and $140.00. As the price is reduced, the number of purchasers increases. At $130.00, thirty horses would be taken. Perhaps thirty horses are for sale at $100.00, so at least thirty horses will change hands, and the price will be between $100.00 and $130.00. At $120.00 there is a demand for forty horses. Forty horses can be had for $110.00, consequently at least that number will change hands at a price between $110.00 and $120.00. At $110.00 there is a demand for fifty horses, but while forty horses could be had at $110.00, fifty can not be had at less than $120.00, seeing the owners of the last ten find them worth more than this to use. Now, fifty horses can not change hands, because the demand for this number is at $110.00, whereas the supply is at $120.00, hence the number sold must be less than fifty; and, as we have seen, greater than forty; the number of horses that will change hands will be between forty and fifty, and the price somewhere between $110.00 and $120.00.

This somewhat lengthy supposition has been written out to familiarize ourselves with supplies and demands *at various prices*, and to see how both the selling price and the quantity sold are finally arrived at by the play of the forces of competition. There is not one, but *many, Demands*, and not one, but *many, Supplies*. We can not tell what the demand is until we know the price at which the exchange is proposed. We can not tell what the supply will be until we know the price offered for the goods.

The Total Demand for any article is commensurate with human wants. It means all that would be used, or taken as a gift. The Total Supply is all there is of the commodity—all the wheat in existence; all the horses fit for use. The Total Supply of any article is simply the quantity of it which exists.

The Demand at any *particular price* is the quantity which would be taken at that price. It can not be greater than human wants, and depends as much on what people have to buy with as on the wants themselves. A starving man can not buy a loaf of bread for five cents, if he have not the five cents. The Total Demand for grain is all that people could use. The Total Demand at a dollar a bushel is all that is wanted *at that price* by people who have the means to purchase it. So there are various Supplies at every possible price. While the Total Supply is all there is, the Value in Use to some owners is so great that they could scarcely be induced to sell. The supply of wheat at even ten dollars per bushel would probably be found to be less than the total supply. That is, even ten dollars per bushel would not call out all the wheat in the world, although one dollar per bushel might purchase half of it. What is called the Visible Supply of an article often means no more than that portion which is offered for sale at a price slightly above the ruling market rate, and means the supply within possible trade limits. The reader can not too carefully distinguish between the different supplies at various prices, as well as between the different demands at various prices. The market rate at which exchanges will actually take place is that price at which demand and supply are equal. When wheat is selling for ninety cents it means that the supply at ninety cents is the same number of bushels as the demand at ninety cents. The supply of wheat at one dollar would be larger than the demand. The demand at eighty cents would be larger than the supply, but it so happens that the amount demanded and the supply at ninety cents are equal; and hence this is the rate of exchange. As the demands and the supplies change, so the market rate changes.

While an increased demand will unsettle the market and require a higher price, no one can tell how much higher. An increased supply will lower the market rate; but no one can tell how much it will lower it, because no one knows precisely what the demands at lower rates are, or what are the supplies at higher rates. Nothing but a practical understanding of the demands and supplies of each article, learned in practical business, will make an accurate judge in each case.

Supply and Demand limit prices even when there is no competition, provided that all articles of the same grade are sold at the same price. Suppose all the wheat of the United States to be in the hands of a combination, so that there is no competition between the sellers. The price will depend on the number of bushels of wheat in existence. There are some persons who would pay $100.00 a bushel rather than not have it, but they would take only a limited quantity. There is more than can be consumed in the United States, and for the purpose of export one can afford to pay only ninety cents. Hence, if all the wheat is sold at the same price, it must all be sold at ninety cents. The owner sometimes finds it profitable to destroy half the supply because he can get more for the other half; or, what is the same thing, to leave half unsold. In manufacturing, he may close half the factories, throw men out of employment, and stop production. There are demands for a certain quantity of the goods at high prices. By destroying a portion, or limiting production, he is able to get high prices for the quantities sold; and a high price for half may give more profit than a low price for the whole. While some persons would pay $100.00 a bushel for wheat rather than do without it, there are others who will substitute something in its place, if it cost more than ninety cents. So that the requirement to sell the whole quantity at a uniform price produces the same effect as competition. This is the object of many government regulations. In railroad business it is now provided by law that all goods of the same class shall be carried for all shippers at the same price. Although the rate may be left to the railroad to fix, and although there are many shippers who would pay several times the regular rates if they could not ship for less, more business, and more income, can be got at the rates fixed than at higher ones. The law is evaded, but if the principles could be enforced, and the railroads compelled to perform proportional services at uniform prices for all parties, nearly all the benefits of competition would be secured, even though there were but one line between two points.

CHAPTER VI.

COST OF PRODUCTION.

We have seen that Exchange Value, the terms on which exchanges are made, is limited by Value in Use and must be between the lowest and the highest values to the parties to the trade. The limits are very wide. If it were possible for a merchant to buy at the lowest Value in Use and to sell at the highest, he would soon have a large portion of the wealth of the earth under his control. Under many circumstances, an article is worth nothing to the seller, and worth a great deal more to the purchaser that he ought to pay.

We have seen that Value in Use is brought within narrower limits by competition, and is usually fixed by Supply and Demand, particularly when demand is made up of many competitors under the condition of free competition.

The next question is, What determines Supply and Demand? We have seen that there are numerous Supplies of most articles, each at a different price; and what we call Demand is made up of many Demands at different prices. Now, what fixes these Supplies and Demands?

Where articles are produced regularly, the supply, and consequently the price, usually depends upon the *Cost of Production*. By the cost of production we always mean, not what it has cost to produce a given article, but what it will cost to produce another like it. It is true that labor and capital invested in the production is sunk, and that the price of the article is fixed by the present Supply; but there will be a future Demand; and if the goods can not be sold this year, they may be retained for sale next year, and thus come into competition with future productions. The goods of this year can not be sold next year for more than it will cost to produce others like them, but, if they do not deteriorate in utility, they will be worth as much as new goods; hence the holder will decline to part with them for much less than the cost of production of others like them; and at a lower price will withdraw his supply from the market. In fact, though the total supply may be great, the supply offered will all be at the cost of producing other goods like the present, less interest, risk, etc. Hence the price at which a supply will come on the market will not be much less than the cost of future production. If the present demand exceeds the supply, this price will be higher.

We may look at the matter with advantage in another way. Most goods are produced to sell. The manufacturer knows they will be of no use to him. He makes them because he believes that there will be a demand at a certain price. If there are indications that there will not be a demand at this price, he will not produce the goods. Now, we have seen that there are demands at various prices. There is a demand for cotton cloth at twenty-five cents a yard, since a large quantity could be sold at that price if it could not be had cheaper. There is a larger demand at ten cents; a larger demand at five cents; a larger demand at two cents. If the manufacturer understands the state of trade, he will not produce goods enough to satisfy the demand at two cents per yard, but he will endeavor to satisfy all demands above the cost of production. If he believes that the supply will be so large as to bring the price below the cost of production, he will shut up his mills. If there is reason to expect that the price will be greatly above the cost of production, he will work his mills to the utmost capacity; and perhaps double the production of goods. Competition among producers and purchasers, therefore, tends to limit the supply to the *demand at the cost of production;* and we may lay down as a general principle that, where goods are produced regularly, and the production can be increased or decreased without great loss, the price or exchange value will tend to be that of the cost of production. It may never settle into this exact price, but it will hover about it.

There has been considerable discussion as to what constitutes the cost of production. For practical purposes under the wages system it is the cost to the producer. It is the wages he pays out, and the interest on the capital he invests, as well as the rent of the land he occupies.

Strictly speaking, the interest should be computed only on what might be called free capital; that is, the sum necessary for the support of the laborers, purchase of material, and general capital which he could turn in some other direction. The cost of production does not strictly imply interest on Permanent Produced Wealth, since machinery can be used for no other purpose, and it may as well be used as to stand idle. Unrestricted competition, therefore, tends to reduce the price to the cost of production, leaving the owner of fixed capital nothing for its use. This is best seen in the case of railroads. Suppose there are two railroads between two points, and they compete freely for business. Since it is better to carry freight for the cost of handling than not to carry it, if there is no agreement or understanding between the roads, unrestricted and complete competition will reduce the rate of freight to a point that leaves nothing for interest on the enormous capital sunk in the construction of the road, and represented either by stock or debts. Competition even tends to reduce rates to a point which leaves nothing for the salary of the general manager, because in each particular instance it is better for the road to accept a rate which covers the cost of carriage than to lose the business.

Here is the weakness of competition. It is well enough where little fixed capital is required; but it is impossible to carry on great business enterprises, railroads, steamships, factories, or anything which requires vast sums of fixed capital, on the principle of unrestricted competition. The competition must be checked in some way, either by agreement, mutual understanding, or common opinion, in order to secure interest on the fixed capital invested.

Practically, however, most business managers refuse

to compete except on terms which will allow interest on fixed capital. There are frequent instances of railroad wars, when, for a short time, goods may be carried at less than the cost of transportation; and even retail merchants have been known, on account of rivalry, to sell at less than the cost of the goods. But it is well understood that this sort of thing can not continue. Railroad wars always come to an end. Most business managers prefer to lose, rather than make a price which will not allow something for interest. They recognize that to do otherwise is suicidal.

Where there is no competition, as in the case of a single railway between two points, excess of supply will never carry the price below the cost of carriage plus the interest on fixed capital. Less business at a higher price would be more profitable. When such a road does make a price at the actual cost of carriage, allowing nothing for interest on capital, it is only to particular persons or for particular classes of goods, with the hope of making its profit from other customers or on different classes of goods. In this case it does not intend to charge all persons the same price for the same service, or proportional prices for proportional services.

As a general rule, therefore, we may say that all prices, under competition, tend to fall to the money cost of production, though this may include interest on capital invested. When they go lower than this, production must be diminished or goods produced cheaper by the lowering of wages, or otherwise.

It is wholesale prices that are here spoken of, because, in regard to them, both buyer and seller are better informed as to the quality of the goods and the extent of the demand and supply. In retail prices, there is room for considerable margin, through the ignorance of the purchaser as to the quality and the cost of production of the goods. If the seller has the reputation of being trustworthy, so that the customer feels sure he is getting goods that are just what he supposes, he will pay a considerable profit rather than go where he can not be sure of the quality of what he buys. Even in retail prices, competition acts through supply and demand, but there is far more margin. It limits the range of prices, but not so closely; so that the same quality of goods may sell for fifty per cent. more in one place than in another. Competition is not inactive, however, when it fixes such limits as these. The limits of Value in Use are very much wider.

The application of the Cost of Production is confined mainly, though not entirely, to the Resources Produced by Human Industry. It, of course, has nothing to do with Natural Resources, which man does not produce, except in the few instances where they can be replaced by the efforts of human industry.

The Cost of Production has much more influence on those goods that are produced and consumed year by year than on those which are of a more permanent nature. Permanent Produced Wealth, such as dwellings, lasts for many years or even centuries. If production ceases, the supply is not, therefore, very rapidly reduced. The same effect is caused, however, by an increase of population, which demands an increase in the supply. Suppose there were more dwellings in a city than could be used. The price would naturally fall below the cost of production. Now, though production were entirely to cease, the supply would still be more than sufficient for a stationary population, until the buildings were destroyed by time; and for more than a generation the price might rule below the cost of rebuilding. This has happened in some villages which have made no growth for years. If, however, population increases, the dwellings are soon insufficient, not for the old, but for the increased population; more must be built, and when the necessity for further production arises, the Exchange Value of all dwellings will be brought up to the cost of producing others as good. Thus the Exchange Value of Produced Wealth *tends* to the Cost of Production, in the long run. Fortunes may be made or lost while the pendulum is swinging to one side or the other, through a period of months or years. It is to be remembered that by the Cost of Production we do not mean what an article cost when it was made—that is a matter of no consequence in determining Exchange Value—but what it is believed it will cost to make another as desirable. The fashions change; a house built a few years ago is out of style. One can now be built for half the money, which, though not so good in some respects, is to most people as desirable as the old. The old is, therefore, worth what this new house would cost. In applying the Cost of Production to values, we consider only what it will cost to make something which will satisfy wants as well as what we have. The cost may be less than half, or more than twice as much.

COST OF PRODUCTION TO THE LABORER.—The cost of production has thus far been considered with reference to a manufacturer who employs labor for wages. The wages are themselves fixed by Supply and Demand, but he has to take account only of what he pays, what the manufactured goods cost him.

Where one produces goods by his *own* labor, as a country shoemaker, or the members of a co-operative factory, the cost of labor is the irksomeness of it. Under such a system there would still be a cost of production which the laborers would have to estimate in the disagreeableness of the labor. One would determine whether he were willing to expend labor enough in the future to replace the article for the price he is offered. If not, while he might be compelled to sell for what he could get, production on his part would cease.

The cost of labor to the laborer is the Value in Use to him of leisure, and increases with the number of hours and disagreeableness of the work.

If all production were conducted by means of co-operation, and no wages were paid, the present wages question would be carried over into the price of the goods produced; the price would depend upon the supply of various forms of labor, and the demand for various kinds of goods. Let us suppose the men of a co-operative shoe factory have produced a quantity of shoes which they place on the market. If they can get no more than the material cost, they would better sell them, since their labor has been already expended and is lost. But if they believe they can get no more, they will cease producing shoes; and the supply being diminished, the price will rise. These men will not willingly remain in idleness; they will seek to produce something which gives the greatest return to labor; and by their production they will increase the supply of something else, and hence diminish the price.

The method by which labor is transferred from one product to another is seen in the case of the average farmer in the Northern States, who raises a variety of crops. One element of the cost of production to him, is his own labor, and the sacrifice of ease it involves. If the price of wheat rules low for a number of years, he turns his attention to the raising of wool or live stock. He may unconsciously estimate the cost of each product in the labor required to produce it. He does not raise some crops, because there is too much work about them; though if the supply is so greatly reduced as to advance the price, farmers will be found to produce these very crops. The price of what these farmers raise will thus be governed by the cost of production to them, measured in their labor. The average price of the commodities which the farmers of a certain State produce will, therefore, be governed by the labor cost of producing them. This is, however, only the relative cost as measured in the various commodities produced by the farmers of this State; and has nothing to do with the cost measured in the commodities produced in the distant factory, or in a State with an entirely different climate. The *relative* prices of wheat and wool and pork will depend on the labor cost of their production.

If there were no friction, and men could freely go from one employment to another, the supply of the various productions of human industry would be controlled so as to be sold at prices which would give the same reward to all laborers of equal ability, in proportion to the disagreeableness of the labor.

In practice the division can never be so simple. We meet first what Professor Cairnes called "noncompeting groups." Two men learn a trade; the one is a printer, the other a carpenter. They may be of equal natural ability, but arrived at middle life neither can do the work of the other without years spent in learning a new trade, which can not be learned as well as in boyhood. Practically there is no competition between these men. Still less is there competition between the watchmaker and the stone mason; the lawyer and the civil engineer; the teacher and the physician. Only in common labor is the full force of competition felt, and here the cost of production to the laborer is estimated in the disagreeableness of the labor and the amount he can accomplish. Every group of laborers, however, competes within itself, and the reward within that group is likely to bear some proportion to the amount one is able to accomplish, or the quality of the work he does. In the professions the quality of the work may be so important a matter that many men have no competition, even in their own group.

CHAPTER VII.
MONOPOLY.

Monopolies are the result of natural advantages, or of legislation, or of the combination of competitors, and are by no means to be condemned indiscriminately.

If a singer is without a rival, though he can not command his own price for singing, he controls the entire supply, and can get what the people consider the full Value in Use of his song. No monopoly will enable one to obtain more than this.

Artificial Monopolies are of two kinds: those granted by act of government, and enforced by its power; and combinations of private parties who would naturally be competitors. Many privileges have been granted by governments to favorites in former times, as well as to private parties in return for some service to the government. Many of these have provoked great indignation. The present patent system of the United States is a monopoly for a term of years. The inventor is given the exclusive right of manufacture—not for the same reason that an author has the right to control the sale of his productions, but as an encouragement to invention.

The author and the inventor should never be confused. The principles on which copyright and patent right are granted are as different as two things can be. The inventor who has bestowed time and capital in bringing out his invention, is entitled to something for his successful labor, put forth for the benefit of the whole people. As a rough measure of his reward, we give him a monopoly of his invention for a limited number of years, on the theory that perhaps no one else would have invented it within that time; and that, in any case, this is a convenient method of rewarding him. Whether there could be a better method is a question of practical statesmanship.

EFFECT OF MONOPOLY ON PRICE.—What price a Monopoly will obtain will depend, first, on whether it is compelled to sell to all persons at the same price, or is able to charge each one all he can afford to pay, regardless of the others.

If compelled to sell at the same price to all, it can obtain only the Value in Use to the purchaser who *can afford to pay the least.* Let one have a monopoly of the supply of flour for a city. There are people who would pay a hundred dollars a barrel, rather than do without it; others would pay fifty, others ten dollars. As it will be impossible to sell his goods at different prices, the holder will fix the price at which his entire stock will bring the most money. If the price be a hundred dollars per barrel, only the wealthy can afford to take it. One will, perhaps, get more money by selling at ten dollars per barrel, and selling twenty times as much. In many cases he who has a monopoly can get more by deliberately destroying a part of his product. If he has all the flour that the city can use, he can get only the price for each barrel that the poorest can afford to pay. If he destroy half of his stock, the poorest of those able to consume it can pay a large price; and his receipts for half may be, therefore, more than they would have been for the whole. Of course, suffering would be inflicted upon the people, and those who obtained flour would pay far more than otherwise; but we are considering Exchange Value. Exchange is heartless; what control it should be subjected to is another question.

Instead of destroying stock, Exchange Value can be as well maintained by limiting production. If the product can be limited, it will be sold at what it is worth to the lowest purchaser, and production can be limited until this value is above cost. The advantage of Monopoly consists in the power to obtain the full Value in Use to the men to whom it is worth least. It may be very much above the Cost of Production, and very much above the price which would have been fixed by Competition.

WHAT PRICE WILL THE MONOPOLIST FIX?— He can not fix a price above the Value in Use to the consumers. Within that limit, his price will depend on the quantity he can most profitably dispose of. When goods must be sold all at the same price, a very small profit on a large quantity may exceed a large profit on a small quantity. Suppose the Sugar Trust to have— what it can not have—an absolute monopoly. There exists a Value in Use, a demand, for a certain quantity at ten dollars a pound; but it would be impossible to wholesale sugar at two prices, and although the ten dollars a pound would be practically all profit, the total sum received might be less than a profit of half a cent a pound on the enormous demand at five cents. Those having an absolute monopoly of this kind carefully estimate the various demands, with the quantity desired at various prices, and fix a price which gives the greatest total profit. Many wants must, of course, be left unsupplied; it is possible that double the wants could be supplied at a lower price, with nearly as much profit, but that is a matter of indifference to the monopoly. What it wants is the greatest total profit, and it rather prefers to make it on a small quantity than a large, since it is less trouble and risk. This is one of the arguments for the control of certain necessary monopolies by the people, of which the post-office is an example. A private monopoly would estimate how it could make the most money. Suppose it concluded that the largest profit could be made at carrying letters at five cents each; at the same time, letters could be carried at two cents, with a total profit nearly as large, because there would be several times as much business. If the government is in control, it will always choose to satisfy the largest number of wants at the lowest price, rather than a smaller number of wants at a higher price, the total profit being the same. Not caring to make a profit at all, it may see that, at an insignificant loss to itself, it can carry ten times the number of letters for the people at half the cost to a private corporation, because the latter would not accept the small loss necessary to gain the enormous business.

When the monopoly is not compelled to sell its goods at the same price to every purchaser, it can charge the *full* Value in Use to each one; and thus secure far higher average prices. It will, under these circumstances, perhaps make even lower prices to those unable to pay more, than the price would be if compelled to serve all alike. It can afford to sell at any price at which it makes a profit, to those to whom the goods are worth least, and may get a hundred times as much from those able to pay more. In this case, the monopoly gets the full Value in Use from everybody; when it is compelled to sell at the same price, it gets only the Value in Use from those to whom the goods are worth least. There are, however, few complete monopolies. Nearly all have something to fear from possible competition or legal enactments; so that it is seldom that the price can be carried as high in practice as in theory. Most monopolies are contented with absorbing the greater portion of the business, and with getting a price very much less than could be had in theory.

The monopolist will naturally endeavor to fix his prices at the point which will give him the largest income. If he have a monopoly of the necessities of life, such as wheat in a famine, he can take all the people have, as did Joseph under Pharaoh; though in modern times, even if the monopolist were not prevented by moral considerations, the people would compel him to sell at some price not far above the cost of production. Few monopolies are of this character. The monopolist knows that people can find some way to do without his service; and, besides, he wishes to reach a large number of consumers, since large profits must depend on large numbers of people. He knows, also, that public sentiment may discourage the use of his goods, even at a price that would be profitable to the user; and the sum which he will add to the cost of production on account of his monopoly is a matter for careful judgment. The theater manager will prefer to sell a thousand seats at three dollars each to selling two thousand at one dollar, but the popular show may find that it can sell a thousand seats at twenty-five cents, when it could not sell a hundred at one dollar. Each man who controls a monopoly will settle these prices for himself in accordance with the circumstances. Moral and other considerations sometimes enter in, and one does not always take all the profit his monopoly makes possible.

CHAPTER VIII.

MONEY.

Money and its substitutes, and credit, are the principal means by which exchanges take place. Without it, very few exchanges would be made. Few questions can, therefore, be more important in Economics than the money problem.

Money is anything which is generally received in exchange, not for the purpose of use, but with the expectation that it will buy anything for sale. The possession of no mere commodity gives this power. One may be rich in land or in cattle, but he will find it very difficult to exchange these things, directly, for what he wants. Money will buy anything; hence, if he wants to buy, he hastens to exchange his cattle for money. The only essential characteristic of money is its general acceptability.

It by no means follows that all money is good money. Some very foolish schemes have passed into legislation, and nations have suffered greatly from the actions of their rulers; but we are not to condemn these schemes by assuming that the circulating medium was not money. It is because it was money, made so by the acquiescence of the people, that the suffering has been so great, and the loss far greater than even the sufferers realized.

Part I.—Qualities of a Good Money.

UNCHANGEABLE VALUES.—The first quality of a good money is *unchangeableness in values*. Money is first bought by the holder with what he has to sell— his labor, farm produce, manufactures, etc.—and then used by him to buy other goods with. He must take into account what he has to give for a dollar, just as much as what a dollar will buy. He does not usually give the same class of goods for money that he buys with money. It is an education to learn how much a dollar will buy—an education which some people never gain. We do not realize the effect of a change in the values of money on the common people when once they have become accustomed to certain values. It is desirable that the average of the values of money shall remain the same, so that the change of any particular value, as in that of wheat, can be explained by a short crop or some other evident cause. There will be a constant change in the values of various articles, due to natural causes; but some being in one direction and others in the other, the tendency is to balance one another. A thousand dollars ought to buy, in the wholesale market, the same average quantity of all the articles in common use by the people.

A change in average prices does not show that the values of the goods have changed (since these values are measured by other goods), but that the values of money have changed; and it is this variation in the values of money which it is all-important to avoid. At one time during the Civil War wheat sold at three dollars a bushel. The price has since been less than one dollar. Does any one suppose that the values of wheat were three times as great then as now? By no means; a dollar is now worth three times as much. The change is not in the values of the wheat, but in the values of the money.

It is the common people who suffer most by changes in the values of money in either direction. One with other business to attend to can not always be making calculations as to how much of each article a dollar ought to buy, or how much more or less it ought to buy than it did a year ago. It has required years, from childhood up, to fix in his mind the values of a dollar at all. It is no trifling part of the education to learn the lengths of a yard, foot, mile, weight of a pound and size of a gallon, so that when any distance or weight is mentioned one will have a vivid conception of it. It requires more years of experience to form a vivid conception of the values of a dollar. The child knows that the nickel will buy so much candy, but it is long years before he gets fixed in his mind the prices of all goods he is likely to want. If, now, the values of the dollar change, the prices of all these goods change, or ought to change, and he has them all to learn over again. He is not likely to do it. He unconsciously estimates the dollar at its old value.

If any one doubts the enormous loss to the mass of the people caused by every change in the value of money, he has only to reflect how difficult it is for even the more intelligent to change habits once formed.

One becomes accustomed to expecting that a dollar will buy about so much of what he wants. If there is a change in the price of any article, he wants to know the reason why. Is it scarcer, or is the dealer making more profit? When the values of money remain the same, he can usually ascertain these facts and act accordingly; but when the values of money are continually changing, the price of all articles must change with it, and he is at sea. He can not figure it out. Not one man in a thousand in the population of the United States can figure it out, and the opportunities for a few men to make money by taking a little from all the people are vastly increased. It is good times for the making of fortunes by a few, rather the lucky than the intelligent, but it is bad times for the people at large. As one does not know what he will have to pay in the future, he does not know how much he ought to have for his labor or the commodities he has for sale.

It must be remembered that a fall in the value of money means a rise in prices; and a rise in the value of money, a fall in prices—always the reverse. A dollar rises in value because it will buy more wheat—two bushels instead of one; but when a dollar will buy two bushels of wheat, wheat has fallen in price to fifty cents. Exchange is like a balance: when one side goes up, the other side goes down. When the value of money goes up, prices of other things go down. When the value of money goes down, the prices of other things go up.

It is impossible, except by more pages of detailed

illustration than there is room to insert, to bring ourselves to realize anything like the loss which comes to the people at large by any change in the value of money. Every change tends to make the rich relatively richer, and the poor relatively poorer. It tends to the failure of great numbers of honest and fairly well-to-do business men, and to the building up of large fortunes. Every change in the value of money opens opportunities for a more unequal distribution of wealth.

Deferred Payments. — Changes in the value of money in relation to debts and credits are more easily brought home to the conception of every one. In our civilization debt and credit are unavoidable. It is by the loan of capital from those who are not in a position to use it to the best advantage, to those who can profitably use it in production or business, that the wealth of the country is greatly increased, and the wants of all better supplied. But when one borrows, what is he to repay? What can he pay? The farmer can pay only with farm produce; the manufacturer, with the products of his factory. If one promises to pay money, when the note is due he must go and *buy the money* with his farm produce or the goods he has manufactured. Only in the rare case of the gold digger can he pay the debt out of the products of his business. He must buy the money to pay with. It is just as important to know how much the money will cost as to know how much money one is to pay. Every borrower unconsciously assumes that it will cost just what it did when he made the loan. If wheat is a dollar a bushel, the farmer assumes that, with ordinary crops, a bushel of wheat will buy a dollar when he has the debt to pay. He is not likely to take into account that, with ordinary crops, it may require twice as many bushels of wheat to buy a dollar as it did when the loan was made. This was practically the state of affairs some years after the Civil War. Men had purchased farms, paying, say half their value in cash, and giving a mortgage for the other half. Paying debts is slow work; and, although the mortgage may have been renewed, or replaced by another mortgage, many farmers paid little more than the interest; and at the end of ten years owed as much as at the beginning. But money had doubled in value. It took just twice as much farm produce to buy a dollar as when the debt was made. The creditor got just twice as much value as he loaned, because a dollar was worth twice as much. The farm which was worth $4,000, for which the purchaser gave $2,000 cash, and a mortgage of $2,000 more, is now worth precisely the face of the mortgage, and the purchaser has lost his original $2,000. Where the mortgage has been paid, and the land is worth as much as when it was bought, it is because of the natural rise in its value; and the creditor has absorbed the value of that rise instead of the farmer. He has also absorbed a considerable portion of the farmer's earnings. Had there been no change in the value of money, the creditor would have got precisely as much as he loaned, and the farmer would be seen to have accumulated more property, or perhaps have lived better in the meantime. The increase in the value of money has thrown the great gain in national wealth into the hands of the few, and built up a few fortunes of millions, which would otherwise have been distributed more equally among the people.

A decrease in the value of money, with the consequent general rise in prices, is also unfortunate. It is the creditors now who lose. The loss in either case is not to debtor and creditor alone; it is to the whole country. It makes business uncertain, teaches the people habits of speculation, and gives fortunes to the lucky and unscrupulous, rather than as a reward of honest industry. There is no national question of so much importance as the unchangeable value of money. Changes in the yardstick and the pound weight would be a less misfortune than changes in the value of the dollar which measures all contracts.

A continued increase in the value of money paralyzes business. It is usually the enterprising manufacturers, farmers and business men who are in debt. They are the life of business; without them the wheels of production move more slowly. Without business men who borrow money, great numbers of men are thrown out of employment, simply because there is no one to set them at work. The capitalist can not do it. He may be a minor heir, an insane man, a pleasure-loving man in Europe, or a good man who recognizes his own lack of business ability. The capital may be in banks, belonging to owners of small sums which they can not use in production. The greater portion of this capital will not be used to keep the men of the nation employed, and to carry on production economically, except in the hands of competent borrowers. How much better for the country when a competent young man runs in debt for a farm with a reasonable prospect of paying for it during his lifetime, than if the same young man is content to remain a tenant!

Nothing is so discouraging to a debtor as to feel that he must pay more than he borrowed, and where money is increasing in value he *must* pay more. The price of goods is continually falling, and men will not do business on a falling market if they can help it. They would rather be out of business and let the production of the country stop; and this means a financial panic, in which rich and poor lose ten times what the creditor has gained by getting a little more value than he loaned.

If there were to be any continued change in the value of money, it would be better to have it slowly *decrease* rather than slowly increase, because business is always active on a rising market. Now, it is not simply that business men, who are mostly borrowers, make a little more profit; the important result is that business is active, and every man in the country has an opportunity to work; all capital is employed. Mills do not stand idle. More goods are produced, and the people have more. Wants are better supplied. It is a question, indeed, if full activity is ever seen except on a rising market, with at least a slight fall in the value of money.

But how about the creditor? Will not he be paid less value in goods than he loaned? Certainly. He loses as much as the debtor gains, directly; but the great gain to the country is a hundred times this, in the activity of business, in the keeping of men at work, and in the prevention of waste. It is probable that most creditors would gain in the constant employment of their capital, and in fewer losses through failures, more than they lose in a slight depreciation. But the real protection to the creditor is in the opportunity of obtaining higher interest, *sufficient to make good the depreciation of his capital.* Money is now loaned on the undoubted security of government bonds at less than three per cent., free of taxes. If money were depreciating in value at the rate of one per cent. a year, the rate of interest would rule at least one per cent. higher. Not so much through an endeavor to keep good one's capital, as from the fact that the greater demand for loans in active business would carry the rate of interest up. So that it is not impossible that the increased rate of interest would actually give the lender returns more than sufficient to balance his loss.

But this has been written only for the sake of making the subject clearly understood. Justice requires that we use our utmost endeavor to prevent any change in the values of money; but, if there is to be a change, it is far better that it be in the direction of a *slight* depreciation instead of an increase. An increase in the value of money means idleness, an enormous loss to a nation, in addition to the small amount unjustly paid by the debtor to the creditor. A decrease in the value of money means a great gain to the prosperity of the country, notwithstanding the small sum the debtor unjustly retains from the creditor.

PORTABILITY.—In a simpler age, the second requirement for a good money was *portability*. As money is constantly changing hands, it is desirable that it be convenient to handle. Paper money answers this requirement best of all, since it is so easily carried. The portability of other forms of money is not of much importance to-day, because in civilized countries they will largely be replaced by paper. Gold certificates are now frequently seen, which say on their face that some one has deposited —— dollars in gold in the United States treasury, which the bearer of this certificate can have by calling for it. He seldom calls, because it is more convenient to hand the paper out in payment. It would make no difference, in this case, whether we consider the paper or the gold the money, so that we do not count both. But, as a matter of fact, the gold is the money, and the certificate the evidence of title. Payments are made by transferring the title to the gold from hand to hand. (This is not true of Government notes, called greenbacks, which are not certificates of deposit, but promises to pay.) An iron or a wheat money would be at once represented by paper certificates. Purchasers in a civilized country would not carry the iron about with them, but would store it in a warehouse and transfer the title by a certificate. The question of portability is therefore no longer of great consequence.

This has a bearing on the use of Silver. It was

formerly claimed that a silver money was objectionable on account of its weight. Even gold has considerable weight, but both it and silver are likely to be represented by paper. The cost of storing silver is no greater than that of gold when the risk of theft is taken into account, because no great value of silver can be carried off secretly. It is an admitted province of all governments to coin money. It is but a step to storing that money and issuing certificates of title to be transferred from hand to hand in place of the money itself. No one has ever objected to the issue by the United States of such *gold* certificates. If silver coin were the only money, it would likewise be thus deposited under our present laws, and the title to its ownership transferred in ordinary trade by certificates. The question of portability, therefore, scarcely enters into consideration.

DURABILITY.—A third requisite for good money is *durability*. It is important that money shall not wear out with the using, or deteriorate with keeping. Gold wears rapidly by the using, and the loss must be borne in the end by some one, in this country by the last user, who must bear the whole loss. A good money must not deteriorate by storage in a bank vault, or suffer too much in actual use. An exception is to be made of paper money. This costs so little to print that we can afford to wear it out and pay the expense of replacing the bills with new. Paper, on account of its portability, convenience, and the ease with which worn notes can be replaced, is certain to be the actual currency which passes from hand to hand in the future. It may be certificates stating that coin is held subject to order, or it may be notes whose redemption is in some way secured. The cost of issuing a second gold or silver certificate, in the place of one worn out, is trifling. The gold and silver whose title is transferred is not affected thereby.

There are other desirable qualities of money, such as *uniformity* and *divisibility*. Cattle have been used as money, but not all cattle are of the same grade, and the debtor will seek to pay in the poorest. Another objection to cattle is the lack of divisibility. An ox is a large piece of money, and inconvenient for small purchases. Paper, of course, has a uniform value; one note, of the same denomination, is as good as another; and issues can be made of any denomination.

The cost of issuing a one-dollar note is the same as one for a hundred dollars, and the smaller note wears out much the more rapidly. No one now thinks of using paper for sums smaller than one dollar. In England the smallest note issued is for twenty-five dollars, though many favor the issue of one-pound notes. Efforts in this country to withdraw the one and two dollar bills have met popular objections, but it would be much better if all paper currency were of the denomination of five dollars and over.

Acceptability is usually named as a quality of good money, but it is this that makes it money. Nothing is money that is not generally accepted, and anything which is generally accepted becomes money, though it may be a very poor money.

It is worth while to notice the difference between paper money and gold and silver certificates. Paper money is of various kinds. It has sometimes been irredeemable on demand, though with an expectation of payment in the future. Our present paper money is redeemable on demand in coin. Here, it is the paper, and not the coin held for its redemption, that constitutes the money. It is not a certificate of title to a given quantity of gold or silver. It is a note, and the reserve is much smaller than the volume of the currency. In estimating the amount of money in circulation, however, we should not count the specie reserve for paper money, since while it is held as a reserve it is no longer used as money. The increase in the circulation due to the paper is only the difference between the sum of the paper and that of the reserve. We did not consider gold and silver certificates as money at all, because it is understood that payment is made by the gold and silver itself, the title to which passes from hand to hand. This is not true of paper money which exceeds the amount of its specie reserve. Of course, if one were to insist on considering the gold and silver certificates as money, we should then be driven to say that the specie to which they are the title is not money. The paper and the specie reserve can not both be money, since the currency is not increased by the issue of the certificates. There is no more money than if the coin itself passed from hand to hand, and the certificates had not been issued.

Part II. What Determines the Value of Money?

We have seen the essential quality of a good money is that it shall have steadiness of value, and we are unprepared to form any opinion about the stability of any form of money until we knqw the causes on which its value depends.

The value of money depends on supply and demand. Gold and silver have values for ornament, and for plate. If neither were used as money, there would be demand for all the gold and silver of the world, but at lower values. Let us suppose that gold is worth five dollars an ounce. Now, let it suddenly be adopted as money, and a hundred million ounces be required for the money purpose. Would not this new demand rapidly raise the value? It might double it. It might make it ten times as great. The increase of the value of gold could increase production only to an irregular extent. If gold were raised as wheat, the new demand would have very little permanent effect, since double the quantity of wheat could be produced at very little increase of cost. But gold is not regularly produced. The amount accessible on the earth is limited. An increase in the value would cause the working of some mines which were before unprofitable, but, at even ten times the price, the increase in the amount to be had is not great. The value of gold is fixed rather by the rules of monopoly, since the quantity is limited. The value of gold will therefore be determined by the balance between the demand for *all purposes*, and the supply. Gold has one peculiarity. Being desired for ornament, the demand may be greater at a high price than at a low price. If it were worth less than silver, it would be discarded by many persons who now use it simply because its cost prevents its being too common. The more valuable it becomes, the more attractive it is to them, and hence the demand may even increase with the increase in value. How much effect the demand for use as money has on the value of gold, no one can estimate. It could be shown only by the general demonetization of the metal by all nations.

The value of silver is governed by the same laws as that of gold, with the exception that the product of silver can be more easily increased. There exist vast quantities of silver-bearing rock of too low grade to work with profit. If the price were greatly increased, the output would also increase. The demand for silver to use as money is one of the demands which give it value. Were it demonetized by all nations, its value would sink precisely as would that of gold.

Paper is the only remaining form of money necessary to consider. What gives value to paper which can be printed at a nominal cost?

1. The anticipation of redemption, either on presentation or in the future. If the promise is to pay on demand, in coin, and the paper is, in fact, redeemed over the counter of the bank without hesitation or trouble to the holder, it is worth as much as the coin. Even if specie payment be suspended, and there is a general confidence that the note will be paid at some

future time, it is worth its face, less such discount as the general opinion may fix for the risk and delay. This was the condition of treasury notes for some years after the war. There was full confidence that at some time they would be redeemed in specie.

2. The quantity in circulation. The value of everything is fixed by supply and demand. If there were, or could be, no money but paper, it would be given a value by the demand for money. The larger the supply, the lower the value.

PAPER MONEY REDUCES THE VALUE OF GOLD AND SILVER.—A paper money increases the total supply of money. It is the same as an increase in the supply of gold and silver, which, of course, reduces their value. The value of gold depends on the supply and demand for all purposes; if paper is substituted for one of its uses, the effect is the same as an increase in the supply of gold.

FIAT MONEY.—A paper money of altogether a different character has been the subject of some discussion in the United States. It is merely stamped paper, with no promise of redemption. Would such a paper be money, and, if so, what would determine its value? Whether it would be money or not, depends on whether it would come into general circulation. If the treasury were to issue paper on which is printed, "This is a dollar," it would be money if it were voluntarily accepted in payment by every one. It could be given forced circulation at the first, by enacting that it be received in payment for debts, and by government officials for their salaries. If such a law were sustained by the courts, the creditor would have no redress, even though the paper were worthless and his claims were confiscated. The government official would have the choice of acceptance or resignation. But this would not make it money. The test of money is its *voluntary* reception by those who have something to sell. If the people should take it, it would be money; otherwise, not.

If it were accepted by the people, what would determine its value? The amount issued, and the extent to which it should be used in exchanges. If it replaced all other money, and were accepted by every one, it would be worth nearly the sum named on its face, *as long as its issues were small*. There is a demand for a certain volume of currency. There would be nothing to replace this stamped paper, except coin, which costs as much as the face of the paper. As there is a demand, and the supply is limited, there is no reason why it should depreciate in value. As soon as the supply became excessive, its value would decrease. The more issued, the less it would be worth. If, at any time, people refused to receive it, and substituted something else, the demand would be so much reduced, and its value so much lower. In case of a panic and a general refusal, it would instantly become worthless.

The nearest approach to this kind of money, of late years, was the Confederate currency. This, to be sure, was a promise to pay, and was first received by the people with the expectation that it would be redeemed. That expectation never quite vanished as long as the money circulated at all; yet the issues were so excessive, and the expectation of redemption so slight, as practically to give it, toward the end, the character of mere stamped paper. It was received because there was nothing else. It was necessary to have some medium for exchange, and this necessity gave it a trifling value.

It is hardly reasonable to suppose that stamped government paper—*fiat money*, as it has been called—could gain a circulation in the United States. Sellers would not voluntarily receive it. If it were once in circulation, and the habit of receiving it formed, a very limited amount might hold its value for a time. But it would be a money very dangerous to stability, and in a panic the loss in the derangement of business would be many times the cost of coin which would have filled its place.

Stamped paper is not to be confused with paper money redeemable in something else than coin, or even redeemable at some future time. A paper money redeemable in interest-bearing bonds would, of course, be worth as much as the bonds. Several such schemes have been proposed, but there are difficulties in the way. Such paper money would have the value of specie, as long as its issue was not excessive, even though the interest-bearing bonds should fall considerably below par. The reason for the fall in the value of the bonds would be the fact that higher interest could be obtained in other investments. The demand for the money redeemable in them would, as long as the supply was not excessive, keep its value up to the cheapest thing which could take its place, which is gold or silver coin. If the volume issued were greater than the amount of coin which would otherwise be in use, the money would depreciate, because the supply would be greater than the demand. The money could not fall below the coin value of the bonds. If the interest-bearing bonds were to rise above par, the currency would at once be exchanged for bonds, and its place would be taken by gold and silver coin.

PART III.—HOW CAN WE SECURE A MONEY OF UNIFORM VALUE?

This is the important quality of a good money. There are many who advocate gold as a standard. But the changes in the value of gold are very great, though not usually very sudden. By the values of any money we mean how much it will purchase in the commodities in daily use by the people, either directly, or indirectly—as steel is purchased to build railroads to carry grain and manufactured goods. The fluctuations of gold are still further increased by the action of governments. Nearly all the annual production of gold is now required for use in the arts; and a larger or smaller demand for use as money tends to rapidly increase or decrease the value of the metal. When the United States resumed specie payments, it was compelled to draw large quantities of gold from Europe. This increased demand could not help increasing the value of the metal, and thus lowering the price of goods. When Germany adopted a gold standard, the effect was in the same direction. France has since been accumulating gold. The Austro-Hungarian empire is now seeking to establish a gold basis for its currency. This bidding of all nations for gold as a reserve for currency can not fail to increase its value—its price as measured by goods. If all the silver-using nations were to adopt a gold standard for their currency, it would send the values of gold up, nobody knows how far, certainly to double those at present.

THE TABULAR STANDARD.—For many years economists have seen that this is the only honest standard of value. It has been proposed to take the wholesale prices of a certain number of commodities, from month to month, and year to year. These should include all the articles which enter largely into the satisfaction of the wants of the great majority of the people. One hundred articles would perhaps give a fair average result. These articles would be taken in the proportion of the values produced each year. Let us see how much a dollar will buy of all of these hundred articles on the first day of July, 1893, and let this be the standard forever after. A thousand dollars is the quantity of these goods which a thousand dollars of our present money will now purchase. Here is strict justice—justice to the debtor, justice to the creditor. A dollar represents a certain quantity of the world's resources. If one lends it to-day, when the dollar is repaid, ten years hence, it should buy just as much, no more, no less, than when he lent it.

On account of imagined difficulties in using a money of this kind, it has been proposed to continue the use of our gold and silver and paper as at present, and to employ the standard only for correction once each year, or term of years; to ascertain how much a dollar will buy each day in the year, and take the average, at the end of another year, to see whether it buys more or less, and increase or reduce the amount of all promised payments accordingly.

A better way would be to use the standard itself. Suppose the United States were to issue treasury notes, *payable in gold or silver*, it being specified that a thousand dollars is as many grains of gold or silver as will buy certain quantities of one hundred named articles at wholesale prices, the amount to be announced from month to month by the statistical office. The wages of labor should be included among other things which money will buy. Every merchant in the world would have an interest in preventing an error of a fraction of a cent, and we may assume that the reports would be accurate. This would be good money. It would be paper money, the most convenient form; its value would be the same from month to month, and from age to age. It could not be issued in excess, because any excess would be returned for redemption in gold. Very little would be redeemed, mostly for those who wished the gold for export, but the certainty of redemption on presentation would give value to the entire issue. One would not know how many grains of gold will be paid in redeeming a thousand-dollar bill a year hence; but he would know that a quantity will be paid which will buy just as much, and no more, in the world's markets, as the quantity of gold which would be paid to-day.

The difficulty with the Tabular Standard is that it is not easy of comprehension, except by those of some education and intellectual habits. It is not an easy system to popularize.

BIMETALLISM.—Next to the Tabular Standard, the most practical plan for lessening the fluctuation in the value of money is bimetallism.

Bimetallism is using both gold and silver at a given ratio of weight. The theory is that by permitting the use of either metal, the cheaper will be coined until the increased demand for it raises its value to that of the other. It is not expected that the metals will fall apart at all, but that if the supply of one increase more rapidly than that of the other, it will be coined the more rapidly.

Suppose, now, that the leading commercial nations agree that they will coin all the gold and silver brought to their mints, free, at an established ratio, say one ounce of gold into the same number of dollars as twenty-four ounces of silver. This means that they must use gold and silver in such proportions as may be necessary to maintain their values at the standard ratio. If the price of one metal for a time rules so high that none of it comes to the mint, these nations increase their currency only by means of the other. In an extreme case, the coins of the dearer metal would be melted up for use in the arts. Nations which agree to bimetallism must, of course, be prepared to go to the length of using *either gold or silver exclusively*, if necessary to maintain the ratio; but this would never happen with a number of commercial nations in the league.

The more nations in such a league the stronger. No league could maintain a ratio beyond the market value of either metal if it were wholly demonetized; but if either metal were wholly demonetized, its value would probably sink to less than half that at present, so that the limits within which bimetallism could be maintained by a union of all the nations in the world are pretty wide. The ratio which should be selected is that which would cause the use of both metals, and of about an equal value of each. Any tendency of either metal to fall will then be counteracted by its increased use, and by a less use of the other. The two metals would be coined in such proportion as would maintain their values at the ratio fixed for their free coinage. The only way to increase the value of either metal is *to use more of it;* and the way to decrease the value of a metal is *to use less of it*.

This would be a **real double standard**, and not an alternating standard as some monometallists would have us believe.

If the United States, or any single nation, were now to open its mints to the free coinage of silver, it should be at some ratio not far from the market ratio of the metals—at present about 25 to 1. It would then have only future fluctuations to deal with.

The object of bimetallism is to limit the fluctuations in the value of money.

CHAPTER IX.

SUBSTITUTES FOR MONEY.

There are substitutes for money, which save the use of money itself. They are not money, because they are not generally received by every one for anything he has to sell; they are not in general circulation.

1. *Bank Checks.*—The substitute which most readily occurs to every reader is bank checks. These are not in general circulation; they usually make but one payment each before being returned to the bank. They are not accepted in complete payment, being merely an order to a bank to pay the money. If the bank pays, well; if it refuses the check, the drawer is liable. Neither is their use general, but it is confined to a limited class. Even a large manufacturing establishment does not pay its employes in checks, but in money. It pays other business firms by means of checks.

Although bank checks are not money, they save the use of money. Each check saves one payment. If it were possible for every person to use checks and make all payments with them, the only use for money would be as a bank reserve.

The advantage of saving the use of money depends on whether we mean gold and silver, or paper money. To save gold and silver is to release them for other purposes. The cost of a metallic currency is the interest on its volume. The cost of paper money is only the printing—not much more than that of bank checks. The reserve for checks should probably be as great as for paper money, so there is no great saving in a general substitution of checks for paper money. They prevent theft, are cleaner to handle, furnish a record of transactions, and are more desirable in many ways for a considerable number of people.

2. *Book Accounts.*—The real substitute for money is book accounts. Bank checks are only a part of a system of book-keeping by which accounts are kept between the depositors of the bank; and, through the clearing-house (the bank of banks), between the depositors of all banks. The simplest form of book accounts, as a substitute for money, is that of a country store. Let us suppose a farmer, who gets pretty much all his family uses—groceries, dry goods, clothing—at this store. The goods are charged to him. He sells his wheat, wool, butter, eggs, to this store, receiving credit for them. There is a settlement, perhaps once a year, at which the balance is either paid in cash, or carried over to begin another year. No money need, therefore, be used between these parties; the book account is a substitute. In this country store the exchanges are made directly, and without the intervention of money. Its only use is a measure of value. The farmer does not know exactly what he will want in exchange for the load of wheat. He trades it for his choice of anything in the store, to be delivered when he is ready for it. As he measures the quantity of wheat by a pound weight, and the

wood he sells by the cord, so he measures the value of this wheat by the dollar value. It is agreed between him and the merchant that, in exchange for this wheat, he shall have the value of a certain number of dollars in goods. He gets the goods for the wheat. The important thing to him is that the dollar measure shall not stretch. He does not want the goods to rise in price after he has sold his wheat.

If the reader is curious to see how the system of exchange by book-keeping is extended beyond the country store, he is referred to almost any good description of banking. The merchant buys his goods without money, and an account is made of them. He ships the country produce he takes in exchange to various business firms. They give him an order (check) on a bank for the value; he transfers this order (directly or indirectly) to the men of whom he bought the goods. He probably divides it up by sending the orders (checks) he receives to his own bank, having it make a book account of them; and then gives his own order (check) to the men of whom he buys goods, and the bank keeps the account. He may not handle a dollar bill in the whole transaction. He sells the farmer goods, without money. He buys the farmer's produce, without money. He sells the produce to a dozen men, and gets no money. He buys his stock of goods of various firms, and pays no money. It is trade all the way through; and the banks keep the account, on the orders (checks) of the parties, as they agree on the terms of each trade. The wholesaler buys of the manufacturer without money, and turns over the orders he has received from the retailer. Even international exchanges are managed by a system of book-keeping. When money is paid, it is gold or silver, and the shipment of one per cent. of the exchanges in gold excites comment in the newspapers. The large transactions, the great business of the world, are done by book-keeping, and not by money. One reason for this is the danger that large sums of money would be lost or stolen.

The reader may by this time wonder if money is used at all. It comes in for the smaller payments. The factory sells its goods for a book account, but it pays its workmen in money. Such country stores as have been described exist, but there are more which sell for cash. The traveler pays in money. He can not give a check for his hotel bill or railway fare. Most of the smaller transactions of life, especially between strangers, are settled in cash. There is usually a balance on settlement of book accounts, which is often paid in cash. Then a vast sum of real money is required as a "reserve," to make good all the demands for cash that arise in this complicated business.

All substitutes lessen the demand for money itself; and, hence, lower its value. If substitutes took the place of all the money of the world, the value of gold and silver money would sink to what the demand for use in the arts would give. The money demand for gold and silver now keeps their value far above this point. Were it not for the substitutes, and for paper money, the value of gold would be several times as high as at present.

3. *Credit.* — Credit has been treated by some writers as a mystic thing, and by others as a material commodity like iron or gold or silver. Like most other popular terms, it has several significations. One is said to have credit at a bank so long as he has money deposited there; that is, his credit is simply his own money left at a bank for convenience. But what is meant by credit in the ordinary sense, is rather the extent to which one can borrow money, or the extent to which he can purchase goods without paying for them on delivery, the sums for which he can " get trusted."

The sooner we understand that credit is nothing more than the willingness of people to give goods to a purchaser on his promise to give something in exchange for them in the future, the better. Their willingness is his credit. The exchange is not completed. One side transfers its goods; the other promises to transfer the agreed equivalent in the future. Whether one will or not, is a matter of opinion. Is he honest? Will he be able? Can he be compelled? His credit depends on the answers to one or all of these questions. One's credit can not be more than the estimate of his ability to pay in the future; it is likely to be much less. His ability to pay can not be greater than the wealth that he now has, with its natural increase, plus the results of his labor power, plus the goods furnished him on credit. It is, of course, possible that one may be able to give back all he has borrowed, if he preserves the goods or uses them without loss. He may also give the results of his labor, less the cost of his living; and if he has any wealth of his own at the time of incurring the debt, he may preserve it until the time of payment. In debating whether they will trust a man, people ascertain—

1. What he is worth, how much property he now has, and estimate the likelihood of his taking care of it. If he has "made it" himself, or has taken care of it without loss for some years, he may be expected to have it at the time for payment of what he proposes to borrow; and he will probably have credit to the extent of a certain part of it. If the property is of such a nature that he can give legal security on it, so that he can be compelled to sell it for the purpose of payment, he is still more likely to have credit. But as few people wish to resort to legal enforcement, one's credit will also be affected by his reputation for honesty, and the likelihood that he will pay without trouble. A rough popular estimate of one's credit from this source is usually something like half of what his property is worth.

2. But if goods are given on one's promise to pay, he has the goods, and may naturally be expected to have them, or their results, at the time of payment. It is possible, therefore, for one who has no property at all to have credit which consists of his reputation and estimated power of labor and management of business. If people generally believe a man is honest, and that he has the power of managing property so as to make it bring the largest returns, he may have credit to an almost unlimited extent. For the goods

loaned him are security, no matter how large their amount may be. If people believe him to be the man we have described, they believe he will have the means of payment when the time comes. So that the extent of one's credit from this source is almost unlimited, and depends entirely on his good name.

3. There is a third source of credit, which is merely one's labor power, independent of the management of money loaned. A merchant will sometimes advance a man food and other means for the support of his family, although he has no property, and the goods are to be consumed at once. The credit of the man in this case is his labor power. He may be working a rented farm, and the merchant believe he will pay when the crop matures. He may be working for wages, and will pay when he receives them. He may be going a-fishing, and will pay from his catch. This kind of credit is not usually given for large sums, though the aggregate in the United States is very great.

The credits by which the business of the world is chiefly carried on belong mainly to the second class named. The manufacturer can not sell his goods directly to the consumer. The goods are not wanted as fast as produced. No one knows just who will want a particular article, nor when he will want it. A reserve stock must be carried somewhere; and it should be where the consumer can easily find it, and examine it when he thinks of purchasing. The manufacturer turns the goods over to the merchant to sell. The latter might sell them on commission, but this plan has not been found to work well for most lines of goods. The manufacturer therefore sells the goods to the merchant, the latter agreeing to pay for them at about the time he hopes to have sold them. Now, if the merchant is honest and competent, it is safe to let him have as many goods as he is likely to sell. When he sells the goods he will have the money. He may steal it, may use it in his living expenses; but, if he is the right sort of man, he will do neither of these things, and will have enough to pay for the goods at their sale. Manufacturers realize the situation, and it is not uncommon, when in the clothing line for instance, there has been a warm winter so that the merchant could not sell the goods, to "carry him over"—that is, to give him time for payment until he can sell them. The extent of a merchant's credit is thus the amount of goods he can obtain on the promise to pay in the future. With the right sort of man the goods may be sufficient security, and there are young business men who have large credit on no other basis.

But the seller also looks to see what property the merchant owns, or what other means of payment he has, so that his credit usually rests partly on the first basis named. The seller also looks to the probability of the purchaser being able to use the goods profitably, either as a merchant in selling, or as a manufacturer in further production. A business man often has credit "for anything he needs in his business," but for nothing more. A manufacturer or wholesaler will let one have all the goods he thinks he can dispose of within the time of payment; but he would not furnish money for living expenses, speculation, or for other uses. Indeed, we should make a broad distinction between the credit of men engaged in business, by which they obtain materials for use in their business, and credit for articles for unproductive consumption, credit for living expenses.

The form of credit mentioned first under this head, is distinct from both of these. Money is there loaned on the property one has, as by a mortgage on a farm; and the disposition of the money or goods loaned is not of so much consequence, since payment is sure in any case. Banks are supposed to deal mainly with the second class of credits. When the manufacturer has sold the merchant goods to be paid for some months hence; the bank buys the account, takes the place of the manufacturer, and receives the payment from the purchaser. It does this partly on the faith that the goods are in existence, and when returns come from them the notes will be paid. Banks dislike to deal in accommodation paper, which is not given for goods.

Credit, therefore—any particular individual's credit —depends on other people's opinion, not only of the value of the property he has, but of the man himself. This opinion is likely to change, and may change suddenly. In a panic, when all persons are frightened, confidence in one's ability to pay may be destroyed. One's credit may expand, or shrink to nothing within a few days, and that through no fault of his own, and for no good reason. Credit is the opinion of the people, and the people are fickle. It depends on the laws of the human mind. Even though the person who furnishes the goods has full confidence in the ability of the second party to pay, the opinion of others, and even of the populace, may make it unsafe to give credit.

The credit of any person is therefore an uncertain and a variable quantity, depending on many causes, some of which it is impossible to foresee; and if we were to conceive of such a thing as the total credit of all people, it would be now of vast proportions, and now shrink to a small fraction of what it was before.

The term "credits" is, however, often used to denote credits already extended; and then means the value of the goods which have been transferred from one party to another on his promise to pay, the exchange being incomplete. More than one credit in this sense may, therefore, be based on the same goods. The manufacturer sells goods to the wholesale merchant; the exchange is incomplete, and credit has been given for their value. The wholesaler sells to the retailer on credit; here credit has been extended to twice the value of the goods—that is, there may be notes out, based on these goods, to twice their value. As a matter of fact, the goods and credits have only been transferred to second parties. It is expected that the proceeds of their final sale will pass from hand to hand back to the original producer.

The advantage of credit is that it puts goods into the hands of those who can use them with the greatest profit. Without it, those who have wealth would be compelled to carry on all the business of the world. Other persons can often use wealth in business to better advantage than its owner. After paying him more for the use of it than he could make himself, they can still make a profit.

How Credit Saves the Use of Money. — Credits make possible a great extension of book accounts, by which exchanges take place without the use of money. A credit itself saves no money, since the payment is only deferred. One gets the goods without the immediate use of money; but, if he pays when he has promised, it requires just as much money to make the payment as if it had been made in the first place. But the credit gives time for the balancing of book accounts which may offset one account by another,. and no money be required. The world becomes one great clearing-house. Every one who comes to it owes other people and others owe him. By a system of book-keeping, debts cancel debts. What one gets is goods for goods. The things he has parted with pay for the things he has purchased. The trade is complete. It is made without money, by the use of accounts. Settlement of accounts, to anything like the present extent, would be impossible but for the time element in credit. The goods received in payment would necessarily be delivered the same day. Where purchases are made on a few weeks' credit, there is time for other transactions which balance the first. The supposed case of the farmer and the general store is possible only where credit is given by one party or the other. They are supposed to have a running account for a year, and during the year the transactions nearly balance each other. If no credit were given, the farmer must take goods on the day he sold produce, and to its exact value, or payment must be made in money. What is true of the farmer and the general store is true of the largest business transactions. Country banks keep a balance in a bank in the metropolis, thus giving them credit, in order that business may be done by accounts, and not by cash. Only through credits can book accounts become a substitute for money to any great extent.

BANK CREDITS. — Credits which are supposed to have the most influence as a substitute for money are bank credits. A bank lends not only its own capital, but its deposits. It can safely lend a certain portion of its deposits on short time—sixty or ninety days—since they will not all be called for at once. But in granting applications for loans, account is taken, among other things, of the amount of money the borrower usually keeps on deposit in the bank. If he gives his note for a thousand dollars, that sum is simply passed to his credit. He may not draw it out on the day of the loan. Part of it may remain in bank until the note is due. Seldom indeed does he draw out the actual money. He probably pays some debt or makes some purchase with a check on the bank. This check may be deposited in the same bank, in which case no money is required; the bank has increased both its deposits and its loans. Even if the check is deposited in some other bank, it increases its deposits, and the loans of one bank thus appear as deposits on the books of another. The granting of loans by banks has been compared to the issue of money. It has been said that the currency can be inflated by bank loans as well as by the issue of paper money. It is rather a substituting of book accounts for money. So long as actual cash is not drawn from the bank by depositors, or by other banks in settlement, the loans enable depositors to do business by book accounts. To a certain extent all banks are one. While the loans of one bank appear as deposits in another, the loans of the second also appear as deposits in the first, balancing one another. If a bank is in real trouble, other banks of the city will frequently come to its aid. A large part of the business of every city is thus transacted without real money, by the aid of book accounts, as previously explained. These book accounts would be impossible but for the system of loans granted by the banks. One can make payments by checks when a bank has guaranteed his checks. Where a large circle of men do business by checks, they offset one another—that is, the exchanges of goods are made by means of book accounts, kept by the bank, made possible by the banks granting credit in the shape of loans.

This policy is sometimes carried beyond the danger line. It is assumed that the bank has some capital, real money of its own, in the beginning, as security. If its loans are made with caution, they will eventually pay the deposits; but the call for the payment of deposits may be so sudden that the reserves will be exhausted before loans become due. In such cases it is necessary for the bank to cease further loans, which disappoints those depending on them, and perhaps completes a financial crash. With the great experience gained in the banking business, and the support banks give to others worthy of it, the system is comparatively safe, and enables book accounts to be substituted for money to an extent otherwise impossible.

The one thing to be remembered is that the real substitute for money is neither bank checks nor credit in any form, but book accounts. They are made possible by credit, and checks are a part of their machinery.

BOOK VI.

THE DISTRIBUTION OF PRODUCED WEALTH.

BOOK VI.

DISTRIBUTION OF PRODUCED WEALTH.

INTRODUCTION.

CHAPTER   I. RENT — THE SHARE OF THOSE WHO HAVE POSSESSION OF THE RESOURCES OF NATURE, ... 355

CHAPTER   II. INTEREST — THE SHARE OF PRODUCED WEALTH, ... 363

CHAPTER III. THE SHARE OF GOOD NAME, ... 375

CHAPTER   IV. THE SHARE OF MONOPOLY, ... 382

CHAPTER   V. THE SHARE OF THE PRODUCER—PROFITS OF PRODUCTION, ... 397

CHAPTER   VI. THE SHARE OF THE MERCHANT—PROFITS OF EXCHANGE, ... 406

CHAPTER VII. THE SHARE OF THE LABORER WHO WORKS FOR HIMSELF, ... 411

CHAPTER VIII. THE SHARE OF THE LABORER WHO WORKS FOR WAGES, ... 420

CHAPTER   IX. THE SHARE OF LABOR WHICH SATISFIES WANTS DIRECTLY, ... 436

CHAPTER   X. THE BOOTY OF THE ROBBER, AND THE WINNINGS OF THE GAMBLER, . . . 441

CHAPTER   XI. THE SHARE OF THE GOVERNMENT, . . 445

BOOK VI.

THE DISTRIBUTION OF PRODUCED WEALTH.

The ownership and control of the means of satisfying wants was treated of in Book III., but the Resources Produced by Human Industry require further discussion, because so many persons and so many interests unite in their production. This book may be regarded as a continuation of Book III. When five hundred men unite in the production of shoes in a modern factory, the distribution of the proceeds is a complicated affair. Only a part of the work in producing the shoes is done by the men in the factory. The farmer who raised the animals from which the skins were taken, and the tanner who converted the skins into leather, had as much to do with the production of the shoes as the workmen in the factory. Neither will men erect buildings, and make costly machinery, without expecting something for their use. How shall the share of each interest be determined? Even if the shoes were divided among all interested parties in just proportion, what would they do with them? They can only exchange them for other products, and their final reward depends as much on what they get for the shoes as on the number of shoes they make. So that the question finally resolves itself into an inquiry as to what share of the nation's product each one who contributes to its production should receive.

Practically, we know, these questions are settled by Exchange. The farmer sells the hide or skins, and thus transfers to the purchaser his right to a share of the finished shoes. The tanner sells the leather to the factory, and with the sale transfers his right to a share in the finished product. Usually the workmen sell their labor, and transfer the right to their share to the employer, in return for wages. The fact that one owns his own labor implies his right to sell it, as well as to use it in production on his own account. The manufacturer sells the goods to the wholesale dealer, and he to the retailer, and he, at last, to the consumer. Each one who has contributed to the production of the goods has thus sold his share; and the price he has received has been determined by Exchange—by the supply of what he had to contribute, and the demand for his service, and for the finished goods. Even if each had not sold out his share as the work progressed, it would have been determined by the laws of demand and supply in Exchange. We see, then, the need of understanding the laws of Exchange before proceeding to distribution. Distribution depends on other principles as well as those of Exchange, but we can not treat of the former without assuming some knowledge of the latter.

In theory, any product of human industry should first be distributed among the interests which have united in its production; then each person would use his share as he saw fit, exchanging it for such things as he most desired, or for the services of others. There would then arise a secondary distribution, by which all the products of human industry would be distributed among the people of the nation, by each exchanging with others. In practice, we know, there is no distinction between the primary and secondary distribution. The members of a co-operative shoe factory would not divide the shoes among themselves; but the factory would sell them for cash, and each would receive his agreed proportion of the money. With the money he must buy such things as he needs, and the quantity he can buy with a dollar is just as important as the number of dollars he receives. It is simpler, therefore, to ask, What share of the nation's products will each receive?

No more can be distributed than is produced. It is true that methods of distribution react on production. Under suitable encouragement one puts forth more effort; with freedom and protection to property, more is produced and saved than under slavery and insecurity. So far, therefore, as methods of distribution react on production, they indirectly increase the sum of goods to be distributed; but in no case can more be distributed than is produced. It is a common though unformulated idea, that there exists somewhere a store of goods from which an unlimited quantity can be drawn. No such store exists. There are those who suppose that wages might be almost indefinitely increased, and everybody be better off. An increase of wages must diminish the share of some other persons, usually of other laborers, unless production is correspondingly increased. If the laborers of a country are all employed economically, an increase of wages does not mean an increase of production. The product to be distributed is, therefore, limited. The method of its distribution, and the share of each, we are to study in this book.

The essential agents of production are the Resources of Nature, and Labor; and in modern production, Capital almost always contributes its aid. The older Political Economists, therefore, taught that all wealth produced was distributed into three shares—land, capital and labor. This statement is correct as far as it goes; but the great share of Labor is subdivided into many minor shares, and some classes of laborers have little in common. Prof. Francis A. Walker was the first to point out the importance of the share of the "Undertaker" of the business, which he distinguished from the share of the superintendent and the laborer. Yet this share of the undertaker of the business is really a part of the great share of labor in the economic sense, which includes all effort of human beings put forth for the purpose of satisfying the world's wants. We shall, therefore, consider: first, Rent, the share of those who control the Resources of Nature; second, the share of Produced Wealth; then the shares of other interests which are to receive anything from a nation's annual product; and, last, the shares of the various classes of laborers, which combined form the largest share of all.

CHAPTER I.

RENT: — THE SHARE OF THOSE WHO HAVE CONTROL OF THE RESOURCES OF NATURE.

The word Rent as used by Political Economists has a narrower meaning than in popular speech. It *never* means the sum paid for the use of a building, but only that which is paid for the use of the ground on which the building stands—the ground rent, as it is sometimes called. The separation of the rent of the ground from the sum paid for the use of the building is easy, and is common in practice. In some cities costly buildings are erected on leased land, with a condition that there shall be a revaluation every five years; and the rent is increased or diminished as the ground is found more or less valuable, by arbitrators or the courts. Rent has to do only with the Resources of Nature, and is the share of the product which the owner receives for their use. The economic rent of a city lot is precisely the same, whether it serves as a foundation for a one-story or a ten-story building. The economic rent of a farm is the same whether there are buildings on it or not. We must always separate the land from the " improvements."

The Resources of Nature are absolutely necessary to production. They are even more important than labor, for land uncultivated will bring forth a limited amount of food for man, and wild animals and fish help to supply the wants of the savage; but labor alone is helpless. A thousand laborers would starve on an island of bare rock. Land is necessary for standing-room and breathing-room, and as a site for a dwelling. If the owner of an island on which a thousand people were shipwrecked could enforce a monopoly of the Resources of Nature, he could put all the people at work and obtain any share of the product he pleased. All that would be necessary would be to allow the people enough to prevent actual starvation. Such an island owner could get a larger share of all that is raised on the island than if the people were his slaves; because under freedom men will put forth greater exertions than under the fear of the lash, and the island owner need allow no more than the necessities of life in either case. This state of things was almost realized in Ireland, but would be impossible where land is plentier.

On the other hand, on our fertile Western prairies, in an early day, land was worth very little. It was owned by the government, and there was more than the people could use.

We can not say that any particular share of the product is due to land, and another share due to labor; in one sense it is all due to land, and in another all due to labor. Both are essential to production; either can afford to give the other nine-tenths of the product rather than do without it. It is, therefore, a question of the division of the product: and the share which the owners of the land receive for its use is named Rent. Our object is now to find how large this share will be.

Rent is entirely independent of the question of private or public ownership of land, which has before been considered. There would be rent, just the same, if all the land were owned by the government; the only difference being that the rent would be paid to the government, and make taxes unnecessary. The question of the ownership and control of the Resources of Nature has nothing to do with economic rent, which is the share that the one in control of the land (whoever he is) can claim, or gain by its use.

Rent is the advantage which the owner of any particular Resource of Nature has from its possession. The older Political Economists drew their illustrations mainly from agricultural rent. They assumed that there was some land which, on account of its distance from market, poor quality, or other reason, just paid the cost of cultivation, so that the owner gained nothing from its possession. Indeed, every farm might have a little such land. All that the best land produces in addition to the cost of cultivation is rent. All grain of the same quality sells for the same price in the same market. If the poorest land pays for cultivation, better land pays something more, and the difference is the advantage the owner has from its possession. This advantage is rent. By poor land we mean, not only poor in quality, but in respect to markets, roads, or anything that makes it less desirable. One man hauls his wheat twenty miles; another, one. The farm near market has an advantage over the one farther out, and this advantage is rent.

Agricultural rent may also be illustrated from diminishing returns, though the thought is not so simple. Let us suppose that a farm just pays when worked to the point of diminishing returns to the labor bestowed on it. With the increase of population, agricultural produce becomes scarcer, prices rise until it pays to work land beyond diminishing returns. The additional product is raised at a greater cost of labor, and the price for which it is sold pays this cost. The other portion of the product is, therefore, raised at a profit, and this profit is rent. Suppose that ten days' labor on an acre of land produces twenty bushels of wheat, and that thirty bushels can be produced with twenty days' labor. Now, unless ten bushels of wheat will pay for ten days' labor, this additional labor will not be bestowed. But, then, the first ten days' labor would also be paid for by the ten bushels of wheat, leaving ten bushels as rent for the land. Every farmer knows that production can not be calculated thus accurately. Much depends on the seasons, and habit. Still, on an average, the tendency among intelligent farmers is to work land about as well as it will pay to work it. When it becomes more valuable, crops requiring more labor are raised, until, near a city, the land is used as a garden and is worth a hundred dollars a year rent. One can as well afford to pay that as to take land farther out for three dollars. Rent is the advantage derived from the possession of a particular piece of land; what a man competent to use it can afford to pay for its use.

Even agricultural rent depends more on location than on the fertility of the soil; and for purposes other than agriculture, rent depends almost entirely on location. Why do merchants go to a city? Because they can sell more goods. The advantages of location may be so great that one will pay a thousand dollars a year for the use of each front foot of land to build upon. For the use of an acre of such land one could obtain $300,000 a year. This is the advantage that its possession would give to the owner. This is rent.

For residence purposes rent also depends mainly on location. For various reasons—nearness to business, good neighborhood, fashion, sanitary surroundings, or all combined—one building-lot is far more desirable than another. In what we may call the second-class cities of the United States there is a great deal of residence land, the annual rent of which exceeds a thousand dollars an acre. This is what some persons are willing to pay rather than live in less desirable locations.

Economic rent is the same whether the owner uses the land himself or leases it to others. The owner of a residence lot has the use of it; the merchant who owns his own store has all the advantage of location in his business; the farmer gets the advantage of good land or land near market, as compared with farms which are just worth working. This advantage is estimated in what such land could be leased for.

Rent is a very large share of the annual product of a nation, and increases with the increase of population and wealth. Rent is not only a large gross sum, but in densely populated countries it is a very much larger *share* of all that is produced than it is in new countries. Labor must therefore have a smaller *share* of the annual production of any country, as population increases, even if it receives absolutely more. Why is the land of New York City in such demand? Because of the great population and wealth west of it. Remove this population, and rents would be what they were in an early day. The immense population and wealth of the United States makes necessary such a city as New York, somewhere on the Atlantic coast; and the coast line and harbors and latitude make the present location the best place for it. A site for business here gives one a great advantage, and that advantage is economic rent; so that the owners of the land on which the city stands are now able to take immense sums from the total product of the country for the annual use of these few square miles of land. If they do business here themselves, they make these profits by reason of their location; if they lease to others, they obtain rent from them. Either way, a large share of the immense business that passes through New York must be given to the men who own the land on which the city stands; and this share must continue to grow larger as the population of the country increases. What is true of New York is true of Chicago and other great cities. The owners of the land on which any city stands receive a large share of the product of the country tributary to it, as rent. It is readily seen that there can be no escape from rent; and that in an old and wealthy country, with a dense population, rent must absorb a large share of the annual product, simply because a part of the land is much more desirable than other parts. Prices of goods must be high enough to pay for using the less desirable land, and the more desirable gains the advantage.

Is there any way by which the total share of rent can be reduced? Evidently by a more even distribution of population. If all the people flock to a few of the largest cities, the demand for residence land must be so great as to give the owner larger and larger rents. The land near the city will also be more desirable. The greater portion of the land of the country has really been placed farther from the people, by reason of the people moving away from it. The cause of rent is the unequal desirability of different pieces of land. If, now, there were more small cities and fewer large ones, so that the people were distributed more uniformly over the country, there would be no such demand for a little land near the center of one great city, and for residence land about it. The demand would be for land in smaller cities; and there being so much more of it, rents must be comparatively low. It is not necessary here to discuss the reason for the drift of population to the large cities; but it evidently means that the people must pay a very much larger share of the annual production of the nation to the owners of city land. What is paid to land can not go to labor.

Where there is no rent, the entire product belongs to the laborers (in the economic sense of the word) who unite in its production, unless they choose to give a portion to the owner of Capital for its use. If an Indian cuts down a tree and hollows it into a canoe, the Resources of Nature are yet so plenty that there is no rent, and the entire canoe belongs to him. Later, if he attempts to fell a pine tree, he will find a man with a legal title demanding a share of the lumber for the removal of the tree. That is rent. That is the advantage one has in the possession of the ground the tree stands on. In a new country, with few people, there is little rent to pay; and the laborer gets the entire result of his labor. He takes timber when he wants it. He pastures his cattle in the highway, or on the commons; or the use of the ground he fences in costs him but a trifle.

It does not follow that people were better off. There is advantage in a population of a certain density—dense, but not too dense. Where population is not too large, the laborer may find the net return for his labor greater, after paying rent, than it was in an earlier day when he paid none. The dense population, however, introduces a class of rent receivers who can live without work, or if they labor, as is more likely, they will have a much larger income. Distinctions are thus introduced into Society, and the laborer *seems* to have less because the others have more. The satisfaction of our wants depends, to a considerable extent, on what we have as compared with others; and it is undoubtedly true that one's satisfactions in life are actually diminished by an increase in the income of those about him.

CHAPTER II.

INTEREST—THE SHARE OF PRODUCED WEALTH.

Labor and Natural Wealth are the only Resources absolutely necessary to production. In the beginning there were no other. Hence, Labor will receive all that is left after paying rent, *provided it asks no assistance.* The product may, however, be increased, sometimes a thousand-fold, by the aid of capital; and the producer may find it profitable to give even a large share to capital, and have more left for himself. He seldom pays the owner of capital as much as its use aids him in production.

Capital is that part of Produced Wealth which is employed in production; but all Produced Wealth—that which satisfies wants directly as well as indirectly—can obtain a share in the world's product in return for its use, and for the aid it renders in the satisfaction of wants.

1. PERMANENT PRODUCED WEALTH.—Notice, first, that which satisfies wants *directly*, such as dwellings. The dwelling continually furnishes shelter day by day, and this is almost as desirable as food. The owner has this advantage over those who have no dwellings. He would not allow another person to use his house without something in return; and one who is engaged in production can well afford to give part of the product for the use of such a dwelling, rather

than do without it. On the other hand, while one will erect a dwelling for his own family, he will not build one for others unless he expects to obtain something for its use.

Permanent Produced Wealth which satisfies wants *indirectly*, of which machinery is the type, vastly increases the product of labor. One man with a machine will frequently produce as much as a hundred by hand. Ninety-nine per cent. of the product is therefore due to the machine, and only one per cent. to labor. If the laborer owns the machine, he is a hundred times better off; if he does not own it, he can afford to give almost any share for its use.

2. CONSUMABLE PRODUCED WEALTH.—The share which the owner of this obtains for its use is no less just, but the reasons for awarding it are not so apparent. The reason for interest is here *the time element in production*. A savage is obliged to supply his wants " from hand to mouth." He catches fish and kills game for the day or week, and the accumulated stores of food are small. Civilized production requires at least a year, and what is the producer to live on in the meantime? The crops are dependent on the seasons. One crop a year is ordinarily the rule. Although a suit of clothing may be made up in a week, this is only the last stage of the production. The cloth must be manufactured from wool or cotton which required a year for its growth. If the farmer or laborer has a year's supply on hand, he may depend on the sale of the product at the end of the year for another year's living. But suppose he has

nothing. If he gets food and the necessities of life for his family as does the Indian, he will have but a miserable living. If he is free to fit the ground and sow a crop, he will get ten times as much at the end of the year. If some one has a supply and will let him consume it, he can afford to return as much at the end of the year, and something besides, perhaps twice as much. The farmer in this condition usually gets his supplies of the country merchant, for which he pays "after harvest"; and the merchant must have a higher price for the goods than if he were paid cash. Even if he sells for cash, the merchant must carry a stock of goods for some time in order to have what the people happen to want.

The present wonderful methods of production would be impossible except that somebody carried a year's supply of consumable wealth. It is said that production is going on all the time; so wheat is growing all the time, yet it is a year from one harvest until another. While manufacturing is a continual process, there are vast quantities of materials and unfinished goods in process of production. This reserve stock enables laborers to be employed to the best advantage. Without it, the United States could not support a million people. We must, then, have this stock of consumable goods, and we must allow the owners interest enough to induce them to accumulate it. It would be better if each man had enough for himself and family to live on for one year. He could then engage in production on his own account if he thought it more profitable than working for wages.

It is worth while here to notice a mistake of Henry George, who assumes that wages are paid out of the product, and not out of previous accumulations. The illustrations he uses are such as, a man going with an employer on a fishing cruise, his wages being paid out of the catch when they return. But how do the fishermen live in the meantime? Why, they take provisions along, and they have clothing enough to last until they return. If the employe leaves a family, its members must live during his absence out of the stock of goods already accumulated. They may get goods on trust at the store. The fisherman may own a house. But it is plain that both the workman and his family must live on goods *already produced* until more are produced. George, like many more careful writers, fails to distinguish between one's living and his wages. If a workman's wages are more than he consumes, he may receive his living out of the stock of goods already accumulated, and wait for the remainder until the production is completed. This is sometimes the case with the farmer's "hired man." The farmer furnishes his living as he goes along, and lets him have what money he needs to use during the process of production. At the end of the year, when production is complete, he pays him the remainder of his wages.

WHAT FIXES THE SHARE OF PRODUCED WEALTH? —We are now ready to ask how much the owner of Produced Wealth will receive for its use. This sum is called interest.

First. The interest on all forms of Produced

Wealth tends to the same percentage. Something is usually added for risk, which may be great in one place and almost nothing in another. Ignorance of the conditions, and friction, as well as personal likes and dislikes, have some effect, but in the same locality interest on all forms of Produced Wealth tends to the same point.

Let us suppose one to have a sum of money, with which he can buy anything, sufficient for the support of a number of laborers for a year. He controls the direction of production. He can build houses, a business block, a factory; or set men to producing machinery, or any other form of Permanent Wealth. Which will be produce? Why, that for which he can get the largest annual return, and competition thus tends to make the interest on all of the investments equal.

But suppose producers of consumable goods want this money to support their workmen? If they offer him a higher rate of interest for it than he can hope to receive from a permanent investment, he will naturally let them have it. Free capital is said to flow where it receives the highest interest, reducing the rate in one line of production and increasing it in another. What really flows is labor. The men who have the means—the stocks of food and goods—on which the laborer must live, are able to direct that labor where it will pay best—now to the production of buildings, now to machinery or railroads, now to the accumulation of a larger stock of consumable goods. The great lines of production go on the same from year to year. The diverting of a little labor from one purpose to another which promises better returns suffices to even up the rate of interest in all.

If there is an excess of any form of Permanent Produced Wealth, interest on it may be very low, and may fall to nothing, until the increase of population makes more demand for it, or a portion is slowly worn out or destroyed by time.

The interest on both classes of capital and on all forms of Produced Wealth really tends to the same point, for the reason that so large a part of all the Produced Wealth in a country is *consumable*—certain to be used up in the support of the people in a year or so, and much of it perishable if not so used. In the last analysis the greater part of this Consumable Wealth is paid out for wages, or used for living expenses of farmers and other producers. Now, the enormous labor power of the country can be turned by wages in any direction, either to the replacement of the wealth consumed, or to the production of any other form of wealth which will pay the largest interest. Competition will tend to direct production to that form of wealth which will pay the largest interest, and hence to bring the interest on all the various kinds of Produced Wealth to the same rate.

The reader will notice that the word "tends" has often been used in these chapters. The actual result in society is almost always brought about by a combination of forces, all of which act with more or less friction, and some of which neutralize others. The simplest way is to consider one force at a time. We may be able to predict what will be its effect when acting alone and without friction; but there may be other forces which modify the result very materially. The friction is also greater in some instances than in others. There is no surer mark of an illogical mind than the supposition that some seeming exception overthrows a principle which we have found to be true by careful investigation. Interest on various forms of Produced Wealth, as a matter of fact, varies considerably. Nevertheless, it *tends* toward the same point. By errors of judgment, too much of one thing is produced. If it be Permanent Wealth, it may be a long time before the population grows up to it, or it wears out. Returns are often higher to one kind of Produced Wealth because others do not know how high they are, or fear the risk of the investment, when the owner alone knows it to be safe. These, and many other influences, cause considerable apparent variation in the rate of interest. Nevertheless, when taxes, compensations for risk, and the share of profit, are deducted, we shall find that the rate of interest in the same locality varies much less on the various forms of Produced Wealth than we might suppose.

Second. Not only does competition tend to reduce the rate of interest on all forms of Produced Wealth to the same rate, but it also determines the average rate of interest, as considered apart from the risk involved in lending. The rate of interest must be high enough to induce somebody to save a year's supply for the people, and to accumulate machinery, and other Permanent Wealth, or wants can not be satisfied in the present economical way. If interest rules too low, the reserve supply for the world's support will be endangered; if too high, competition will bring it down.

A high rate of interest is a great inducement to saving. A farmer knows that a ditch would increase the product of a field fifty per cent. He has not the time to dig it, but the inducement to work more hours, or to save money to hire it dug, is strong. A workman is paying $200 a year for a little house which he could build for $500, and he is likely to deny himself, and save money to get a home of his own. A manufacturer sees that a new machine would increase his profits fifty per cent. of its cost. The machine would pay for itself in two years. If he can not borrow the money, he will make every effort to save it. If one can rent a house for four per cent. of its cost, there is less inducement to build one; and if a manufacturer can borrow money at four per cent., he will not make the effort to save that he made when he was paying fifty. So, if one can lend money at three per cent. a month, he will deny himself, and save to lend, since a very moderate fortune will give him an income on which he can live. When he can get only four per cent. a year, the inducement to save is less strong. More people are, therefore, saving where interest is high, and numerous small fortunes are accumulated. If interest were fifty per cent., it is probable that a very large part of the people would scrimp themselves in living, in order to save a year's supply of the necessities of life, and avoid the payment of interest to others. As interest becomes lower, few people are willing to save, and the majority will consume all they receive. Yet experience has shown that a few will continue to save all of this sort of wealth which the world needs, if they can gain even five or six per cent. for its use—an insignificant sum compared with the advantage which the world gains. It is because interest is so low that laborers do not save more.

It is undoubtedly true that there would be a certain amount of saving even if there were no interest. Men wish to lay by for a rainy day. But it would be very little. Interest, in the economic sense, is not merely the sum paid for the use of money, but the return to the owner from any form of Produced Wealth. This would mean that when one built a house he could get for its use only what the annual repairs cost, and a sum which would replace the building when it is destroyed by time. It would be safer to bury his gold in the earth. What would be the inducement to make machinery if one hoped to get back only the cost of the machine when it is worn out? It is true that the desire to accumulate a hoard of wealth for future needs, or for posterity, would lead to considerable saving, especially by the wealthy, and the saving might take the form of machinery and buildings; but we can hardly imagine that such saving would be sufficient to keep the world going. The stock of Produced Wealth would diminish, and wants would be satisfied at far greater cost of labor.

How high a rate of interest is necessary to maintain the existing stock of wealth, depends on the character of the people, their progress in civilization, and the relative amount of wealth in the country. The accumulation of a great reserve requires time, and is in the beginning a slow process. Because interest rules, for a few years in a new country, at twenty per cent., it does not follow that this rate is necessary to induce people to save; but they have not had time to save the capital needed. Produced Wealth is worth this high interest to use, and there is so little to lend that there is no competition among the lenders. Wait until time has been given for accumulation. In England, Holland, and the United States, interest, exclusive of taxes and risk, has fallen as low as two per cent.

The annual share of Produced Wealth is comparatively a small one, and the share of that portion which is used in production, called capital, is smaller still. If we roughly assume that the manufactured products each year equal in value the capital invested, the producers will pay to capital interest on the investment, say six per cent.; which would be six per cent of the product, since we assume the product equals the capital employed. Certainly laborers have no reason to complain if capital receives six or ten cents out of every dollar's worth of goods produced in mills where one man turns out a hundred times as much as he could by hand. It is not expected that capital will receive anything like what it contributes to production.

In concluding this chapter it must not be forgotten that the sum paid for the use of a building includes both rent for the ground, and interest on the value of the improvements; also that a large portion of Permanent Produced Wealth is used by the owners, who do not pay interest to others. Its possession contributes to production or to the satisfaction of their wants directly, and this benefit is a part of the share of Produced Wealth.

The share of Produced Wealth is called interest, and the rate of interest is determined by competition. It tends to that point which will induce people to accumulate enough Produced Wealth to enable the world's production to be carried on with the greatest economy. If interest is too high, it is a spur to accumulation. If it is too low, the increase of Produced Wealth goes forward less rapidly than it would otherwise.

Put in another way, the average rate of interest is determined by what additional Produced Wealth is worth to use. When it is relatively abundant, additional wealth is of little value. If we have all the cotton factories needed to supply the wants of the people, an additional factory would have no *value in use*, and would pay a very low rate of interest on the investment. As new machines are invented, or as we discover new methods in which Produced Wealth can be made to yield a return, interest tends to rise. The combined result of all tendencies, to-day, is toward the lowering of the rate of interest. The average rate may yet sink to two per cent.

Interest is usually reckoned as though it were on money. But the real things that the manufacturer wants are not money, but labor, machinery, etc. What the laborers want is food, clothing and other comforts and luxuries of life. Money is only a convenient way of estimating the relative value of all these things and keeping the accounts. In the last analysis it is goods, dwellings—real things. We have, therefore, considered the substance and not the shadow. We are much more likely to get at the truth by dealing with real things, the things that satisfy wants, than by suffering ourselves to be confused by the idea that it is money we are seeking for. The return from all forms of Produced Wealth is interest. Even the satisfaction the owner gets from a costly painting is supposed to equal the average rate of interest on its value; else he would sell it, and invest money in something else.

CHAPTER III.

THE SHARE OF GOOD NAME AND ESTABLISHED BUSINESS.

A "good name" and an established business are usually classed with capital, but they are not Produced Wealth, because all wealth is material. Here we see the advantage of looking at things as they are. When we talk of Produced Wealth there is no danger of failing to understand precisely what the term covers, and the division is a natural one.

A " good name" and established business are frequently the result of great labor, and are often of great advantage to the world as well as to the owner. In any case the owner is entitled to the benefit they confer upon him. One's name is a part of himself, and the good name of a business is a guarantee of its character which saves others trouble of investigation and risk of loss.

Suppose one is engaged in the production of shoes. He can wear very few of them. The rest are worth only what he can get for them. The satisfaction of his wants will depend on Exchange, on how much money he can get for the shoes, and how much he can buy with the money. Now, when two factories make shoes equally good, why is it that one will receive a higher price for his goods than another? Leaving out differences in the ability of the salesmen, the higher price comes from the reputation, or the good name of the shoes. There are two brands of soap on the market which have for years enjoyed a large sale. It is said that soap equal in every respect to either can easily be made. But can it be sold? Not at the same price except by increased cost of selling. These soaps are known. They have a good name. A great many people have used them, and know them to possess certain qualities, and have been led to believe they possess other qualities which can not be so readily ascertained.

No one not an expert is a judge of all goods from their appearance. He must buy largely on the reputation of the maker or the seller. If he has bought something of a certain brand and found it to be good, he feels safe in buying another article of the same make. Another manufacturer may make precisely the same goods, or those equal to them, yet the purchaser does not know that they are as good; and can tell only by purchasing and using. Consequently, he will pay a little more for the well-known goods than for those he knows nothing about. If the price be the same, he is more likely to choose those he knows.

One unfamiliar with the complications of modern business, can have only a faint idea of the enormous advantage this gives the well-known maker. It may prevent another from doing business at all. The only way in which the new manufacturer can compete with him who has a good name established, is by making a name for himself. Perhaps he attempts to do it by advertising, in which he must spend large sums. Perhaps he does it by allowing the retailer larger profits. Perhaps he sends men about the country to explain the merits of his goods to merchants who will explain them to others; or, as for example in the early sewing-machine trade, he sends men to the customer, direct, to explain the merits of his goods. The manufacturer whose goods are well known may do all these things in order to maintain his reputation, but nevertheless he has a great advantage over the other. If the reputation of his goods gives him a large trade, this may enable him to manufacture cheaper; and thus, though he sells at the same price as his competitor, he may gain larger profits. We have seen the advantage of the division and recombination of labor, and of manufacturing on a large scale. This great gain to the world from the increased efficiency of labor may be absorbed by the large manufacturer on account of his *good name*. The reputation of his goods enables him to do a large business, by means of which he can manufacture cheaper, and sell at the same price as those who do a small business. The reputation of his goods may also enable him to get a slightly increased price, which, in his large manufacturing, may mean great profits. One cent from each of the inhabitants of the United States would mean $600,000.00, and while no person can deal with every one of this great population, he may deal with vast numbers of them; and a few cents additional from each may mean a great fortune annually. All this is the result of his reputation and good name. Numerous instances could be cited where the good name of an article or business could not be purchased for a million dollars. This good name may have cost the owner all or more than it is worth to him, or it may have cost less, or be the result of accident; its advantage is the same in any case. The reputation of some goods has been made by expending vast sums in advertising. This advertising may have cost all the reputation is worth. Sometimes reputations have been built up by distributing samples of the goods free, and thus inducing the people to use them and ascertain their merits. More often it has been made by the slow process of selling as one can, and trusting to the quality of the goods to make their own reputation; and their good name may represent years of patient industry and effort.

However it may have been obtained, a good name is of great value to any producer, and enables him to take a share of the product; sometimes a very large share; often a much larger share than interest. His competitor must either sell cheaper, or sell less, or expend great sums in convincing the people that his goods are equal to the other. This share of a good name is a species of monopoly. There are good and bad monopolies, which will be considered in the next chapter.

Under the head of "good name" may, for convenience, be included the business terms "good will," and "business," since they all follow the same law, and are economically part of the same share. The words "business," "name," and "good will," frequently occurring in sales of property, are parts of one thing.

The prospect of receiving this share is frequently sold, or "capitalized," and is considered worth a sum which if put at interest would yield the same annual return. That is, if the "good name" of a business is worth $80 a year, and the rate of interest is taken at eight per cent., the "good name" is capitalized at $1,000. A large soap factory was recently sold for something over six million dollars. It is not likely that the plant cost half that sum. The rest was in the "good name." In this case the "good name" had been gained partly by advertising, and had cost fabulous sums. But the business had the "good name," whether it cost more or less than it was worth. The new company, by keeping up the quality of the goods, was almost certain of the share which came from the "good name" of the article.

We are to remember that when "good name" is thus capitalized, it is not Produced Wealth. Wealth is always a material substance, and we have been at great pains to use the term Produced Wealth in place of the indefinite one of "capital" where there was danger of misunderstanding. It is best to look at things as they are. Produced Wealth, material substance, is one thing; the prospect of getting a share of future production on account of the good name of a product or an established business, is another. They should never be confused. The one is the share of the Resources Produced by Industry; the other is the share of "good name." The nature of the share is not changed because some persons estimate it in terms of a principal sum which would bring as much if placed at interest.

The share of " good name " is sometimes included in the share of profits, and sometimes in that of interest; it should be included in neither. It is a share by itself. In an ordinary business which one has built up for himself, he thinks of the share of "good name" as a part of profits. He pays rent, and interest, and other expenses, and lumps the share of " good name " in with his own services and compensation for risk. In many lines of business one can not practically do otherwise. He makes more than his neighbor; and perhaps flatters himself that the result is due to his superior business management. In reality, his larger gross profit is in consequence of the good name of his goods, or his own reputation. Since this "good name" is probably the result of his own business efforts, there is perhaps no reason why it should not be classed with profits, as compensation for his past efforts.

When " good name " is " capitalized," the share is wrongly credited to interest. Let us suppose a soap factory which is sold to a company at a capitalization. In addition to the present value of the plant —what it would cost to replace it by a new one as well adapted to the purpose—a considerable sum is added for the value of the " good name " and " business." The new company is expected to pay dividends on the entire stock, that which represents the value of the plant as well as that which represents the capitalization of the " good name." Here the share of the " good name " is called interest. Wherever a " good name " and business is thus capitalized, its share is included under interest. It should be separated.

The share of " good name " is, however, very closely related to that of Produced Wealth, and in all stock companies is classed as capital. It may have cost as much as the plant; and the stockholders should have interest on it. In the one case, labor has been expended in building a factory and making machinery; in the other, labor has been expended in making a good name for the goods, and arranging with others for their sale. The labor would never have been expended except for the hope of reward. One can not make enough in one year from the good name to pay what it has cost, but he, or his successors, may make the *interest* on what it has cost, forever. In this case " good name " is as justly entitled to a share as Produced Wealth.

Property in "good name," " business " and "good will " should always be distinguished from property in material wealth.

CHAPTER IV.

THE SHARE OF MONOPOLY.

The price at which goods can be sold under monopoly was necessarily considered under exchange. Whatever is obtained in addition to the natural price under competition, is due to monopoly.

There is monopoly in production as well as in exchange. One may be the only producer in his line, and be able to prevent others from engaging in the manufacture of his class of goods. The share of the world's productions which he will thus be able to obtain will be gained through exchange, in a higher price for his goods than he would otherwise receive. This higher price, in the end, comes out of the consumer, who is probably engaged in some other form of production.

NATURAL MONOPOLIES.—The monopolies most important to consider at present are what have come to be known as Natural Monopolies. By this term we do not mean the monopoly of natural talent, to which every one is entitled of right. We mean *necessary* monopolies—necessary because, in the nature of the case, there can be no real competition; necessary, because the service can be so much more cheaply performed by one company than by two that it is practically necessary to give it into the hands of one. In the case of these monopolies we must abandon the idea of competition, because it logically leads to combination and higher prices. The term, Natural Monopoly, is now fixed and generally understood in this sense. It would be useless to attempt to change it.

There are certain services, required by the larger portion of the people, which can be done on a large scale so much cheaper than on a small one, that they are certain to be gathered into the hands of one company. Competition can not act because the small concern can not, in the nature of the employment, compete with the large one. Such is the supplying of water to cities. Not every person, but a large portion of the people, desire water furnished through a system of pipes. In a crowded city, it is necessary to require its use by all, for the health of all. If several companies attempt to supply the city, it necessitates several systems of pipes, each costing nearly as much as one which could serve all equally well. If the companies divide the city into districts, each laying its pipes in that district alone, then each of such districts has a monopoly; since there can be no competition with companies whose pipes do not reach that territory. Hence, rival water and gas companies usually fight until one destroys the other, at a great waste; or they combine, openly or secretly.

The most important necessary monopolies are: in the cities, water, gas, electric light, street-car lines; in the nation, the post-office, telegraph, express business, and railroads.

Doubtless there are many other lines of business in which a monopoly can do the work somewhat cheaper than competition, but the advantage is not sufficient to make a monopoly certain. It is not true that the grocery business can be carried on very much cheaper in large than in small establishments. There will always be competition in this business, without government interference. When competition acts, it can usually be trusted to give low prices. The old praise of competition was not as an end, but because it was believed that it was the best means of securing fair prices. When in the nature of the case it can not act, as with Natural Monopolies, some other means of regulating prices must be found; and there are many who see no method save in government control.

The share of the world's productions which one will be able to obtain on account of a complete or partial monopoly, depends on the principles set forth in considering monopoly as affecting Exchange. One of the most important of these is the principle that the price which the monopolist can fix will depend, in the first place, on whether he is compelled to perform the same service to all persons on the same terms, or whether he is permitted to charge different prices to different people. In the former case, he can obtain only the value in use to those to whom his services are worth least; in the latter, he can obtain the full value in use from every person with whom he deals. This statement is so important as to bear repetition; and it is one which has usually been overlooked by political economists. In other lines of production competition requires all goods to be sold at something like the same price. A good illustration is a railroad which has a monopoly of transportation at a certain point. It can charge different shippers different prices for the same service. It will, therefore, seek to get as near the value in use to each one as it can. If it is convinced that one person can not afford to pay more—that is, that he will not ship, or will go out of the business which necessitates shipping at the established rates—it will give him a reduction; seeking to get from every person as much as he can *afford* to pay, or the value in use. Here is, certainly, a proper field for legislation, which Congress has entered within the last few years, against great opposition. The principle is that the Monopoly must sell to all at the same price; that it must perform like services for different persons at the same rate, and that when such services vary, the rate shall not vary in undue proportion.

A monopolist frequently meets with competition at some one point. Rather than lose the profit to be made here, he may sell the goods as low as he can afford. If now he can be compelled to sell everywhere at the same price, his power to obtain excessive prices is partly or completely destroyed. Again the best illustration is a railway. At railway centers rates are low, perhaps too low, because of competing lines. But every road passes through many towns in which there is no other road; and here it can charge monopoly prices, which are " what the traffic will bear." If, now, the road is compelled to give the same or similar rates to all the towns on the line that it gives to railway centers, the benefit of competition is extended to every station on the line. If it gives low rates anywhere, it must give them everywhere. If the competing roads at railway centers find rates are too low, they must raise them; but they must not compel other stations to make up what is lost at a railway center. Competition at the railway centers is pretty certain to make rates low enough; and the extension of these rates to every station on the line would change many railways from monopolies to competitive business.

This principle is the foundation for the famous "long and short haul clause," of the Interstate Commerce law. This clause provides that a road shall not make a greater charge for a less distance in the same direction, and has met the chief attack of railroad managers. Yet no juster measure could be devised. There may, indeed, be cases in which it actually costs the road more to leave a car fifty miles short of its terminal than to carry it through, but not very much more. Now, the principle of the law is, as near as possible, the same price to all for the same service; by which a road is compelled to fix uniform rates for those who, in their distress, or from lack of competition, might be compelled to pay any price the road chose to ask. It is thus intended to carry the benefit of competition at terminal points to every one who does business with the company. It is true this may cause a raising of rates at competing points; but it is more important that every one have an equal chance, with one price to all, than that rates should be low to anybody. The Interstate Commerce law is a question of practical statesmanship; and while it has not ac-

THE SHARE OF MONOPOLY. 387

complished all that might be desired, its principles are steps in the right direction for the control of monopoly. It is introduced here only for the purpose of illustration, and not for complete discussion.

Most *Natural Monopolies* may properly be placed under government control. Such control may be either by government ownership, or by legislation prescribing under what conditions the monopolies may be carried on by private parties. Either course apparently narrows somewhat the sphere of private enterprise; but such monopolies would otherwise be conducted by great corporations, with the management in the hands of a few officers, and the number of people who would thus be prevented from managing a business of their own is insignificant. Every business which is of the nature of a natural monopoly has been owned and controlled by government in some civilized country. In the United States, the post-office has always been regarded as better in the hands of the government than in those of private parties. There is no necessity for rival post-offices in the same town. The business is much more economically managed under one system. No private corporation would have given us our present magnificent postal system. The government has regard for the interests of all the people, to the extent of making a uniform rate for all parts of the United States; and, although there is considerable difference in the cost of carrying a letter from Boston to New York or to San Francisco, and a still greater increase in the cost of carriage to out-of-the-way places, the encouragement to communication, and the desire to make the country a more desirable place of residence, are arguments which justify a government in charging something more than cost in the one case, and something less in the other. The difference is more apparent than real, because a uniform rate enables the entire service to be carried on much cheaper. Concerning the control of this most important Natural Monopoly by government ownership, there is no question anywhere.

Railroads are frequently owned by the government in European states. In Austria the country has been divided into zones, and a uniform rate made for each zone without regard to distance, something on the principle by which letters are carried in the United States. The uniform rates, of course, simplify the business, so that the cost of carriage is less. The railroad service is not a complete Natural Monopoly, since there will always be considerable competition at large cities; but it is practically so at local stations, and any government would undoubtedly be justified in undertaking the management of all the railroads in its territory, *if no other means of control can be found.* The magnitude of the task in the United States should make this course a last resort. It would be far more difficult with us than in England, on account of the condition of our Civil Service. It would be intolerable that the vast number of railway employes should be at the mercy of a political party, and so many places regarded as the spoils of an election. If men were appointed, as in England, on the merit system, wholly without regard to politics, the task would be easier; but, even then, it is one we may well shrink from.

The second means of control of a Natural Monopoly is by prescribing the conditions under which it may be carried on. The State may even require that certain things be done for the good of the whole country, although a railroad may be compelled to charge more than cost of carriage in some instances to make up the loss. For example, it is greatly to the interest of the United States to build up the smaller towns, and to prevent the massing of dense populations in cities. We may, therefore, require a railroad to perform the same service for all persons at the same price, to give a small town the same rates as a larger one for the same distance, and to make the same price to him who ships a single car as to him who ships a dozen. The road can make its average rates high enough to cover the cost. The solution of the railroad question is likely to be found in the principle that roads must perform like services for all persons on the same terms; and must not give lower rates to either large cities or large shippers. The entire traffic of the road will thus be regulated by the rates at railroad centers, where competition will be likely to keep them within reasonable limits. The courts of some States have gone further, and ruled that rates must be *reasonable*. What is reasonable is, of course, a question of fact for a jury. This legislation is based on the old common law for common carriers; but the economic principle for its justification is found in the fact of the Natural Monopoly, which practically prevents competition from regulating rates at all points, and to all persons. There is competition enough at some points; but for the greater part of its stations, the road has a Natural Monopoly. The tendency is also toward consolidation, and while competition exists at railroad centers, at present, all roads may at some time in the future form parts of one great system. If so, the Natural Monopoly would be complete.

If it be asked why similar regulations should not be made in all lines of business, the obvious reply is, that outside of monopolies competition is a sufficient regulator of prices, and that such regulation might destroy the business. If the law compels a Natural Monopoly to perform some service for less than cost, that all citizens may have an equal chance, the very fact that the monopoly is without competition enables it to fix its average rate high enough to cover such loss. We do, however, make other regulations for various lines of business when the public interest demands it.

In the United States, the post-office and the railroads may be said to be at the two extremes of Natural Monopolies. The first we are controlling by government ownership; the other we are attempting to control by such regulations as the Interstate Commerce law. Between these two lie water-works and gas-works for cities, street-car lines, the express business, the telegraph, etc. It is now pretty generally agreed that water-works are best under city management. A few cities have recently built their own gas-works. In others, legislation practically fixes the price of gas. The last is an unsafe plan; there is danger of practical confiscation of the property on the one hand, and of allowing enormous margins for profit on the other—profits which no man could make in a business influenced by real competition. Street-car lines are controlled in most cities by roughly fixing the fare at five cents; a convenient sum to handle, but one which gives great opportunity for profit or loss. There is yet considerable competition among telegraph lines, but they are a Natural Monopoly which could be carried on much cheaper under one management. There has, on this account, been a strong demand for a postal telegraph, which means government ownership.

GOVERNMENT CONTROL OF NATURAL MONOPOLIES NOT SOCIALISM.—It is probably good statesmanship to bring all Natural Monopolies under government control, but government control does not require government ownership or management. The Interstate Commerce law brings the railroads to a considerable extent under government control. It would be possible to leave them in the hands of private owners, and at the same time secure fair rates of charges. The essential thing about fair rates is not so much low charges as equality, so that no person or corporation can secure an improper advantage over another. We may require railroads to do business in a certain way for the good of the people; but beyond necessary regulations, they should be free to manage their business as they please. We may say, We expect you to make a reasonable profit; but you must make it in certain ways, and you must not make it by methods contrary to the good of the whole people. In return for this limitation, the government is able to protect different companies from the effects of their own natural competition, where it would be destructive, either to the roads or to reasonable profits.

This is not Socialism, which would destroy every one's power to engage in business for himself. It takes only a limited number of lines of business out of the hands of private control; and those lines are certain to go into the hands of some monopoly, any way. If a business is of such a nature that it must be controlled by a monopoly, most people will prefer that that monopoly be the government. Individualism does not prevent the formation of partnerships. When a city is to be supplied with water, it does not destroy Individualism for the people to engage in a partnership to furnish themselves with water. Individualism only demands that all lines of business which are adapted to private management shall be reserved for private enterprise. Government ownership of railways may be very objectionable, but such ownership is not Socialism, nor a step toward Socialism. A railway employe would have the same liberty in the service of the government as in the service of a great corporation. The equalizing of rates would give opportunity for many small lines of business where the production is now in the hands of a monopoly. Government ownership of railways would probably tend to an increased number of independent producers. The objections to it are the necessary extension of governmental powers, the vast increase in the number of offices to become the spoils of every political election, and the opportunities for swindling the government which it would afford. Government ownership is common in Europe, and is a question of practical statesmanship; but the American people hope to find a better way of securing just and equal rates for all.

The price at which any monopoly can sell its goods depends on the principles set forth in the chapter on "Monopoly," in the book on "Exchange." A part of this price—usually the greater part, and frequently nearly the whole of it—is what would be obtained under competition. The excess, only, is the share of Monopoly. But while the percentage of the price which is due to monopoly may be very small, the aggregate share of a monopoly is frequently very large.

A recent form of monopoly is known as the Trust, which is simply a combination of men who would naturally be competitors. The prices which they can obtain for their goods are shown under "Combination," in the book on Exchange. All that is obtained over the natural price under competition, is the share of Monopoly.

CAPITALIZATION.—Monopolies are sometimes capitalized, though not so frequently as "good name." Some forms of monopoly are not so certain to return a future income. When a patent right is sold, the monopoly is capitalized, but as it is expected to expire in a few years, the capitalization must be such as is expected to pay, not only interest, but the principal, within the time the right has to run. To a certain extent, this is true of all capitalization. If one has a monopoly of any kind of production, or any service which he can transfer, it can, of course, be capitalized and sold.

The truth that must not be forgotten is, that such capitalization is not material wealth. It does not come under the head of "Resources Produced by Human Industry," which are always material. Such capitalization represents only one's right to a share of the world's production, or perhaps only his power to take a share. It does not increase the resources for the satisfaction of wants. The apparent wealth of the country is often vastly augmented by the mere drawing of certain papers, but there is no more real wealth than before. One may be making great profits out of a soap factory, by reason of its " good name " and monopolies secured by letters patent and otherwise. Now, to call the " good name " and monopoly of this factory worth a million dollars, does not increase the wealth of the country. If we call it capital, then capital is not always material wealth. It was for this reason that we treated of the "Share of Produced Wealth," in a former chapter; and did not treat of a share of Capital. Capital is too indefinite for our purposes. By "Produced Wealth," or the "Resources Produced by Industry," we know what we mean.

We do not always separate the share of Monopoly from the other shares which may fall to the same individual or company; and the share of Monopoly is not found in the product, as it comes from a factory, but in its exchange for other things. Of the money (representing a share in all the world's products) which the monopolist receives in exchange for his product or service, a considerable part represents rent; another portion is the share of interest; the largest amount, probably, represents labor, or wages paid for labor; and another share, the profits of business management. The share which comes to one on account of monopoly is clear gain; it is so much more than other men can make in the same line of business.

There are good and bad, just and unjust, monopolies. The monopoly of personal talent is the highest right in the world; it is the right of the laborer to the result of his own labor. Nobody begrudges Joseph Jefferson the income he receives from his monopoly of playing Rip Van Winkle as no other living being can play it. No one is compelled to see him; and the actor can honestly make the price of witnessing the performance as high as he pleases. The monopoly of "good name" is not only the right of the possessor, but is in the highest degree conducive to the interests of the people. It encourages honest goods. The producer is anxious to make a name which will lead people to buy of him again. If all men were honest, and the stamp on any piece of goods a guarantee that they are precisely as described, a good name would be worth less than now, because more common. The share of the world's produce which it pays for the good name of certain goods, is partly a penalty for the unreliability of dealers. It is the cost of protection against the swindlers and the incompetent.

The share of Natural Monopolies is a very large one ; not because they are numerous, but because they serve so many people, and take something from each one. Frequently, the sum they draw is much larger than that of all others combined, except the share of labor. Next to the rise in value of land, they are the chief means by which large fortunes have been accumulated.

CHAPTER V.

THE SHARE OF THE PRODUCER — PROFITS OF PRODUCTION.

We now come to the great share of economic labor. Rent must be paid. Interest on Produced Wealth used in production is justly due, and must be paid if the stock of Produced Wealth is to be kept up, and production is to be carried on economically. The owner of a good name will be able to obtain a larger share of the world's goods in exchange for the goods he makes on account of it; and is justly entitled to this share. The monopolist can always take a share, larger or smaller, on account of his monopoly; and is often justly entitled to it. Usually, however, we seek to reduce this share; but it is frequently impossible to do away with it, without destroying the right of property, and losing more than we would gain. Methods of reducing it, and abolishing it in some cases, have already been considered.

After these shares are taken, all else belongs to Labor. But it is to be remembered that we are using the word "labor" in the economic sense, not in the popular sense of "workingman." It includes every effort of mind or hand for the satisfaction of wants. The classes of laborers in this sense are so many, and so widely separated, that it does not help us much to say, as did some of the older economists, "so much belongs to the laborer." In this and the following chapters we shall, therefore, study the shares of the various classes of laborers. It will be necessary to use the term "laborer" sometimes in the economic sense, and sometimes in the narrower popular meaning; but the connection will be such that the reader can not misunderstand.

After paying rent and interest, the shares of land, Produced Wealth, good name and Monopoly, all else belongs to the Producer, to him who engages in production, taking its risks for the sake of its profits. If the manual laborers themselves engage in business enterprise, as in a co-operative factory, they *are* the producers and this share is theirs. The farmer usually owns his land and stock, and carries on business for himself; hence the entire product belongs to him. If he is a "renter," he pays rent for the land, and probably interest; and the remainder of the product is his. If he works the land "on shares," he may give as much as a third of the product for rent.

When the undertaker of any business employs men, paying wages for their labor, he steps into their place, succeeds to their rights, and has labor's share of the product. The ownership by each man of himself, and his right to his own labor, implies the right to sell that labor as well as to carry on production on his own account. Often he can get more for his labor than he could produce; and there is no difference in principle between selling his labor and the product of his labor. A shoemaker in a small shop makes and sells shoes; the shoemaker in a large factory sells his labor to be employed in making shoes, because he can get more for his labor than he could for all the shoes he could make by himself. Said a Socialist, "That building belongs to the workmen who built it." Said a man in the crowd, "I laid brick on that building for four dollars a day, and the building belongs to the man who paid me the four dollars." Certainly; what else did he pay him the four dollars for? If the workman wanted to put up a building for himself, who would hinder? But what idiot would pay four dollars a day for nothing?

The man who pays the wages concentrates in himself all the risk, and all the chance of gain of perhaps a hundred laborers. He must sell the product under the laws of Exchange; and many men are compelled to sell it for less than they have paid in rent, interest and wages. If this loss or profit were divided among the hundred laborers, it might be only a small percentage on the yearly wages of each one; but when it is concentrated into single hands, and falls on one person, the loss or profit may be very large. The taking of such risk seems necessary. It is not gambling, though the chances are sometimes as great as in gambling. It is legitimate and honest business, conducted for the good of the nation. When one engages in business, he must take the chances of a good many things he can not control, as well as of his own ability in management. A very little variation may make the difference between bankruptcy or a fortune. Co-operation is the only way of avoiding the throwing of this risk on a very few persons, and co-operation has not yet demonstrated its practicability. It is easy enough for one to divide his profits, when he makes any, among his employes, but no one will consent to share his losses; and no one can afford to take risk without the chances of profit.

By the Producer, we understand the one who undertakes the production of goods, succeeding to the share of all laborers to whom he pays wages. It is not easy to find a good name for him. In French he could be called the *entrepreneur*. Prof. Francis A. Walker suggested that he could naturally be called the "undertaker" were this word not now used in the sense of funeral director. The word "undertaker" may yet come into use to signify the one who undertakes any business on his own account, taking its risks, being responsible for it, and having its control with all loss or profit after paying rent and interest, and other shares. He has here been called the "Producer," because he engages in production, and succeeds to the share of all other laborers to whom he pays wages. The share of the Producer is what is left after paying all other shares and wages (either in the payment of labor direct or as represented in the purchase of material), and is called Profits.

Profits consist of two elements; the first is compensation for the risk of business, and includes "good and bad luck"; and the second is the result of one's own skill and business management. The risk of business we have already seen. There is a certain amount of good and bad luck in the world. Of two men who work equally hard and manage equally well, one succeeds through good luck, and the other fails through bad luck. The result comes from unforeseen causes, often causes which nobody could . foresee. There is an effort among business men to reduce the risk from fire, and loss by sea, by means of insurance; but insurance can not touch those more remote happenings on which the success or failure of business often depends. And the failures are numerous. We are dazzled by the success of the few, and do not notice the failure of the many.

The second element of profits is the direct result of the economic labor of the "undertaker" of the business; and he is as much entitled to it as any laborer to his own labor. He adds so much to the satisfaction of human wants. Men differ widely in their ability to manage a business. Enterprises are continually failing; and others just live along, paying rent, interest, and current wages, but afford the owner perhaps less than he could get as wages. Still, the demand for goods maintains the price just high enough to keep what we may call these no-profit establishments running. But in some corner of the country we see a man, who is producing the same kind of goods of equal desirability, paying the same wages and selling at the same price; but who is making a fortune each year, when others can hardly make both ends meet. This man may not labor two hours a day. It does not matter, so that he manages that great business as he does. Goods are probably cheaper than they would be without him. Laborers get more than they could make for themselves. His management enables more goods to be produced with the same effort. This is the result of his economic labor. This is his profit. The Producer does not get wages, but profits. He pays all other shares, and takes what is left; and what is left depends, apart from risk, on his own economic labor in the direction of the business. His management may make this residue fabulous sums, and nobody else have any less than if the management were in less competent hands, with no profits at all.

Of two farmers with the same kind of land, and who work equally hard, one gets rich, and the other barely makes a living. In a factory with an expense of a hundred thousand dollars a year, one owner may save ten per cent. over any one else in the business. The difference is in the men; and each man owns himself, and his own labor.

From this it is evident that there will always be profits as long as there is a difference in the business ability of men. The entire production of a nation can not be carried on by half a dozen of the most superior "undertakers." No one knows who are the most competent except after long trial. The risk of all business in the hands of a few men is too great. It is far better for the country that production should be in many hands. New men of ability are continually being developed, and others are dropping out. Production is already concentrated in too few hands. It would be better if we had more small concerns. But if the concerns managed with a fair degree of ability just pay expenses, all below them will fail; and all which are better managed will pay a profit. The goods will sell in the same market at the same price. The most superior management will secure large profits, which represent its superiority over the factory that just pays expenses. If we could arbitrarily raise wages, or lower the price of the goods, the factories just paying would be forced into bankruptcy; and there would not be goods enough to supply the demand at the new prices; else the best factories would increase their output, and the production be concentrated into fewer hands, until they were few enough to become a Monopoly—and then we have monopoly prices. This element of profits represents the difference between the ability of different Producers.

Profits are limited by competition. The share of Monopoly is not profits, and has been considered in a previous chapter. Men are so anxious to be in business for themselves that they are willing to do business on very small returns. Wherever there is a chance to make large profits, there is a rush of producers. It is this competition which keeps profits down, so that the ordinary man must conduct his business with no more than ordinary wages, and often with less. The extraordinary profits are due to great superiority in business management, and to the good luck which comes to some men as a result of the risk which ruins others. The man who makes an improvement in business methods usually gains a corresponding profit for a few years or months, until his methods can be imitated by others, when his profits sink to the normal, and the gain all goes to the consumer.

The management spoken of in this chapter is that of the owner, or "undertaker," of the business—the Producer. He may employ many superintendents, whose salaries will be fixed by the laws of Exchange.

Other minor elements enter into profits, and, therefore, the only definition which covers them is, *What is left after paying all other shares.* What at first may be thought to be included in profits may belong to good name or monopoly.

The question may be asked, Do not profits include the enormous gain from the Division of Labor, and from modern methods of production? Not at all. This great gain shows itself in lower prices of goods, in balancing the continually increasing share of rent, and in higher wages. The people should get the benefit of improved methods of production, and they get it in lower prices, except where the business is protected by monopoly; and, even then, the monopoly can seldom get more than a small fraction of the gain. Under competition there will always be business conducted with no profit, no matter how great the improvement in production may be. Prices will simply be lower. Profits will be found in the better managed and more fortunate establishments, which are able to make something at the same prices at which some establishments just pay expenses, rent, interest, and wages to the employes.

Profits are not always legitimate. If the shoe manufacturer uses pasteboard insoles instead of leather, the little that he may save is the result of fraud. He has robbed the consumer, and taken a larger share of the world's production than belongs to him. It is probable that the great success of many men in amassing wealth is due to swindling rather than to legitimate profits. The swindle lies, not in making as good goods as other people at less cost, but in making articles which, while they appear to be as good, are really not worth half the money. They do not wear as long as honest goods, or do not satisfy wants as well while they last. Yet the customer can not distinguish by their appearance before using. Let there be two trunks, for example; one will stand twice as much handling as the other, and perhaps required fifty per cent. more labor to make. But, while they could readily be distinguished by an expert, a customer, who buys a trunk only a few times in the course of his life, can not detect any difference. Of course, he takes the cheaper. He pays a little less, but he has been swindled out of half his money. The manufacturer has not made as much as the customer has lost, but he has made nearly fifty per cent. more than his honest rival. Wealth accumulated in this way is simple robbery. What one gains another loses, and the victim usually loses twice as much as the swindler gains.

CHAPTER VI.

THE SHARE OF THE MERCHANT — PROFITS OF EXCHANGE.

In the last chapter we considered the share of the producer, and now turn to the share of those who conduct the world's exchanges. Both are profits. Yet the work of exchange is so different from that of production, that unless the two kinds of profits are distinctly separated, the reader is in danger of overlooking either the one or the other.

The share of the merchant is partly a share of Labor, and partly compensation for risk. The merchant is a laborer in the economic sense; that is, his efforts aid in the satisfaction of wants. He is the distributer of the world's productions to those who need them. And this labor is no less important than that of the producer. The Chinese grow tea, nearly enough for all the world. But how is a family to get the pound it desires for present use? Some one must go to China, get the tea, bring it to America, and distribute it to those who desire it, giving to each that one of the many varieties he prefers. More than this, he must tell the people what the taste of each pound of the tea will be. A consumer can not try it before buying; but the merchant tries it—employs men to draw it and taste it for the consumer. The merchant sees to it that the teas are properly classified—by taste.

THE SHARE OF THE MERCHANT. 407

The right of the members of a co-operative shoe factory to the result of their labor means the right to the shoes they have made; but their right is only to the *shoes*, and not to anything produced by other people, or to any specified sum of money. Now, the labor of distributing these shoes to those who want them, convincing them that they are the sort of shoes they need, and getting money for them, may be as great as that required to make the shoes. There are many lines of manufacture where the labor of selling is actually greater than that of making, especially where a new kind of goods is introduced, and their merits must be explained. This is the labor of exchange. The cost of exchange—of getting tea from China, and distributing it to the consumers; of taking the product of every factory, and distributing it with as little loss as possible among those who want it; and conducting the exchanges so that each man shall be able to get something of everything he wants in exchange for the products which he manufactures — this cost of exchange consists of rents on the land used by stores and railways; of interest on the enormous capital invested; and of a vast amount of highly skilled labor, that of clerks in retail and wholesale stores, book-keepers, bank clerks, etc. The business ability required in carrying on the exchanges of a country is, perhaps, greater than that demanded in the production of all its goods.

Profits in Exchange are precisely what they are in Production. They are what the merchant has left after paying all other shares and expenses. The owner of a ship in the Chinese trade pays rent for the land he may use at a private dock, pays interest on the cost of the ship, pays the wages of the captain and the crew, pays the Chinese producer for the production of the tea; and sells it for what he can get. If he has anything left after paying the expenses, that is profit. The retailer buys the tea of the wholesaler; pays rents for the ground on which his store stands, pays interest on the capital required to keep a stock on hand until it is wanted, pays for the labor of transportation, pays for the labor of his clerks; and retails the tea at a higher price than it cost him. After paying all expenses out of the difference, what he has left is net profit. It is compensation for his risk, and a return for his own skill and labor in the management of the business—in selecting such goods as his customers are likely to want, buying them low, keeping them in good condition, etc.

Merchants usually speak of the difference between the wholesale and the retail price, as profit. For convenience this may be called *gross* profit; out of it must be paid all the shares of rent, interest, labor, etc. The remainder is net profit—which is the only profit in the economic use of the term.

The profit or share of the merchant is determined by competition. Nowhere else can competition be so fully trusted to regulate prices and profits. If a retail merchant is doing well, another is pretty sure to set up a store by his side. The number of men who wish to get into the mercantile business is so large that it is claimed ninety out of a hundred fail, and meet with loss instead of profit. Surely, this goes to show that the profits of these men are none too large. But nowhere does business management count for more. One merchant in a hundred, serving his customers equally well or better than others, selling goods as cheap, and keeping the variety they desire, makes thousands of dollars a year, profit, when others are failing by his side. He knows what to buy and how much, and what not to touch. His net profits represent so much real addition to the satisfaction afforded a part of the community. Without him goods would not have been so well distributed, or customers would have paid a higher price for them, or been less perfectly satisfied. These increased satisfactions are the result of his economic labor, and he is as much entitled to the profit as the workman to the shoes he has made. That he makes large profits under competition (assuming that he is doing an honest business), shows that he is doing more to serve the world, more to aid in satisfying wants, than others who are making nothing. If any one else can perform the same service for a less share, the opportunity, under competition, is open to him. Competition can safely be trusted to keep merchants' profits down to the minimum. The mercantile business is not a natural monopoly, and never can be.

The question arises whether profits contain other elements than "good luck" and business management. There are undoubtedly sometimes minor elements, and hence the only definition of profit is, "what is left after paying all other shares." Yet almost all elements beyond "good luck" and business management which are popularly supposed to belong to profit are not profit at all. Let a man start a new business in a line where competition has free play, and all the profit he makes the first year will be likely to be due to his management of the business, and his good fortune.

Profits, then, whether made in Production or Exchange, are what the producer or merchant has left after paying all other shares and expenses. It has been assumed that he pays laborers a fixed sum, as wages; although he sometimes bargains with them to take a share of the profits in the place of wages. This is usually where he has very intimate relations with the employe, and fully trusts him. In some lines of business it would be fatal to have one's profits known. In a poor year, when he made nothing, the fact might injure his credit; and in a good year rivals might be tempted to engage in the same business, supposing that all years are good. The competition of trade is so severe that in many lines considerable secrecy in the method of managing one's affairs is necessary to success. Where a clerk has a share of the profits in place of salary, it is necessary that he know what the profits are, and all details connected with them. Such information made public may prevent the making of any profit at all the next year. Partners divide the profit among themselves on terms previously agreed upon, as their compensation.

CHAPTER VII.

THE SHARE OF THE LABORER WHO WORKS FOR HIMSELF.

The laborer who works for himself is in the place of the "Producer" of Chapter V. He receives the total product after paying rent and interest. If his labor is of a kind that satisfies wants directly, he receives its advantage in the satisfaction of his own wants, or those of his family or friends to whom he gives his services. If his labor is of a kind that satisfies wants indirectly, he has the goods produced, to sell or exchange for such things as he needs. With the growth of large factories, more men work for wages than formerly, but the largest line of production, that of farming, is carried on by men who work for themselves. The farmer works for himself. He may pay rent to a landlord, and interest on borrowed capital. He may pay wages. But after paying these shares he has the remainder of the product. He does not get wages.

Where the laborer works for himself, his reward is determined by the price he gets for the product, under the laws of Exchange. The farmer often feels that the price of grain is too low and the prices of goods are too high. He pays more for his agricultural implements because the iron workers receive what often seems to him a fabulous price for their labor. He does not know why everything is so high and the price of grain so low, and likely blames the merchant and the grain-buyer because these are nearest to him. But the contest is in the prices of grain and goods, where it should be. He knows he gets all he produces; and has only the difficulty of every other man in the world who wants to sell dear and buy cheap. But he fights it out in the province of Exchange, where there is some hope of settlement, and where substantial justice is likely to be done under the influence of competition. He is more independent than the wage laborer, because he works for himself.

In the early history of this country the greater portion of production was carried on in this way, and the line of small producers is not yet extinct. In many branches of business there will always be men who will work for themselves and sell the product. But in other lines of production, the small producers have been crowded out by large factories, made necessary by the improvements in machinery. Here, the only means by which laborers can work for themselves is on the plan of co-operation. Co-operation is said to have been tried and failed; it will probably fail a good many times before it succeeds, yet it presents the only escape from a much larger wages class than is desirable.

By co-operation we mean the union of those who would have been small producers on their own account a few generations ago. It is not so uncommon a thing as we imagine, since it is only an extended form of partnership. Two, three, or four men now unite in the ownership and management of business, each one giving special attention to the branch which he is best fitted to attend to. Why may not the number be extended to twenty or a hundred? Co-operation demands as much judgment and business sense on the part of each member as was required of a small producer a hundred years ago. But there are thousands of men capable of carrying on a business, who can not own a plant costing hundreds of thousands of dollars, and there is perhaps nothing else left for them to do but to work for wages. If a hundred of them could unite, they might carry on a business which would rival that of the largest producer in their line. Of course, each one must know how the business is managed, and what are the profits and losses. They must pay all expenses, and take the total product for their share in place of wages. They will probably employ men and pay wages, but they will be satisfied with their own share, even though it is less than the wages they pay, since they know it is all there is.

The advantages of co-operation are two; first, to Society; and second, to the workmen.

The advantage of co-operation to Society is that the workmen know that they get all there is, after paying rent and interest. A great deal of discontent would be avoided, and vast losses by labor troubles prevented. The members of a co-operative factory are also likely to be more independent members of society, and to take a broader view of its interests. No matter how high the dispute may run over prices, the independent producer will not stop work, as men go on a strike. He can gain nothing by that. If prices are too low, men may close their factory, and engage in some other line of production; they would hold back their goods from the market if they thought anything could be gained by it, but they would not stop work, and would not engage in the destruction of property, or attempt to prevent other men working. The battles under Exchange are not so destructive to the interests of society as under the wages system, and the warfare is more likely to be of intellect than brute force.

ADVANTAGES OF CO-OPERATION TO THE WORKMAN.—The workmen would gain, not only natural wages, but the share of profits; and in time that of "good name"; and, in some cases, that of monopoly. They might get everything except rent and interest. The poorest managed factory that could exist would pay only wages; the more successful would pay profits.

Successful co-operation, as success in any large business, depends on good management; and good management depends largely on one good manager, just as the success of an army depends on a general. The best known interest of co-operation in the United States is the fishing industry of New England, which has been managed in this way from the beginning. Each man received a share of the profits, though a whaling vessel might be gone two years. Such ships, however, had a captain, whose authority was no less than when seamen are paid wages; and whose share was as large in proportion to those of the men as the salary of other captains to the wages of a common seaman. It is useless to talk about a co-operative factory run by a committee of the workmen. There must be some one in control, and he must receive either as large a salary as a private corporation would pay him, or a large share of the profits, else he will transfer his services to private companies.

Good management, however, by no means depends on one man alone, and here would be the strength of the association. The foreman of every department, and many of the workmen, would be members, and receive profits instead of wages. The *details* of the business would therefore be well managed. Good work could be put out, which would sell goods in the future. The book-keeper and the traveling salesman would be members of the body, their compensation depending on its profits. Although a considerable number of men might be employed at wages, there would be enough members of the firm in every department to see that there was no waste—that everything was done as it should be, and that the business was economically managed. The laborers would also secure the share of "good name" as soon as they made one. No new firm has a name which is worth anything. It must be built up, often by years of effort.

If engaged in business where competition is free, the only monopoly the co-operative factory is likely to deal with is that of patents. So far as patented devices are in general use they must pay royalty the same as others. But there is every opportunity for minor inventions in their factory by men who are interested; and patents owned by themselves, and trade secrets, are monopolies of which they derive all the benefit.

The chief difficulty in the way of co-operation is the unwillingness to pay a general manager what such a man can command from private companies. A good manager will sometimes double the net income of a factory, though he may labor fewer hours than any other man employed about it. There is every reason to believe that managers for co-operative factories could be secured for much less than they could make in carrying on business for themselves. There are vast numbers of men competent to manage business, who have not the capital, and can not borrow it without security. A body of laborers with a good reputation, and a business manager with an equal reputation, might more readily secure the use of capital than one man by himself. A small contribution from each man would furnish a part of the necessary capital, which would be security for what they needed to borrow. A number of positions of this kind will tend to develop more managers out of the ranks of the workmen and clerks.

A co-operative factory, then, gets the shares of profits, good name, and perhaps monopoly. Its members receive the total product of their labor, out of which they have to pay only rent and interest—rent for the land occupied, and interest on the money borrowed. The co-operative factory gets something more than the natural share of wage labor, because it contributes something more than wage labor. On the other hand, receiving profits, it must bear losses. The failure of most co-operative factories results from a lack of stamina to meet losses, and to accept half as much as could be made in wages, for one year, in the hope of getting more the next. There is also a failure to appreciate the advantage of owning one's own business, and of steady employment in a bad year at even half wages, as contrasted with the chance of being thrown out of employment altogether. Few co-operative men realize the value of the "good name" and business they might build up during the best years of their lives, which would almost support them in their old age. In short, the very qualities are demanded for co-operation that are possessed by successful business men of "nerve," and it would probably be unsafe to admit any man to membership in a co-operative company who would not have been capable of carrying on a small business of his own in the days when there were no great factories.

Co-operation would not abolish the wages class. It could do no more than unite men of considerable business ability, nerve, self-restraint, and judgment, into companies for production. They would naturally fill the more important positions, of superintendents, foremen, book-keepers, traveling salesmen, etc.; though there is no reason why the men of the least mechanical skill, and those whose manual labor counts for the least, should not be members of the company, receiving the smaller share to which they are entitled, provided they have the intellectual and other qualifications necessary.

Laborers who work for themselves—farmers, small producers, members of co-operative factories, etc.—receive, therefore, the total product of their labor after paying rent and interest, with perhaps other minor shares. Their ultimate reward depends on what they sell the goods for, and what they pay for the goods they buy for their families. It is merely a question of exchanging what one makes for what other groups of laborers make. The real contest is between various groups of laborers—between the farmers, the makers of agricultural implements and machinery, furniture workers, house builders, and woolen and cotton spinners and weavers: it is a contest of every class of laborers with every other. If one class gets more, another must take less. There is only so much to be distributed. Shall the farmer's share be increased and the iron worker's share diminished, or *vice versa*. Many laborers would receive a good deal in consequence of "good name." The small farmer near a city often gets double price in consequence of the reputation of his produce. There would be something paid to monopoly, but almost the entire product of the nation's industry, after deducting the shares of rent and interest, would be divided among the groups of laborers working for themselves.

The merchants are one group of laborers, and since they come in contact with all other groups, every one lays the blame for its own small share on them. Hence we hear so much about the "middle men." The truth is, the merchants are as necessary as the producers. What is the product of a shoe factory worth to the workmen, even if they have the whole of it? Why, precisely what they can get for it. But no one family wants more than a few pairs of shoes; and if the workmen were to attempt to peddle them out by house-to-house visits over the country, it would take them longer than to make the shoes. The selling of a product is just as important to the producer as its production, and the merchants can usually sell it with less labor than he can. They understand the business of selling, as he understands the business of manufacturing. If, however, the merchants get a large share of a nation's products for distributing them, other groups of laborers must get less; if all others get more, the merchants must take less. Unless we can increase production, there is only so much to be distributed, and it is a question of what laborers shall get the most. We have seen that competition fixes the share of the merchant; it would also fix the share of every other group of laborers. The real contest would be between groups of laborers—farmers, carpenters, masons, workmen in each branch of manufacturing, railway employes, merchants' clerks, etc. The more one class receives, the less other classes must have, since there is only so much to divide. Each class would seek to sell its product as dear as possible, and to purchase as cheap as possible, and the play of competition would determine what share each would obtain. Competition would also determine the share of each member of a group of laborers in a co-operative factory, relative to the total share of the factory.

CHAPTER VIII.

THE SHARE OF THE LABORER WHO WORKS FOR WAGES.

It is not within the plan of this book to enter into any extended discussion of the " wages question," which would require a volume by itself. An important phase of the labor question was treated in the book on Exchange, in the labor cost of production. The object of the present chapter is mainly to show the place of the wages question in the general system. Wages are a question of Exchange, and the practical wages questions are applications of the principles laid down in the book on Exchange in this volume. All that has been said of utility, value, supply and demand, competition, combination and monopoly, finds an application in wages as well as in prices.

The wage-worker differs from the man who works for himself in that he sells his labor, whereas the latter sells the goods he produces. One can more easily see the laws which fix the prices of goods than he can see those which fix the price of labor. The farmer sells wheat, and its price depends on supply and demand. The wage-worker sells labor, and its price depends on supply and demand. Both are questions of Exchange. The majority of wage-workers can probably get more for their labor direct than for the goods they would produce in working for themselves, even if they were able to borrow the capital necessary to engage in production.

While wages depend on supply and demand, it is the supply and demand for *labor*, and not for goods—an important distinction. But one element in the demand for labor is the anticipated demand for goods. Nobody will pay wages in production unless he expects to sell the goods the laborer helps produce; unless he has reason to expect a demand for the goods, he will not employ labor. An increase in the number of laborers may, however, cause an increase in the demand for goods, since the laborers themselves constitute a demand, and with their wages will buy either the goods they themselves help produce or those produced by other laborers.

But the wage-laborer does not propose to produce goods and sell them when finished, farmers and co-operative factories do that, he is looking for a man who will pay him wages every week or month, and take the risk of selling the goods for enough to pay the cost of production. The wage-laborer's employment depends on finding such a man. Wages, therefore, depend directly on the number of employers, and the number of men they believe they can profitably set to work. The wage-worker must have one more man, or company, between himself and the consumer than the laborer who works for himself. It is an old saying that "When two bosses are seeking one laborer, wages will be high; when a multitude of laborers are seeking one boss, wages will be low."

Highest Permanent Limit of Wages.—The highest permanent limit of wages is what the goods produced sell for, less rent, interest, and enough profit to induce producers to continue business. Let us give a moment's thought to this proposition. The wage-worker can not *permanently* receive more than his labor produces. No one will pay him wages unless with the hope of selling the goods he makes for enough to reimburse himself. Anything else would not be wages, but charity. The workman can not, therefore, get more than what the goods he makes sell for. But rent is paid for the use of a profitable location, rather than take one where production would cost more. Capital can not be had without interest. If the employer uses a patented process or machine, he must pay royalty to the monopoly. Now, the goods produced must sell for enough to pay all these charges, or the employer must stop business. In no case can the laborer continue to get more than what is left after paying rent and interest.

How about profits? There will be some manufacturers who will continue to do business without profit. In their factories the wage-laborer may get all the goods sell for, less rent and interest. But there are better business managers who will sell their goods at the same price as the others, pay the same wages, and make large profits. There is no reason why they should sell their goods for less, since the same quality of goods will bring the same price in the same market. There is no reason why they should pay laborers any more than the factory which is making no profit. They might discharge their own hands, and hire those of the no-profit factory. Wages, as well as the price of goods, tend to the same rate for the same service. Suppose wages should rise so as to take the profits of the best managed factories; then those managed with less ability would be compelled to close, for they were before making nothing—paying out in wages, rent and interest, all the goods sold for. Now that wages are higher they can no longer run without loss. But the closing of so many factories would throw many laborers out of employment. Hence there must be profits, sufficient to keep the wheels of industry in motion, and these profits must be paid out of what the goods sell for.

It is the same with the share of "good name." There will always be factories which have no good name to speak of. They must pay expenses, or their workmen will have nothing to do. But the factory with a good name can sell its goods higher, and will not give this additional price to labor. Why should it? It is the good name of the brand of the goods of the factory, not of the workmen employed. It could take the workmen from the factory which has no good name, and still sell its goods higher.

The poorest managed factories with no reputation must, therefore, pay rent and interest out of what the product sells for, and the wages of the workmen can not exceed what is left. The best managed factories will pay the same wages, but will have something left for profit. The best managed factories with a "good name" will pay the same wages, but sell their goods at a higher price than the others, and have something left for profits, and something for the reputation of their goods. Wages will be practically the same in all factories; and the highest permanent rate is what the no-profit factories, which the demand for goods keeps running, have left after paying rent and interest.

RAISING PRICES.—The foregoing shows the highest limit of wages possible without raising prices. Assuming that the furniture workers of the country are receiving this highest natural limit of wages, if they could get their wages doubled, the price of furniture, so far as wages enter into it, would also be doubled. Profits would be doubled. All workmen who buy furniture would then pay more for furniture, and the furniture workers have doubled their wages at the expense of the consumers, nearly all of whom are other workmen. The farmer, the iron-worker and the printer pay so much more for their furniture, and their real wages or incomes are reduced.

For it is not "nominal," but "real wages," that we are seeking. Nominal wages are those paid in money. Real wages are what the laborer can buy with the money received. If the rise in the wages of any trade has the effect of increasing the price of the goods manufactured, these workmen gain at the expense of other laborers. It often happens that the natural fall of the prices of goods in consequence of improved methods of production does not take place, because wages are advanced. In this case the workmen in that particular line reap the benefit that would naturally go to the public.

It is probable that the farmers are at present the greatest sufferers. They can not increase the price of wheat, because it is fixed by the foreign demand. They get no more money than before. The wages of workmen in many lines of production carried on in factories have been increased; and the farmer pays more for the goods he buys. It is true he suffers from monopolies, but high wages affect him ten times as much. Railroad steel and machinery cost more, and railroad charges are consequently higher; so that the farmer gets less for his grain than if wages in rolling-mills, and among railroad men, were lower. *Economically*, no two interests are more opposed than those of farmers and mechanics. It is for the interest of every class of laborers to have wages in other lines of production as low as possible, in order that its own wages may buy more goods. It is for the interest of farmers that the wages of all workers in factories and on railroads should be low, in order that the money received for farm produce may buy more goods, and that freights may be cheap. There undoubtedly exists an idea among workingmen that the more wages any class receives the better for the others. Nothing could be farther from the truth. When one class gets more than the highest rate of wages consistent with present prices, other classes must receive less of *real* wages, because of higher prices. High wages do not increase production, and there is only so much to divide.

Even where wages sink to their lowest limit, *and there is free competition*, other laborers reap the chief benefit. In the "sweat-shops" women often make clothing for a mere pittance; but this clothing is sold cheap, and is presumably bought by other laborers. The millionaire has his clothes made by a fashionable tailor, whose workmen receive the highest wages. The clothing that is made by starving women is bought chiefly by laborers, and they get the benefit of the low wages the women receive. Here is undoubtedly an instance where one class of laborers, the sewing women, should receive more and other laborers less; but it shows how wages are a division of the greater part of all that is produced. We can not have high wages and cheap clothing at the same time. Recent investigations in London have shown that the sewing women who work for the lowest starvation wages are employed by men almost as poor as themselves; that the relations of employer and employe are friendly, and that the employer makes little more than the men who work under him. Wages are so low because the clothing is sold so cheap; and the low price is the only thing that enables other poor persons to keep themselves comfortably clad. In American cities, however, it is claimed that employers in "sweat-shops" make something. Wages must be paid out of the annual production of a country. A large annual product, with a small population to divide it among, affords the opportunity for the highest wages.

It is true that the method of manufacture of clothing by the "sweating system" in London may not be the most economical, and that the work could be done cheaper in a factory; but this does not affect the principle involved. In the case of monopoly we may have high prices of goods with low wages; but where competition acts, either wages rise or prices of goods fall to the limit of lowest profit which will keep up sufficient production. We often fail to realize that cheap goods are of as great advantage as high wages.

It should be remembered that it is only the highest natural rate of wages that can not be increased without raising prices, and taking from other workmen. We assumed that the workman was receiving all that the product sells for, less other necessary shares. One difficulty with the wages system is that a workman can not usually know whether he is receiving this highest natural rate of wages or not; and we are all likely to think that we are receiving less than we should. One of the advantages of co-operation is that the workmen get all they produce, less rent, interest, etc.; and *know* that they get it. This knowledge is the most important of all. It gives contentment to a man to know that, small as his income is, he gets all that is justly due him, all that he produces. If competition were unrestricted, and there were no friction, wages would tend to this highest natural rate. New factories would spring up, and employers would seek laborers whenever wages were below this standard.

A monopoly may, however, not only sell its goods at the highest price the public can afford to pay; but employ laborers at the lowest rate at which they can afford to work. Even where there is not a complete monopoly, there are frequently partial monopolies; and there is always a good deal of friction in economics, as in mechanics. Hence wages often fall below the highest rate that current prices would bear.

In every effort to raise wages it should be asked first, Is it expected that the proposed increase will raise the prices of the goods, and thus be paid by the consumers,—nine-tenths of whom are other workmen,—or that the additional wages can be paid by the employer without increasing prices? Where competition is active, any general increase of wages is likely to raise prices; where there is a monopoly, an increase of wages may come out of the share of monopoly, or may result in raising the prices of the goods, according to the circumstances of each case.

The wages of all laborers of the same grade, in the same line of production, tend to the same rate in the same locality. But there are, as J. E. Cairnes showed us, non-competing groups, and the wages of the men in each group will be determined by the supply and demand for labor in that group, without much reference to other groups. Brickmasons do not compete with jewelers, or jewelers with printers. There might be a great scarcity of blacksmiths, but carpenters could not take their places. If laborers are scarce in one line of production, the prices of the goods they make are likely to rise; and their wages will be increased at the expense of the *real* wages of other classes. If the ranks of labor in another line of production are overcrowded, and competition is free, wages will be forced down; and the prices of the goods they make will proportionally fall, so that all other laborers who use these goods will gain at the expense of the laborers who make them.

It might be supposed that laborers would at once be transferred from the line of production in which wages are low to that in which they are high. This happens in the numerous employments denominated " common labor," where no previous training is required; and the wages for a great many lines of employment, therefore, remain the same. It is because the wages are the same, that the employments are classed together in the popular mind as " common labor." In employments which require previous training, transfers are not so readily made. A man does not easily learn a new trade after middle life. Young men, however, in learning new trades, naturally select those in which wages rule highest, or in which the labor is most desirable. The full force of competition is not felt, even here, because many boys learn not the trades they choose, but the trades they must. Frequently one takes the first opportunity open to him, and the selection is almost a matter of accident.

The question is frequently asked, " What can be done to increase wages?" and it suggests another, " Are not the interests of the farmers, the grocery-keepers, and the innumerable small producers who work for themselves, as important as the interests of the men who work for wages?" The economist has at heart the interests of the whole people.

With the improved methods of production ought not the wage-laborer, as well as others, to get more? Most certainly; he does get more, more nominal wages, and still larger real wages as measured in the goods he buys. He may not get as much as he should; but he certainly gets more. He gets more because he produces more; but he can not get more than he produces, with the deductions before mentioned. Improvements in production show themselves in reduced prices, which benefit all classes, the wage-workers as well as others. The improvements in production have, fortunately, resulted in lowering the prices of such goods as the laborer uses to as great an extent as those consumed only by the wealthy.

There are two reasons why the laborer feels that he has not gained as much as he should:

(1.) The improvement in his condition does not appear to be as great as it is, because of the gain to all classes. One's wants are, to a certain extent, relative. He compares his condition with those about him. If all other people have as much more as he has, he seems to himself no better off than before. If everybody wears coarse clothing, it is the fashion, and one feels as well dressed as his neighbors. If other people have luxuries, one feels his poverty, even though he may have absolutely twice as much as before. One considers his relative, rather than his absolute, income. Yet the hope of society is to elevate all of its members; and if all receive more, the laborer may feel as poor as before. With the great increase in wealth of a very small class of society, the laborer is inclined to measure himself with it rather than with the average of the people.

(2.) The laborer has not received as much as the

improved methods of production would warrant had there been no increase in the value of land, and in the great share of rent. In a new country the share of rent is very small; as the population increases, the proportion of the product which goes to rent continually grows larger. It is not only that the laborer must often pay more for the land on which to build a house than the house will cost; but the rent of the priceless land on which great buildings in cities stand, the rent of valuable land at harbors and railroad centers—all rent must come out of the nation's product, and leaves less for labor. He pays more for lumber for building a house. In a new country he could build a house of logs on land which he could buy for a few dollars. Even lumber cost little, because the timber had not been cut off.

The early history of this country was the golden age of the laborer, in comparison with all that had gone before. Land was plenty, and if one could not get wages, he could get a farm. Labor was scarce compared with land; now, land is scarce compared with labor. The high wages of this country have been due, almost entirely, to the abundance of land, and the low rents as compared with the densely populated lands of Europe. With the increase of population, wages must continually become a smaller *share* of the nation's annual product, though not absolutely smaller for the labor performed. The *share* of rent will grow larger; and the *share* of wages, smaller. Thus far, improvements in production have more than balanced the natural decrease in wages through the growth of population. With unlimited immigration there is no such thing as maintaining high wages for all classes. To increase wages does not increase production; and no nation can have more than it produces. A high scale of living for all the people must mean a relatively small population, with abundant capital; so that the Resources of Nature can be made to produce more goods in proportion to the people.

One of the most unfortunate things about the wages system is the temptation to spend all of one's wages, whether high or low. A wage-worker has the money every week, and there are so many opportunities of getting a present satisfaction out of it, that it requires more than ordinary command of one's self to save. The farmer, on the contrary, often has to save. He can not get the money each week. When the crop is sold he has something saved. He is also compelled to save in the improvement of his land. This is one of the arguments for a true plan of co-operation. Workmen could not safely allow themselves more than half of the ordinary weekly wages. At the end of the year they should have something saved, which would be needed as capital.

The principles on which high wages depend are the following:

1. Other things being equal, wages are always highest in a new country, or a country with a small population relative to its Resources, because the share of rent will be less, and there will be more to go to labor. It was for this reason that real wages were so high in the early history of the United States as

compared with Europe. In England the share of the land-owners is enormous, far greater than in the United States.

2. Wages can be increased through increased productiveness of labor. The same number of laborers produce more, and there is more to divide. This is the second reason for high wages in the United States, where labor is more effective than in any other country in the world. It is also the principal reason for higher wages in England than on the Continent, since English labor produces more than in any other country of Europe or Asia.

3. Wages will be highest where there is freest competition between employers in all lines of production, because laborers may then get the share that would otherwise go to monopoly.

4. Wages will be higher in a country like the United States, where there are numerous employers, and many men anxious to get into business for themselves. In an enterprising country, with thousands of men on the lookout for a chance to make something, and willing to take risks, the demand for labor will be brisker than in a slow country where few new men think of undertaking production, and everything is left in the old channels.

5. Success of co-operative factories would tend to increase the wages of laborers by withdrawing many wage-laborers from the market. If co-operative factories could be managed as well as private enterprises, they would soon absorb the best and most intelligent laborers of the country.

PROFIT SHARING has been put forward prominently during the last few years as a means of increasing the income of the laborers. Its advantages are those of co-operation as far as they go. If, for example, wage-workers could accept half wages, and half profits, we might realize the advantages of co-operation. Living on half wages, they might in many cases save the profits, which they would receive at the end of the year.

Profit sharing, as the term has come to be used, however, does not contemplate any reduction in wages. Its advocates are particular to insist that the employer shall also pay the very highest wages. How, then, can a producer in competition with others pay as high wages as they, and give away part of the profits, which have been reduced to the lowest possible sum by competition? The answer is, that the producer expects that the offer of a share in the profits will be an inducement to extra exertion and saving on the part of employes, so that more will be produced at the same cost, and he will have a larger profit, which he can divide. That is, he expects to pay employes something extra out of increased production due to their exertions. Suppose a large corporation to make $10,000 a year, net profit. By carefulness and extra exertion on the part of every employe, that profit might be increased, and the corporation make $12,000. It could then give its employes $2,000, and have as much left as before. Profit sharing in theory should lessen the danger of strikes, although strikes occur under it. Now, a strike inflicts a good deal of damage in any business. Even though the employer can not afford to yield, and his men return to work in the end, he has lost heavily. Any manufacturer would pay something to an insurance company to be guaranteed against loss from strikes. If profit sharing were sure to prevent them, the employer could afford to give a portion of the profits to employes to be protected from the damage they and their associates have the power to inflict upon him. This is an application of the principle that the way to increase the wages of laborers is to increase production.

Profit sharing is capable of much further extension than co-operation. It is not limited to men who have saved capital, or who have the ability to manage a business for themselves. A very serious objection to profit sharing is the fact that few private employers can afford to make a statement of their business without risk of ruin, and the plan of offering the employes a share of the profits without telling what per cent. that share is, can hardly have permanent success. Semi-public corporations, which are now compelled to make public statements of their business, appear to afford the most favorable field for the experiment.

CHAPTER IX.

THE SHARE OF LABOR WHICH SATISFIES WANTS DIRECTLY.

The share of labor which satisfies wants directly differs decidedly from that which satisfies wants indirectly, because it is not measured by material products. When a hundred men have engaged in the manufacture of shoes, any one can see that their reward must come out of what the shoes sell for.

The share of labor which satisfies wants directly is determined by exchange. This labor does not produce material commodities to divide. The boy who blacks one's boots, the girl who serves in the kitchen, the lawyer who argues one's case, the singer whom thousands flock each night to hear—all these satisfy wants directly. If they satisfy their own wants, as when one blacks his own boots, or cooks his own food, they are thus far independent of others. The circle of wants and satisfactions is complete within themselves. But when one devotes his time to the service of others, he expects to receive a fair share of the world's products in exchange for his services. The teacher and the lawyer and the physician are at first paid in money, but this merely represents goods and the personal services of others. Money, here as elsewhere, is only the means by which the exchanges take place.

How Will the Share of this Class of Labor be Determined?

1. Partly by competition; the supply of labor and the demand for it. The limits between which the compensation will fluctuate are the least the laborer can possibly accept, and the most others can afford to pay. The wages of servant girls are mainly fixed by competition. The girl must have shelter in the house of the employer, meals, and a sufficient sum of money for clothing. It is impossible for her to do this sort of work for less, and this is all that some girls receive. One servant may, however, be worth four times as much as another; and may thus receive, through competition, higher wages. There are girls who make such poor servants that no one will give them even board and clothing; the supply of better help is sufficient to avoid the necessity of employing them. Competition does not mean that every laborer will receive the same wages; but that wages will be in proportion to ability, and that the wages of a certain grade of service will be fixed at a given rate. The wages of servant girls are by no means wholly fixed by competition. Other motives enter in, such as a desire for their welfare, custom, public opinion, etc.

Instead of competition, the reward of some labor is fixed by monopoly. This is partially true of all persons who stand so high in their own department that no one can exactly take their place. Joseph Jefferson played Rip Van Winkle as no one else could. He charged monopoly prices; that is, the highest sum the public would pay. An eminent physician may charge monopoly prices, without even the limitation that the price shall be the same to all. He may put his regular charge so high that only the very wealthy can pay it, and serve some less wealthy patients for what they can afford to pay. The laborer of rare skill is entitled to monopoly prices by the highest right in the world, that of each man to his own labor. If he does nothing, the world is no worse off than it would be without him; and his services are worth what he receives, else people would not pay his charges. When a woman sings as no other woman in the world can, her power is her own. She has the right to its absolute control. She is entitled to whatever anybody is willing to pay to hear her song.

A partial monopoly of labor is found in a profession in which most of the members agree not to charge less than a certain sum; or fix rates which they regard as reasonable, below which nobody is expected to go. Men who do not belong to this association may charge lower prices, and competition is perfectly free; but the fact that a considerable number, perhaps the majority of the best members of the profession, refuse their services at less than a certain price, has its influence. This method would not make it possible to raise prices above a certain rate, probably not to maintain them above what the wealthier class of people regard as reasonable; but it modifies the influence of competition, even though there is a large number of fairly competent men in the same profession practicing with lower fees. It is understood that the laborer's power of labor is his own, and that his right to what persons are willing to pay for his services is unquestioned.

Any attempt to prevent other men from practicing at lower rates, by force, would be instantly, and justly, condemned. Any man has the right to serve others for as low fees as he chooses to accept, and that right must not be interfered with.

3. The share of labor which satisfies wants directly is sometimes determined by what those one serves think he *ought* to have; and sometimes by the cost of living in the way which the service requires. The salary of a minister is worth a moment's study. His congregation and duties demand that he shall live in a certain way. In a city the people would not expect him to appear in the pulpit unless fairly well dressed. As a teacher, they desire him to have books and periodicals; and it is to their discredit if he lives below a certain standard. Unless the minister has means of his own, his congregation understand that they must pay what it costs him to live *in the way they demand;* and few congregations pay any more. When his salary is fixed, the minister usually accepts the lowest sum he thinks he can live on, *in the way he will be expected to live.* Competition is more likely to show itself in the case of young men. Some congregations are always seeking for a young man; because he can live, in a way that will be creditable to them, for half the money which it will cost a man with a family. Young men are, however, inclined to insist on the same salary that the church would have to pay

a man with a family; and there is no reason why they should not receive it.

What those interested think one ought to have, and the cost of living in the station required, has more influence in fixing the reward of labor in other callings than the political economist often imagines. In some kinds of labor it makes no difference, as a matter of business, to the employer how or where a workman lives, or how he appears; but a salesman must dress and live in a certain way, and his salary must be high enough to cover the cost of living. In conclusion, we may say that the share of labor which satisfies wants directly is determined by exchange; and that competition, combination, monopoly, custom, public sentiment, and the cost of living in a way which the service makes necessary, all have their influence.

CHAPTER X.

THE BOOTY OF THE ROBBER, AND THE WINNINGS OF THE GAMBLER.

If during the process of production or distribution, before the product reaches the consumer, a robber or thief succeeds in making way with a portion of the goods, some other share must be diminished. In the case of the robbery of an express company, the rates for carriage are intended to cover the risk; and hence the loss is likely to be distributed.

Open seizure of goods is, however, not so common as other forms of theft. A few years since, a young man with a little money was enabled to buy stock in a well-paying railroad. By borrowing money on the stock as fast as purchased, and by other devices, he soon got a large nominal interest in the road, and had himself elected to a position which gave him the practical control. He at once proceeded to rob the company; and, although detected and put out of office before the road had been brought to ruin, he succeeded in stealing large sums. This loss probably came out of the share of interest and the profits of the stockholders. If the rates for transportation were raised to help cover the loss, it fell, also, on shippers and producers, and through them on labor. Railroad wrecking has been common in the United States, and many large fortunes have been founded by the sheer theft of property.

The adulteration of food, and the deception in the manufacture of goods, give the largest field of robbery. What are called "shoddy goods" are those made to deceive the ignorant buyer. They do not satisfy his wants as well as he had a right to expect; and all the profit the manufacturer, or dealer, has made by the deception is so much stolen. In most cases it seems to be stolen from the consumer; but the consumer is probably a producer, or at least a laborer, and the final return for his labor is the goods he gets. If these goods are less satisfactory than he would have received through an honest dealer, his share of the world's product is so much less.

The swindler does not usually make as much as the others lose, because the manufacture of "shoddy" goods is not economical, and it costs something to make what is of no utility. It costs something to deceive the purchaser. The robber also causes actual destruction. A gang of sheep-thieves once invaded the field of a farmer and killed a number of sheep for the pelts, which they took off and made way with. The pelts would not bring fifty cents apiece, while the sheep were worth four times as much. The thieves had, therefore, destroyed four times as much property as they got. It is usually true, both in production and distribution, that the booty of the robber or swindler takes far more from the other shares than he himself receives. It would be cheaper for society to support him in idleness.

It is not necessary to stop to investigate the various methods of swindling, or theft and robbery; but no treatment of "Distribution" would be complete without calling attention to the vast quantities of the world's products which are stolen outright, and to the diminished shares of other persons on account of the dishonest methods of manufacture and trade.

The booty of the robber is frequently disguised under the claim of "profits"; and it is sometimes impossible for the public to know whether receipts are profits, or the result of swindling. If the swindle is not detected, the gain of the swindler is likely to pass for profits.

It is well understood that gamblers can not live off each other. They must win from men who are engaged in other business, although what one thus wins may be passed back and forth among his class. Gamblers produce nothing; they do nothing to satisfy wants. They must be supported by the labor of others; and their support often costs the modest income of a good many families. The Louisiana lottery has made great fortunes for its owners, while the expenses of its management have been wasted. A great many millions of dollars are actually taken from the other shares of production by direct gambling, such as lotteries, races and gambling-houses. We may next add to this the gambling of the boards of trade in the leading cities. Not that there is no honest and necessary business conducted there; but that it is generally recognized that mere betting on future prices of grain and stocks equals or exceeds the legitimate transactions. How much of the purchase of stocks by outside parties may properly be classed with gambling, it is impossible to say. All business contains an element of risk; but the risk of mining, of raising a crop of wheat, or of manufacturing, is in no sense to be classed with gambling, as it is sometimes done by unthinking persons. Gambling is *getting* money as distinguished from *making* money; and though few men have gotten rich by playing cards, the number of great fortunes founded on other forms of gambling is larger than is usually supposed. Gamblers waste more money than they save.

CHAPTER XI.

THE SHARE OF THE GOVERNMENT.

The share of the annual production of a country which falls to the government consists chiefly in what it takes by taxation. The cost of government must be met in some way, and in return for the benefits conferred it takes the cost of its maintenance. A civilized government, such as the United States, is worth more to any individual than it ever takes from him, under even a bad system of taxation; but this gives it no right to take more than is absolutely necessary for the maintenance of the service it furnishes. Government may be regarded as a great co-operative institution whose cost must be paid by the members, and whose benefits are shared among them. It should not unnecessarily trespass on the freedom or the income of the individual.

A distinction should be made between the expenses of government proper and the cost of carrying on any business in which the government may be engaged. Among the former may be mentioned: the cost of the national defense; legislative, judicial and executive departments; the public school system; asylums for the insane, the blind and the deaf; and hospitals for the poor and unfortunate. All these and other expenses are borne with no expectation of return.

The second class comprises all government business

enterprises, which should ordinarily pay their own way, and in some instances a profit. The government should seldom or never undertake any business which is not a natural monopoly. The expenses of such business should never be charged as government expenses, and the receipts should not be entered as government income. The accounts of each business enterprise should be kept separate, and only its profit and loss entered among the goverment expenses. If the post-office does not pay expenses, the small loss should appear in government reports as a necessary expense of maintaining such a convenience for the people. The people should understand how much they are paying for law and order, and how much for loss on business enterprises. This method of book-keeping would reduce the nominal national expenses, and prevent much confusion. It would also make extravagance more difficult. It is true that in the United States there is some separation of accounts at present by which a book-keeper can get at the facts; but the expenses of the post-office should not even appear in the general government statement—only the net loss.

The method by which government revenue shall be raised forms the general subject of taxation, which is a question of practical statemanship based on the principles of economics. However interesting and important such a subject may be, its consideration here would carry us too far from the purposes of this volume. The object of this chapter is to call attention to the share of the government, without discussing methods of levying it or the other shares from which it may be taken.

GOVERNMENT PROPERTY.—The government, as the natural trustee for the people, has in its keeping a large part of the Resources for the Satisfaction of Wants. It is the trustee for all that the people hold in common—the air, the water of lakes and rivers, the highways and public parks, buildings for public schools, all public institutions, buildings for the use of government officers, ships and arms for national defense, etc. Every one must be free to run his steamboat over government waters under the same restrictions. The streets of a city and the highways of the country are parts of the land which is recognized as government property. So also are public parks. The name "Boston Common" has become known all over the United States, and calls to mind the New England idea of reserved common wealth. Any income from the rent of such property is, of course, a part of the general share of the government.

INDEX.

Accumulation of permanent wealth, 262.
Adulterations of food, 442.
Atmosphere, the, 26.
Bank credits, 346.
Ballot, 191.
Bellamy, Edward, 152.
Bequest, right of, 186.
Bimetallism, 333.
Book accounts, 336.
Booty of robber, 441.
Buildings, 38.
"Business," 378.
Capital, 242.
Capitalization, of good name, 379; of monopolies, 393.
Child labor, 221.
Chinese, 140.
City, proper density of population, 70; model city, 253.
Combination, 288.
Competition, 287, 383; weakness of, 299.
Confiscation of property invested in the resources of nature must not be permitted, 166.
Control of Society, 189.
Co-operation, 412; constant employment under, 208; would not abolish the wages class, 417.
Consumable Wealth, 261, 364.
Consumable Natural Wealth, 29.
Consumable Produced Wealth, 364.
Copyright, 182.
Cost of production, 296; to the laborer, 303.
Credit, 339; bank credits, 346; how credits save the use of money, 345.
Crime, influence on population, 130; criminals, 252.
Currency, see Money.
Danger of immigration, 142.
Deferred marriages, effect of, 126.
Deferred payments, 316.
Demand, 290.
Dense population, advantage of, 362.
Diminishing returns, 78.
Discovery of Resources of Nature, 68.
Desire and want compared, 17.
Division of labor, 214, 110.
Distribution of Produced Wealth, Book VI., 351; how distribution takes place, 352; primary and secondary, 353.
Economical use of resources, 201; of Labor, 203; of Nature, 225; of Produced Wealth, 242.
Economy, definition of, 9.

(449)

Emigration, 113, 135.
Exchange, Book V., 271; beneficial to both parties under the circumstances, 275; cost of, 273; difficulty of, 270; distinguished from production, 273; exchange value, 277, 280; how exchanges satisfy wants, 271.
Exchange Values, 277, 280; limits of are fixed by value in use, 285; not the cost of production, 284.
Famine, 124.
Farm or Factory, 82.
Fish, 28, 233, 235, 240.
Finished goods, 42.
Financial panics, effect of, 207.
Forces of nature, 27; discovery of, 68.
Forests, 28, 239.
Forestry, 239.
Gambling, 443.
George, Henry, mistakes of, 178, 366.
Geometrical progression, 118, 131.
Good luck, 400.
Good name, share of, 375.
"Good will," share of, 378.
Government, 445; may require land to be brought into use as fast as needed, 228.
Government land, 176.
How to build a city, 227.
Immigration, 113; refusal to permit, 137.
Improvements on Land, 40.
Inheritance, of wants, 14; of property, 185.

Interest, 363; an inducement to save, 370; usually reckoned on money, 374.
Interstate commerce law, 386.
Irish land tenure, 179.
Irrigation, 210.
Labor, 32; a changing force, 34; child labor, 223; consumers of direct, 259; constant employment of, 203; definition of, 32; development of, 221; difference in laborers, 89; division of, 214; advantage of, 215; how far should it be carried? 217; tends to belittle the laborer, 219; direction of determined by employer, 258; hours of, 211; irksomeness of, 209; labor power depends on ability rather than on the number of the people, 35; ownership and control of, 160; prohibition of certain forms, 223; purposes for which it shall be used, 257; relation to population, 87; satisfies wants directly or indirectly, 36; satisfies wants directly, 260, 267; unemployed, 205; use in satisfying wants directly, 260; utility of, 53; value of, 92; value to laborer, 93; wasted labor, 209; when a drug in the market, 88; woman's labor, 224.
Laborer, cost of living, 205; golden age, 431; improvement in condition of, 212, 430; laborers the purchasers, 206; must live, 206.

INDEX. 451

Laborer's ownership of himself, 160; reasons for, 160; apparent exceptions, 161.
Laborers, proportion to idlers, 90.
Land, 22; for residence, 22, 70; factories, 23, 76; agriculture, 24, 77; government control of, 228; improvements on, 40; practical methods of use, 172; quality for residence, 70; for factories, 76; for agriculture, 77; speculation in, 227; value of, 169.
Land Laws of Moses, 168.
Laissez faire, 195, 196.
Law of increase of population, 116.
Liberty, desire for, 160.
Limit to natural resources, 69.
Limiting production, 295.
Limits of Exchange Value, 285.
Long and short haul clause, 386.
Machinery, limited use, 244.
Malthus, 116, 118.
Marriages, deferred, 126.
Materials, 43.
Merchants, share of, 418.
Minerals, 28.
Mill, John Stuart, on Socialism, 156; proposed plans of dealing with land, 178.
Money, 312; durability, 322; fiat, 327; gold, 325; how to secure uniform value, 330; increase in value, 318; paper money, 324, 326; portability, 312; qualities of good, 313; silver, 321; value of, 326; substitutes for, 335; tabular standard,
331; what determines value of, 325.
Monopoly (see also natural monopoly), 306, 382; capitalization of, 393; effect on price, 307; share of, 382.
Monopolist, price he will fix, 308.
Morality by legislation, 254.
Moses, land laws of, 168.
Natural wealth (see Resources of Nature), definition of, 30 31.
Natural monopolies, 194, 382–396; government control of, 387; not Socialism, 391.
Needs and wants compared, 17.
Non-competing groups of laborers, 428.
Not right to satisfy all wants, 17.
Ownership and control of resources, 151; of labor, 160; of resources of nature, 165; of resources produced by industry, 181.
Opening of new employments to women, effect on population, 127.
Overcrowding of population, 123.
Paper money increases value of gold and silver, 327.
Parks, 238; reservation of, 180.
Penn, Wm., and the Indians, 184.
People the purchasers, 206.
Permanent natural resources, 225.
Permanent Wealth, 262–266, 363.
Personal interest in scientific study, 165.
Poor laws, effect on increase of population, 129.
Population, Book II., 65; appli-

cations of laws, 135; assumed to double in 25 years, 118; checks to increase of, 120; in the United States, 142; classes who should people a country, 138; effect of education on, 147; law of increase of, 116; number of people per square mile in cities, 70; population and labor, 87; population and society, 103; population and Produced Wealth, 96; population and Resources of Nature, 60; room for increase of, 139; stationary, 133; tendency to rapid increase fortunate, 122.
Population and Labor, 87.
Population and Produced Wealth, 96.
Population and the Resources of Nature, 66.
Population and Society, 103.
Practical business, 251.
Price, 281.
Price of a dollar, 275.
Profit sharing, 434.
Profits of production, 397; limited by competition, 403.
Profits of exchange, 406; gross and real profit, 408.
Private Property, natural right of, 151; what resources may become, 157.
Private Property or Socialism, 151.
Produced Wealth (see resources produced by human industry), consumable, 364; definition of, 45; economical use of, 242; how much needed, 96; permanent and consumable, 244; permanent use of, 363; saving of, 101; utility of, 52; value of, 100; what fixes share of, 366.
Producers and Non-Producers, 36
Productions of Human Industry, 38 (see Resources Produced by Human Industry).
Produced Wealth, 45.
Production of consumable goods, 261.
Profits, definition of, 404, 410; consist of two elements, 400.
Profits of Exchange, 406, 408.
Profits of Production, 397.
Profit Sharing, 434.
Prohibition of certain forms of labor, 221.
Property, 153, 182; disposition of after death, 185; moral right of, 182; natural right of, 153; not robbery, 185; what resources may become, 157.
Public opinion, effect on marriages, 128.
Purposes for which labor shall be used, 257.
Purposes for which resources shall be used, 256.
Purposes for which permanent Produced Wealth shall be used, 243.
Railroads, 387-389.
Rent, 175, 355; does not depend on public or private ownership, 357; how rent may be reduced, 361.
Resources for Satisfaction of Wants, Book I., 21.

INDEX. 453

Resources of Nature, 21; can not be increased, 66; classification, 28, 30; consumable, use of, 231; discovery of, 66; economical use of, 69; how many people will they support? 70; limited, 69; must be separated from those produced by industry, 166; ownership and control of, 165; permanent and consumable, 29; Permanent, 225; practical methods of using, 172; public use of, 236-241; public and private use of, 234; satisfy wants directly and indirectly, 30; use of inferior, 226; used by private parties, 235, by the State, 235; utility of, 51; value of, 84.

Resources produced by human industry, 38 (see Produced Wealth); economical use of, 242; how much needed, 96; ownership and control of, 181; population and, 96; utility of, 52; value of, 100.

Right of property, 154, 181, 182; what it includes, 183.

Rights, of children, 161; criminals, 162; idiots and insane, 162; paupers, 162.

Risk in production, 399.

Roads, 39.

Sale and purchase simpler than barter, 278.

Savings, 101, 247, 250.

Share of good name, 375; of the government, 445; of laborer who works for himself, 411; of laborer who works for wages, 420; of laborer who satisfies wants directly, 436; of the merchant, 406; of monopoly, 382; of Natural Wealth, 355; of Producer, 397; of Produced Wealth, 363.

Society, 46; a million people compared with more, 106; control of, 189; definition of, 46; depends on the wants and character of the people rather than their number, 105; limit to the number of people desired, 107; negative utility, 55; population and, 103; satisfies wants by its presence, 104; satisfies wants directly, 46; indirectly, 47, 106; utility of, 54; use in satisfying wants, 252; value of, 109.

Socialism, 151, 193; danger of, 182; definition of, 151, 193; distinguished from other organizations of society, 193; destruction of independence, 157; not a means of saving society, 156; private property and, 151; slavery to society, 157.

Substitutes for money, 335.

Suffrage, who should have the privilege of, 190.

Sunday work, waste work, 213.

Supply and demand, 289, 297.

Support of workmen, 207.

"Survival of the fittest," mistake in popular conception of meaning of the term, 139.

Swamps brought into use late, 229.

Taxes, 163.
Telephone exchange, 278.
Timber, 28. 232.
Title by exchange, 184.
Tools and machinery, 39.
Total demand, 290.
Total supply, 289.
Use of Resources, 201.
Use of the resource of society, 252.
Utility, 49 ; Jevon's view, 49.
Unchangeable value of money, desirability of, 313.
Undertaker, 354, 398, 400.
Value in use, 49, 57 ; decreases with quantity, 60; means scarcity, 57 ; measure of, 59 ; shows relation between wants and resources, 65; of Resources of Nature, 84.
Value of money, 283.
Values of a dollar, 282.
Visible supply, 293.

Wages, 420; depend on supply and demand, 421; effect in raising prices, 424; nominal and real, 424; principles on which high wages depend, 432 ; when high, 432 ; why increase in has not been greater, 430.
Wages system, 420; unfortunate, 432.
Wants, 10 ; all should not be satisfied, 17 ; creation, development and suppression of, 11 ; spiritual and religious, 15.
Wants and Resources, relation between, 65, 95.
War, 120.
Water, 25.
Wealth, 1 ; natural, 31; produced, 45.
What shall be produced ? 256.
Who shall people this land? 138.
Wholesale and retail, 301.
Wild animals, 28.
Woman suffrage, 192.

www.ingramcontent.com/pod-product-compliance
Lightning Source LLC
Chambersburg PA
CBHW032006300426
44117CB00008B/918